To my good friend George

thank you, [illegible]

instructive and truly

memorable year.

Graham.

THE GREAT STRIKE

A History of the Penrhyn Quarry Dispute of 1900–1903

JEAN LINDSAY

DAVID & CHARLES
Newton Abbot London North Pomfret (Vt)

British Library Cataloguing in Publication Data

Lindsay, Jean
The great strike : a history of the
Penrhyn Quarry dispute of 1900–1903.
1. Industrial relations——Wales, North——
History 2. Trade-unions——Stone-cutters
——Wales, North 3. Slate industry——
Wales, North——Employees
I. Title
331′ .0422354′094291 HD6976.S7/

ISBN 0-7153-8635-2

Typeset by ABM Typographics Limited, Hull
and printed in Great Britain
by Billings Limited, Worcester
for David & Charles Publishers plc
Brunel House Newton Abbot Devon

Published in the United States of America
by David & Charles Inc
North Pomfret Vermont 05053 USA

Contents

To
The Staff and Pupils
of the
John Bright School
Llandudno
1974–1986

Acknowledgements

In writing this book on a subject which is still controversial, I have been singularly fortunate in receiving much help and much kindness not only from archivists and librarians but also from descendants of both parties to the dispute.

I owe a particular debt of gratitude to Lady Janet Douglas Pennant, who allowed me full access to the large collections of Pennant papers at the Gwynedd Archives in Caernarfon and at the University College of North Wales in Bangor. I am also very grateful to Lady Janet's husband Mr John Douglas Pennant and their son Edmund, who together located and made available a valuable collection of additional documents.

Gwynedd Archives was my second home for many months, and it is a pleasure to recall the assistance and hospitality offered to me by Mrs Mary Aris, Mr Randolph Ellis, Mrs Angharad Jones, Mrs Anne Lovell, Mr Bryn R. Parry, Miss Anne Venables and Mr Gareth Williams. I am especially grateful to Mr Martin Davis, who helped me to interpret the Minutes of the N.W.Q.U., and to Mrs Catherine Hughes, who introduced me to many scholars working in the Archives on related subjects. I greatly appreciated the advice and encouragement I was given by Mr J. I. C. Boyd, Mr Eric Ffowkes, Dr. R. Merfyn Jones, Mr Frank Rhys Jones, Mr Gwynfor Pierce Jones, and Dr Michael Lewis.

In my research for this book, as in my earlier work on the North Wales slate industry and the Pennants' Jamaican estates, I have made extensive use of the library and archives of the University College of North Wales. I am especially grateful to the former archivist, Mr Alun Giles Jones, and the present archivist, Mr Tomos Roberts, for their practical help and enthusiastic support. I should also like to thank Miss Diana Clarke for her patient and always cheerful assistance. Many members of the academic, library and administrative staffs of the College have shown an interest in the progress of my research. I cannot name them all, but I must in particular acknowledge the encouragement I received from Dr Cyril Parry of the Department of History and Professor William Tydeman of the Department of English.

ACKNOWLEDGEMENTS

My colleagues and pupils at the John Bright School in Llandudno have lived with my interest in the slate industry for many years, and their advice, especially on linguistic and topographical points, has been invaluable. Mr Maldwyn Hughes gave me the benefit of his knowledge as the son of a Penrhyn quarryman. Mr Gareth Jones, Mr Fôn Parri, Miss Jaci Parry and Mrs Elsie Williams helped me to understand the distinctive society and culture of the quarrying villages. Mr Hilary Chapman and his father-in-law Mr R. H. Roberts enlightened me about some oral traditions concerning the dispute. I should like to thank Mr Iwan Jones, Mr Trefor Lewis, Miss Jaci Parry, Mr Derfel Roberts and Mrs Margaret Williams for their advice and assistance over matters of translation and Welsh idiom.

In my search for places connected with the events of 1900 to 1903, I received willing help from many residents of the Bethesda area. I am grateful to them all, and in particular to those who enabled me to identify what is now a bingo hall as the site of the strikers' weekly meetings. When I was seeking information about the early life of the second Lord Penrhyn, I received valuable assistance from Mr Patrick Strong of Eton College and Mr Norman Holme of the Royal Welch Fusiliers Regimental Museum. Dr Clare Taylor of the University College of Wales in Aberystwyth took a keen interest in my work and gave me the benefit of her expert knowledge of the history of Jamaica. The staff of the Manchester Central Library responded to my various requests with unfailing courtesy and efficiency.

The preparation of this book has involved substantial travelling expenses, and I am grateful to the British Academy for awarding me a grant which helped to cover these. The work could hardly have been completed without the encouragement provided by a guarantee of publication, and I should like to thank the Penrhyn Trust for the generous subsidy which made this possible. The twelve illustrations were chosen from the large collection of historical pictures in Gwynedd Archives, and I am grateful to the archivist for granting me permission to use these. I have also to thank Mr Evan Hughes of Caernarfon for supplying the necessary reproductions.

My husband, Dr David Lindsay, has found time even in the beleaguered life of a British university teacher to disentangle many problems of conflicting evidence and obscure chronology. Our two children, Cora and John, have followed the book's development with friendly interest, scarcely hinting that they would have approached the task differently. I am deeply grateful to them, and must therefore emphasise that I alone am responsible for the views expressed or implied in this study.

JEAN LINDSAY
Bangor

1
The Origins of the Dispute: 1782–1874

In 1885 George Sholto Gordon Douglas Pennant took over a large slate quarry at Bethesda in North Wales, with a workforce of about 3,000 men. His father, Colonel Edward Gordon Douglas Pennant, first Lord Penrhyn, died in the following year. The new owner had come into his inheritance at a difficult time. The role of the aristocracy was being undermined by the growing power of the other classes, and laissez-faire was being eroded by parliamentary legislation. Prosperity was threatened by industrial recession at home and by increased competition from abroad. The social discontent prompted by economic circumstance was being voiced by militant trade unionists, who in North Wales could enlist nationalist sentiment in support of their cause. In 1886 the new Lord Penrhyn was fifty. He had succeeded his father as Conservative M.P. for Caernarfonshire in 1866, lost his seat in 1868, regained it in 1874, and finally lost it again in 1880 when the Liberal Party gained ground at the expense of the Tories. Discipline was all-important to him, and he had been in his father's confidence during the last years of the latter's life. He could not accept the growth of trade unionism, which he saw as a device not to advance the men's interests but to destroy the owner's control.

The Pennants were connected with the medieval abbots of Basingwerk, and had lived in Caernarfonshire since the early eighteenth century. Their links with Wales had been tenuous, however, for some generations before George's time. George's father was a member of the Scottish aristocratic family of Douglas. He had inherited the estate through his first wife, George's mother, Juliana Isabella Mary Dawkins Pennant, who died at the age of thirty-four. She was the daughter of George Hay

Dawkins (1763-1840), who had taken the surname Pennant as a condition of inheritance when his cousin Richard Pennant (?1737–1808) died without heirs. Dawkins Pennant was responsible for the building of Penrhyn Castle, which was begun about 1827 on the site near Bangor of an earlier house designed by Samuel Wyatt. The Castle has a Norman keep 115ft high, and its sumptuous interior includes a hall of Anglesey marble; though it has been much maligned, it remains a powerful affirmation of wealth and authority. Dawkins Pennant's claim to the estate came from his paternal grandmother Elizabeth, daughter of Edward Pennant of Clarendon in Jamaica. The Dawkins family was itself very wealthy, and drew much of its income from the Jamaican sugar-plantations.

The founder of the Pennant fortune was Edward's father Gifford, the second son of Henry Pennant, whose grandfather Thomas had been Abbot of Basingwerk. In the 1660s Gifford Pennant emigrated to Jamaica, where he received grants of land from the British government and like other planters employed black slaves transported from Africa. Although the Pennants like many owners of Jamaican estates had become absentee landlords by 1750, both Edward's son John Pennant and John's son Richard Pennant left extensive records showing their concern for the plantation workers[1]. All British slaves were emancipated in 1833, and in 1835 Dawkins Pennant received £14,683 compensation for the 764 slaves on his estates; but an Anti-Slavery Society had existed in Caernarfonshire in 1828, and an interest in slavery lingered in the county[2]. Although George Douglas Pennant was born three years after emancipation, his descent from slave-owners was used as a weapon against him by his political opponents. The Pennants continued to run their Jamaican estates until the 1930s, when they were sold by Hugh Napier Douglas Pennant[3].

Richard Pennant inherited the family estates in 1782. In 1783 he was created Baron Penrhyn of County Louth, an Irish peerage which died with him; and as Lord Penrhyn he was renowned as a public benefactor. The profit from his sugar plantations was used to give employment to many hundreds of

Welshmen in a new slate quarry, known in Welsh as Cae Braich y Cafn, which was situated at the entrance to Nant Ffrancon in Snowdonia. In 1790-91 he established a harbour on the outskirts of Bangor, which is known as Port Penrhyn; and in 1801 the quarry and the harbour were connected by means of a six-mile tramway used by horse-drawn wagons. Penrhyn Quarry on the eastern side of Elidir Mountain and Dinorwic Quarry above Llanberis on the mountain's western side were to become the largest slate quarries in the world. Slate was also quarried on a large scale in the Nantlle and Ffestiniog areas of North Wales, but the owners of Penrhyn and Dinorwic paid no rent or royalties and had greater capital resources. In 1882 these two quarries produced 198,595 tons of slate, valued at £468,212. Penrhyn and Dinorwic were similar in location and early history; but it was Bethesda and not Llanberis which in the years 1900-1903 became the focus for one of the longest and bitterest disputes in the history of industrial relations.

Some of the journalists who reported that dispute presented their readers with an image of Bethesda as a harmonious and tranquil community reduced to division and desolation by the tyranny of Lord Penrhyn. Bethesda was indeed both divided and desolate during the dispute; but its problems were not entirely new. The quarry's earlier history had been punctuated with strikes and revolts; and although the Welsh language was a unifying factor, the community had long been split both in religion and in politics. Because of its close links with the building industry, the slate industry was continuously affected by changing economic conditions; and labour relations were made peculiarly difficult by the piece-work wage-system and the varying quality of the slate, which together created large opportunities for bribery and favouritism.

At Penrhyn Quarry as elsewhere, quarrymen worked in crews, usually of four men, who were partners in a 'bargain' or operation. Wages depended on the price of slate and on the number of slates produced, and the total wages bill was shared among the four partners. The slates were classified according to their sizes; and from the time of Hugh Warburton in 1738 the three largest sizes had been called Duchesses, Countesses and Ladies. These large slates were sold by tally, per mille of 1200, whereas the smaller 'ton' slates of all sizes were sold by weight. The bargain-setter was in a position of some power, as he allocated to each crew an area of slate, usually about 60ft high and about 30ft wide, whose character effectively determined the men's earnings. An attempt was made, however, to compensate for bargains that turned out badly by paying an allowance inversely proportionate to the quality of the rock; this was known initially as 'price and a quarter' or 'price and a half', and later simply as 'poundage'. The skilled quarrymen undertook the training of boys entering the trade, and it was usual for a father to act as instructor; boys were often admitted only if they had fathers working in the quarry. These boys were known as *rybelwyr*, but this term was also applied to men who had failed to become quarrymen and who continued to do jobs in the galleries on a free-lance basis. The 'badrockmen', who usually worked in groups, were responsible for clearing the waste rock or 'rubbish' from the galleries, and for building the tips of waste rock. Other employees included blacksmiths, carpenters, counters, weighers, loaders, plate-layers, engine-drivers and clerks. Some of these men worked at Port Penrhyn, where the main quarry offices were situated[4].

The work on the rock face was particularly dangerous, especially in the early days; a small beam was fastened to the top by two ropes at each end, and four or five men stood on this beam with crowbars and sledgehammers, chipping off the slate in pieces two to eight feet thick[5]. Some improvements were introduced in the time of Dawkins Pennant. A huge drainage scheme was created with underground tunnels; and a slate-dressing machine worked by a treadle was designed by the quarry manager John Francis. The risk of casualties was reduced in 1831 by Bickford's invention of the safety fuse; and fixed hours for blasting were established in 1857[6]. Such innovations, however, could not eliminate accidents, most of which were caused either by human error or by falls of rock.

The life-expectancy of Penrhyn quarrymen seems to have

been surprisingly high. On 11 February 1892 the quarry manager E. A. Young told the Commission of Enquiry into Labour that the average age of the quarry's thirty-nine pensioners was 78½, and that the average age of the quarrymen who had died in the years 1882-91 was 59. Employment in the quarry, however, involved exposure to slate dust and to bad weather at high altitudes; and many quarrymen had long walks to and from work. These conditions commonly resulted in poor physique with little resistance to disease, and tuberculosis in particular was widespread. The problem was aggravated when a diet of strong tea and white bread was preferred to the traditional Welsh diet of barley bread, oatmeal and buttermilk. These factors distinguished Bethesda from Penrhyn Castle; but bad drainage and inadequate sanitation were problems in both places, and the second Lord Penrhyn suffered frequently from rheumatism and influenza[7].

The first recorded strike at a North Wales slate-quarry occurred at Penrhyn in 1825. It was quickly ended when Dawkins Pennant refused to alter conditions or negotiate with the men[8]. At about the same time, the Dinorwic quarrymen rebelled against a ruling that they should work till 4 p.m. instead of 1 p.m. on Saturdays. This protest, unlike the Penrhyn one, was successful. Both quarries were controlled by wealthy and paternalistic landowners, and in most respects they developed on similar lines. The Assheton Smiths, who lived at Vaynol Hall between Bangor and Port Dinorwic, gave "well behaved' Dinorwic quarrymen eight to fifteen acres of land each on leases of thirty to forty years; and a similar practice was followed on the Penrhyn estate. In 1893 the Penrhyn estate agent, the Hon William Sackville West, explained that the early quarrymen had built cottages on the estate, with the Pennants providing the slate for the roofs. When the leases expired, the nominal rents were slightly increased, as happened also at Dinorwic[9]. The increased rent was still low, averaging £3 per annum inclusive of rates. According to Sackville West, this barely covered the cost of repairs, and some cottages were 'a dead loss'; but many workers naturally resented paying additional rent for houses they had built themselves[10].

The Bethesda Congegational Chapel, which was built in 1820 and rebuilt in 1840, took its name from the pool by the sheep market in John v 2, where 'a great multitude of impotent folk' waited for 'the moving of the water'. This chapel in turn gave its name to the small town where, in the later nineteenth century, most Penrhyn quarrymen lived; and the town acquired other ecclesiastical buildings, among which the Jerusalem Methodist Chapel was the most imposing. Bethesda was built not on Pennant land but on the freehold of the Cefnfaes estate, an area of about 128 acres in the parish of Llanllechid for which W. J. Parry (1842-1927) served as estate agent. On 19 June 1901 Lord Penrhyn complained to the Rev T. Eiddon Jones, 'a prominent Nonconformist advocate of the Temperance cause in North Wales', about the many public houses which had been opened in Bethesda:

> It is well known to you that Bethesda does not belong to me and that its numerous public houses (17 or 18 in all) which you doubtless have seen standing in some cases two or three together adjoining each other (the majority of them within a space of 200 yd) are all on property which us under the control of Mr William John Parry (of Coetmor Hall). I can well imagine the sort of outcry which, perhaps justifiably, would have been raised against myself, if all those public houses were on my estate; and I may perhaps be allowed to draw your attention to the fact that in this whole district there is only one public house or hotel which belongs to me. I need hardly point out to you how desirable it is that the inhabitants of the locality, more especially the working classes, should be relieved from some of the temptations to which they are exposed in that plague spot of drink called Bethesda, and I hope to hear that your efforts are concentrated on the amelioration of the conditions of things prevalent in that village[11].

Lord Penrhyn made no reference to the fact that Bethesda's public houses, though numerous, were outnumbered by its chapels.

Building leases were granted in Bethesda from the 1830s. An Act of 1854 (17 and 18 Vic c 101) provided for the paving, cleansing, lighting and drainage of the town; and Colonel Edward Douglas Pennant, later the first Lord Penrhyn, became the first chairman of the Bethesda Improvement Commissioners. He contributed £1,000 towards the water supply, lighting and drainage schemes; and he also gave £300 for drainage tanks at the nearby village of Gerlan, which like Bethesda lay outside the Pennant estate. These improvements helped to reduce the incidence of cholera, typhoid, and typhus fever; but sanitary conditions in Bethesda remained poor, and continuing population growth necessitated more work on drainage and water supply. This was undertaken in 1882 by the local Board of Health, at a cost to the ratepayers of £13,000. On 12 May Lord Penrhyn agreed to lease the Board a plot of land for use as a reservoir; and he also gave four acres near Coetmor Mill for filtration to prevent pollution of the river[12].

On 30 May 1872 Lord Penrhyn summarised his experience as a landowner in a letter to H. Barber, a solicitor who had considerable knowledge of the Penrhyn estates:

> There is not much encouragement to purchase land in Carnarvonshire whatever the nominal rent may be. I find that as soon as it comes into my possession the calls on me for immediate repairs, new buildings, drainage, enclosure, churches, schools, Parsonage houses, and Stipends for incompetent incumbents equal if they do not exceed the total nominal rental and the purchase money is a dead loss in a pecuniary point of view, while any supposed territorial or political advantage in its possession is a fiction.

The Penrhyn estates included 41,348 acres in Caernarfonshire, 5,377 acres in Northamptonshire, 2,625 acres in Denbighshire, 121 acres in Kent and 77 acres in Buckinghamshire. These 49,548 acres were valued at about £71,000[13].

J. Edmund Vincent, a barrister and *Times* correspondent, believed that the problems of Penrhyn Quarry were misinterpreted by outsiders who did not understand their social context. He emphasised the long-standing politico-sectarian bitterness in the quarry community, where some of the employees were Conservatives and Churchmen but the majority were Radicals and Nonconformists. The connections between religion and politics, he argued, were much closer than in England, where Nonconformists were not necessarily expected to be Radicals. In the quarrying districts, the sect a man was born into affected his whole attitude to life; and quarrymen under the influence of Nonconformist preachers and Radical trade unionists were inevitably hostile to a quarry-owner whose Anglican and Conservative views were well-known. Vincent composed a pamphlet presenting the proprietor's case on labour relations at Penrhyn Quarry; but in July 1903 Lord Penrhyn decided against its publication[14].

Religious life in Wales was punctuated with 'revivals'. A revival initiated at Beddgelert in 1818 led to the building of new chapels, and the Temperance Revival which began in 1835 persuaded many people to renounce alcohol. Social attitudes in the quarrying districts were further modified by the appearance in 1843 of the Welsh newspaper *Amserau*, which in 1859 was amalgamated with *Y Faner*. In reading the *Baner ac Amserau Cymru*, which later reverted to the title *Y Faner*, the quarrymen developed their sense of identity and their political consciousness. The 1867 Reform Act enfranchised small farmers, small shopkeepers and some wage-earners; and the old rivalry among landowning families like the Pennants and the Bulkeleys was gradually replaced by conflict between political parties. The New Liberalism, which drew much of its support from Welsh Nonconformists, attacked Church Establishment and 'feudal landlordism'; and Liberal values were promoted by Welsh periodicals, including *Yr Herald Cymraeg* (established 1831) and *Y Genedl Gymreig* (established 1877)[15]. The shortage of elementary schools revealed by the 1846 Royal Commission was partly remedied by the development of National Schools for Anglicans and British Schools for Nonconformists. After 1870 grants were provided for the creation of nondenominational Board Schools, but the National Schools continued to receive support from Lord Penrhyn and other landowners.

After 1885, when George Douglas Pennant became owner of the quarry, he and his new manager E. A. Young were commonly represented as ruthless oppressors of their workers; and it was often suggested that George was entirely different from his benevolent and well-loved father. In reality the first Lord Penrhyn incurred almost as much hostility as the second; and both men responded to personal attacks with stoicism and a dry sense of humour. On 3 July 1872 the father received an invitation from the 'Committee of the Welsh Choir Reception', who assured him that 'no *gentleman* connected with the principality' would 'meet from his Countrymen with a more hearty welcome'. In a letter to Barber he commented:

> Rather amusing!! This came the same day and by the same post as the article from the same political party source – describing me as 'an alien in blood, language and feeling'. Which am I to take as the real expression of feeling?[16]

On 30 March 1874, when his son wanted him to challenge a 'pure falsehood' in *Y Faner*, Lord Penrhyn wrote to Barber again:

> I have myself for so many years been accustomed to attack in the Welsh local publication that am perhaps somewhat case hardened, but at the same time I think that whenever a *good* opportunity offers for making these Editors feel (which they only do when their pockets are hit) it ought to be taken advantage of. Perhaps this is not one – but a contradiction ought to be given I think[17].

The slate industry made a leap forward in economic terms in 1831, when all the quarry-owners petitioned vigorously and successfully for the repeal of the slate duty. The development of railways at about the same time stimulated a boom in industrial investment, especially in building. The increased demand for slates affected all the quarrying areas, including the Ffestiniog district and the town of Blaenau Ffestiniog, where slate-mines began to develop and prosper. There was a recession in the 1840s, however, and trade declined again.

Working conditions in the slate industry were always dangerous. There were 258 fatal accidents in Penrhyn Quarry between 1826 and 1875; and the number of fatal accidents was proportionately even higher in the Nantlle district, where the quarries consisted of pits with almost vertical sides. Little provision was made for the victims' families; the quarry-owners usually made donations, but the granting of pensions was rare.

Some of the workers at Penrhyn Quarry came from as far away as Anglesey or Llandudno; and 1,030 of the 7,967 people living in Bethesda in 1841 had been born outside the area[18]. A significant aid to recruitment was the Penrhyn Benefit Club, which granted pensions to aged quarrymen of good standing. This Club had been founded by Richard Pennant in 1787, and re-established with new rules in 1825. In 1874, after W. J. Parry had revealed that the quarry agent and one of the managers had been guilty of serious malpractice, Lord Penrhyn gave £2,000 to cover discrepancies in the accounts, and effective control of the Club was given to the quarrymen. The benefits provided thereafter included sick pay of 5s a week for twelve months, and a small pension for any member who had to retire because of old age, accident or illness. Quarrymen who suffered serious injury could receive treatment at the Quarry Hospital, which had been established in the 1840s and was supervised by the quarry manager[19].

Expansion in the building industry after 1855 resulted in a renewed demand for slate and a general rise in wages; but there were grievances about pay and conditions at Penrhyn Quarry. These led in 1865 to the formation of a Quarry Committee, whose original members were Robert Parry, Robert Thomas, Richard Evans and Richard Pritchard. The Committee, which was to play a large role in later disputes, wrote to Colonel Douglas Pennant; but they received no reply, and on 31 July the men came out on strike. The Committee sought the help of W. J. Parry, thus forming an alliance which was to have large consequences. Parry's father was a Penrhyn quarryman who owned a house in Bethesda High Street and served as a deacon in the Congregational Church. After his father's death Parry became a pupil at Llanrwst Grammar School, where the medium of instruction was English. By the time of the 1865 strike he had become an Associate of the Society of Auditors of England[20]. The range of his later business interests may be deduced from an undated advertisement for 'W. J. Parry Limited' of 'Coetmor

Yard, Bethesda':

> Estate Agent to the Cefnfaes Estates, Wholesale Ironmongers and Builders' Merchants, Implement Agents, Powder, Oil and Dynamite Merchants. All kinds of Quarry Tools Etc . . . Every description of Farm, Household and Garden Ironmongery[21].

When the members of the Committee met Colonel Douglas Pennant and his estate agent Captain Pennant Iremonger, the young W. J. Parry accompanied them as interpreter. There were three meetings, and according to Parry Colonel Douglas Pennant promised to grant concessions; but because of 'the attempt then made to divide them' the men resolved to establish a trade union for Penrhyn Quarry employees. The union was created in September 1865, and more than half the workforce joined it. On 2 December Colonel Douglas Pennant warned the men that such an organisation would 'establish an ill-feeling between himself and his workmen which both parties would soon regret.' He proclaimed his intention of closing the quarry and re-opening it only to those who 'declared themselves averse to any such scheme as a Trade Union.' On 22 December 1,229 of the employees informed Colonel Douglas Pennant that they had given up the idea of a trade union, and expressed the hope that there would be no 'severity or revenge.'

In 1866 Colonel Douglas Pennant became the first Baron Penrhyn of Llandegai; and according to Parry his son George 'stepped into his father's seat as representative of the County of Carnarvon, which seat was then looked upon as an appendage to the Penrhyn estate.' In 1868 the seat was contested in the Liberal interest by T. L. D. Jones Parry, who won by 148 votes and thus proved that Caernarfonshire was not a 'pocket Borough'[22]. Jones Parry had presented his campaign as a fight against 'bondage', but J. E. Vincent argued that George Douglas Pennant had in fact been defeated 'by another landowner who knew how to take full advantage of the Nonconformist vote.'

W. J. Parry later claimed that Lord Penrhyn had in March 1869 avenged his son's defeat by sacking two and downgrading two of the thirty-seven quarrymen who voted Liberal in Bethesda. Parry asserted that he had written to Lord Penrhyn about this 'victimisation' on 20 March and received no reply; but in fact Lord Penrhyn's reply was written on 25 March and has survived. It began with a comment on Parry's role as letter-writer:

> I am quite aware that you have on several occasions written to me in the name of persons living in or in the immediate neighbourhood of Bethesda – but I cannot for a moment recognise you as a medium of communication in reference to the management of my property.

Lord Penrhyn undertook to investigate the case of the two men who had been dismissed; but with reference to the two who had allegedly been 'turned from their bargains' he declared that men were often 'transferred to other parts of the work either temporarily or otherwise according to their Character, Efficiency or good Behaviour'.

On 27 March 1869 Captain Pennant Iremonger reported, on the authority of the quarry manager John Francis, that two of the men concerned had refused other work after the completion of their bargains. Of the two men dismissed, one had been employed in a part of the quarry which would not be worked for some years; and the other, according to Iremonger, owned a large shop in Gerlan and was 'frequently in the habit of losing time'. Deploring Parry's assumption that Lord Penrhyn would listen to complaints from 'every Radical firebrand at Bethesda', Iremonger argued that a complaint should be communicated by the men themselves:

> With all due deference I think it a pity that you should enter, as you have done, into any explanation with Mr Parry. I do not see that it is any business of his whatever and if you are to be accountable to every one for your reason for not employing men on your property you will be persecuted beyond measure. Also it is ridiculous to suppose for a moment that you should be held responsible by those meddling lawyers' clerks[23].

Labour relations at Penrhyn Quarry continued to deteriorate. Wages averaged 24s a week, whereas in other quarries they averaged 30s; and weak management allowed bribery and favouritism to flourish. Slack trade led in 1870 to the dismissal of eighty workmen; and it was alleged that they were being punished for their roles in the 1865 strike and the 1868 election. On 9 July 1870 Lord Penrhyn told Barber that other quarry-owners had also dismissed men, and that 'every care' had been taken in his own quarry 'to select those on whom the dismissal would fall the lightest'. While acknowledging that the constant 'scurrilous' attacks on him would be believed by 'the mass of the lower orders in the County', he declared himself to be 'perfectly indifferent' to this:

> I have done my best for the people, and in no other part of the Kingdom would such attacks be tolerated; but if Welshmen like to encourage these writers in making them I cannot prevent them. I can only punish the authors when I catch them in anything actionable[24].

Lord Penrhyn blamed W. J. Parry for some of these attacks; and on 28 September 1870 he told Barber that Parry had been 'persistently troublesome' and had 'bullied and frightened' the men into the strike of 1865. To the strikers themselves Lord Penrhyn was less hostile:

> When the strike was at an end I told the deputation who asked me whether they were to suffer for it, that I would not punish them for what was passed but I told them that if anything happened in future they must take the consequences.

Parry, whom Iremonger had described as 'resentful', was said to have announced his intention of 'worrying Mr Francis'; and Lord Penrhyn was convinced that he was 'a thorough bad one' who viewed events from 'a Welsh tenant's view i.e. getting all he can from a Landlord and doing nothing himself'[25]. A more detached view of Parry's role was offered at a later date by Richard Morris, an overlooker at the quarry, who described him as 'the adviser of the Committee' and continued:

> He was often up at the Quarry and was a man of great influence throughout the whole place – being supposed to have both the Committee and Mr Wyatt [Lord Penrhyn's shipping agent] under his thumb. He was voted £150 by the Committee for his services during the Strike [of 1874]. He was also appointed Secretary of the

Benefit Club at a salary of £80 a year – and he supplied explosives and materials to the Quarry[26].

The situation in the Ffestiniog area was very different. Samuel Holland, who owned much of Blaenau Ffestiniog and employed hundreds of men in the Rhiwbryfdir slate mine, was a prominent Liberal. As M.P. for Merionethshire from 1870 to 1885, he was supported by most of the quarrymen; and although working conditions were often worse than at Penrhyn, relations between workers and management were friendlier[27]. The formation of the North Wales Quarrymen's Union in 1874 was given a lukewarm reception by the Ffestiniog quarrymen, who felt it to be unnecessary. By 1877 the Union had recruited 91% of the slateworkers in Bethesda, 83% of those in Llanberis, and 25% of those in Nantlle; but in the Ffestiniog district the figure was only 10%[28].

It was the quarrymen at Dinorwic who in 1873 revived the idea of a trade union. Because wages were failing to keep pace with the cost of living, they formed a Society for the Defence of Slate Quarrymen; and after a meeting at the Queen's Hotel in Caernarfon on 18 March 1874 this became the North Wales Quarrymen's Union. In order to avoid victimisation, outsiders were chosen as officials. The president was Morgan Richards, a Bangor tradesman who later wrote a book on slate quarrying; and the treasurer was a bank manager named Hugh Pugh. The secretary was W. J. Parry[29]. On 17 July 1874 Lord Penrhyn complained to Barber about the reports which were appearing in the press. On a *Liverpool Courier* statement that Penrhyn quarrymen were 'the worst paid of any in the country', he commented:

> I do not think that any body of Workmen ever were better looked after as to their comforts and their circumstances . . . . It is painful to think that three such men as Mr Pugh, Mr Morgan and Mr Parry of Bethesda can produce so much mischief in the county and it makes me despair of any permanent good being effected in it[30].'

Lord Penrhyn clearly expected nothing but trouble from the Union. Some of its supporters wanted to promote the cause of Radical Liberalism, and believed that for this purpose 'the power of Penrhyn Castle and the Vaynol had to be broken, and with that power the silver manacles of their paternalism[31]'. Without consulting Lord Penrhyn, the manager of Penrhyn Quarry joined the other major employers in Caernarfonshire in arranging a meeting at Caernarfon; and a circular issued after the meeting declared that

> every quarry proprietor in North Wales should refuse to employ any man who is ascertained to be a member of the union, and . . . every proprietor or his representative should give notice of such determination to his men at the earliest opportunity[32].

Lord Penrhyn regretted this decision, and explained his views to the press. On 2 June 1874 he told Barber that he strongly objected to being led into 'entering . . . an Union . . . and forbidding others to do so', and he complained that the decision had been taken 'without any communication whatever or consultation' with himself[33].

The first quarrymen to join the union were those at the small Glynrhonwy Quarry on the opposite side of Llyn Padarn from Dinorwic. The manager, Captain Wallace Cragg, duly locked out his men on 21 May 1874; but as he could not afford to lose production at a time of buoyancy in the slate market, the men were allowed back as unionists after three weeks. At Dinorwic itself the men complained about the regulations on punctuality which had been introduced by the newly-appointed chief manager, a brother of Lord Penrhyn's shipping agent Arthur Wyatt. On 17 June 1874 Lord Penrhyn wrote to George William Duff Assheton Smith, who had come of age only five years earlier:

> I think you are quite right in getting rid of these Union men, so long as they continue under the dictation of others, because it seems to me that they are not only dictating to you, how you should work your own Quarry, but also who should be your Head Manager of it, and you may depend upon it, no man will be employed by me without a certificate of character from his last employer. How any of these quarrymen can be such fools as to place themselves under the dictations of those three men who are named as the principal officials of the Union I cannot understand[34].

On 18 June Assheton Smith informed his men that Dinorwic Quarry would be closed unless the Union was abandoned; and this threat was followed by a lock-out which lasted five weeks.

During this lock-out the quarrymen at Penrhyn collected £206 for the Dinorwic men; and Lord Penrhyn was alarmed by this evidence of their sympathy for an organisation which told owners and managers how to work their quarries. On 14 July 1874 he threatened to lock his men out if they maintained their support for the union; and they responded by establishing a union lodge with about 2,200 members. On 31 July they came out on strike; and some members of their Committee then had a meeting with Lord Penrhyn's estate agent, who in 1872 had changed his name from Pennant Iremonger to Pennant Lloyd. Pennant Lloyd arranged for the Committee to meet Lord Penrhyn; and this meeting took place on 21 August 1874. Lord Penrhyn told the men's representatives that he could not increase their wages because the quarry would not then pay its way; and he reminded them of the schools he provided and of the low rents he charged for their cottages. The men were in no mood for conciliation, however, and told Pennant Lloyd that they would give up these 'charities' for the sake of higher wages.

The fact that the industry was still prosperous at this date facilitated negotiations; and in September 1874 Lord Penrhyn and the Committee accepted what was later known as the Pennant Lloyd agreement. This provided that only the chief manager should have the power to take on and dismiss men; that all the men were to be re-admitted to the quarry; that complaints about letting were to be referred initially to a Committee appointed by the men, who would decide whether to put them before the chief manager; and that any quarryman who failed to earn 27s 6d a week for two consecutive months should be entitled to put his case to the Committee, and through them to the chief manager. This agreement gave the Committee considerable authority in dealing with the men's grievances.

In the meantime the lock-out at Dinorwic Quarry had come to an end, with Assheton Smith accepting the trade union on the understanding that it would not molest non-unionists or interfere with the rights of management[35]. The men who had returned to work at Penrhyn Quarry, however, claimed that the Pennant Lloyd agreement was not being honoured. The chief manager at this date was John Francis, son of the earlier manager who had invented a slate-dressing machine; his assistants were R. Morris and O. P. Jones. The workers put serious complaints against these men to Arthur Wyatt; and then, while Pennant Lloyd was on holiday, they came out on strike again. Lord Penrhyn's comments, made on 8 September in a letter to Barber, suggest that their complaints had some substance:

> There is no doubt that great roguery has been going on in regard to the sub-agents employing men on their terms etc but with the example set them, it was not to be wondered at – But in regard to John Francis it is difficult to blame him for not showing up his father[36].

Seeking financial support for the strikers, W. J. Parry claimed that 2,200 men had taken action after asking for an increase in wages, and that 300 old men had then been turned out of the quarry[37].

On 28 September 1874 Lord Penrhyn's son George, who had regained his seat as M.P. for Caernarfonshire earlier in the year, wrote to his father from Bournemouth. Having read in that day's newspaper that the men had broken off negotiations, he declared that he was 'shocked beyond all measure', and that his father had 'dealt all along too tenderly with them[38].' Lord Penrhyn agreed, but found it difficult to make a strong stand. On 20 October he told Pennant Lloyd that when the enquiry into the men's complaints had reported he would 'act, and give the option to all . . . to return to work'. He went on:

> The Committee is the obstacle to everything. They pretend that they are not urged on or influenced by Mr Morgan Richards and Mr W. J. Parry, but I see them myself going to Mr Morgan Richards' house every day, and I see him haranging them and Mr W. J. Parry comes down with them when they come down to the Port, although he does not come into the office and *all* their letters are in *his* handwriting. At the same time I have no doubt that *great abuses* have been going on[39].'

On 4 November 1874 the two arbitrators submitted their report, which endorsed all but one of the men's eighteen complaints. The unpopular managers resigned, and John Francis was succeeded as manager by J. J. Evans, who had previously been manager of Dorothea Quarry in Nantlle. The men returned to work, and the Committee increased its power over both men and management. Evans established good relations with both Wyatt and Parry, but the campaign against Lord Penrhyn continued. On 26 March 1876 Lord Penrhyn complained to Barber that *Yr Herald Cymraeg* had represented him as opposed to plans for a railway to Bethesda, when in fact he had given them 'every encouragement'. He also claimed that an Anglican clergyman had accused him of trying to extinguish the Welsh race, and had urged him to return to Scotland if he could not support the public campaign over a new title for the Prince of Wales. He was accused of bias, too, in his role as Lord Lieutenant with responsibility for appointing magistrates. On 29 January 1881 he told Barber that, although most Caernarfonshire landowners were Conservatives, he had appointed many Liberals to the Bench, and had made his recommendations 'on the footing of respectability and character and quite independent of party politics'[40].

The Pennant family was a close-knit one, and these attacks on Lord Penrhyn were keenly felt by his son George. In July 1893, seven years after Lord Penrhyn's death, the vicar of Llanuwchllyn wrote to the *North Wales Chronicle* proposing a subscription for a statue of him in Bangor. George, as a director of the newspaper, advised against the publication of this letter:

> I think one cannot do better than leave all the good works which he did during the fifty years of his life in Wales . . . to speak against those men who systematically reviled him for being what they called 'an alien' in blood, language and feeling[41].

2
A Golden Age: 1874–1888

Penrhyn quarrymen of a later period saw the years following 1874 as something of a golden age. During this period Arthur Wyatt acted as chief manager, with J. J. Evans as his assistant. W. J. Parry was secretary of the Benefit Club, and for part of the time president of the North Wales Quarrymen's Union. Most of the union's members were Welsh-speaking Nonconformists, and the political force behind it was the Liberal Party. In 1874 its 7,916 members represented more than half the workforce in the slate industry; whereas even in 1892 the total trade union membership in North Wales was only 8,820 or 1·96 per cent of the population, and the total trade union membership in England and Wales only 1,318,000 or 4·5 per cent of the population.

Legislation passed between 1868 and 1875 resulted in large-scale slum clearance and new housing schemes; and the consequent demand for slate contributed to the industry's prosperity in the late 70s and the early 80s, although competition from tiles and foreign slates had already begun. At Penrhyn Quarry the Pennant Lloyd agreement, which was regarded as the quarrymen's charter, enabled the Committee to play a large role in managerial decisions. In 1876 Parry was succeeded as secretary of the union by W. J. Williams, who was to remain in office until 1897. Parry served as president of the union from 1877 to 1879, and again from 1884 to 1889; and he was also a major force in local politics, although he did not achieve his ambition of becoming a Liberal M.P. His hostility to the Pennant family was muted during the last years of the first Lord Penrhyn's life; but it emerged again in 1886, when George Douglas Pennant dismissed Wyatt and revoked Parry's contracts for supplying the quarry with explosives[1].

George was born at Linton Spring in Yorkshire on 30 September 1836, and his mother Juliana recorded his birth in her diary:

> Linton Spring September 29. I began to feel unwell at about 2 o clock in the morning and at ½ past 6 on Friday morning the 30th my little boy was born and a very fine fat child different to little Emma who was at first most miserably thin, he was christened on Tuesday the 15th of November at Wetherby Church by Mr Jacob Marsham and called George Sholto Gordon – Papa and Lord Morton being his Godfathers and Lady Bridget Bonacre his Godmother – Vaccinated 1st on 17 December but it did not take but after another 18 January it took very well.

The bill for the first vaccination was 10s and the bill for 'Wallace the wet nurse' was 12s per week[2].

In 1842, when George was only six, his mother died in Pisa. Four years later his father married Lady Louisa Fitzroy, daughter of the fifth Duke of Grafton. There were celebrations at Port Penrhyn and at the village of Llandegai by the gates of Penrhyn Castle, and the employees of Penrhyn Quarry were given a brief holiday with pay. The second Lady Penrhyn lived until 1912, thus surviving both her husband and her stepson. George had a younger brother, Archibald Charles Henry, who died in September 1884; and he also had four sisters and five half-sisters. He was educated at Eton and at Christ Church College, Oxford; and in August 1856 he became a lieutenant in the Royal Carnarvon Rifles, later renamed the 4th Battalion Royal Welch Fusiliers, of which his father was Honorary Colonel. In December he resigned his commission, following his marriage to Pamela Blanche, daughter of Sir Charles Rushout Rushout.

A rare glimpse of George's personal feelings is offered by the ivory Book of Common Prayer which he gave his future wife on 23 August 1860. In this prayer book she recorded the births of their seven children:

> Kathleen born June 2 1861, Alice born June 23 1862, Pamela Georgina born May 28 1863, Edward Sholto born December 24 1865, Ina born Dec. 5 1867, Violet Blanche born Jan 31 1869.

Beneath these entries George wrote:

> On Feb 5th 1869 it pleased the Almighty to take away my own true darling wife. May God in his mercy help me in my misery. G. Douglas Pennant.

The prayer book was placed in a small box with an envelope containing a quantity of his wife's dark brown hair. The marker in the prayer book is at the ninth Sunday after Trinity: 'Grant us Lord we beseech thee, the spirit to think and do always such things as be rightful[3].' George married again in October 1875, his second wife being Gertrude Jessy, daughter of the Rev. Henry Glynne, rector of Hawarden near Chester. From this marriage there were two sons and six daughters; both sons were killed in the first World War.

As Lord Penrhyn, George was to have four residences in addition to Penrhyn Castle: Mortimer House, Halkin Street, S.W.; Wicken, Stoney Stratford, Buckinghamshire; Glan Conway, Bettws y Coed; and Cairnton, Banffshire. His main concerns were his estates and his quarry; but he took a keen interest in race-horses and horse-racing, and like other landowners enjoyed hunting, shooting and fishing. The records show that he was a devoted son, father and grandfather; and the letters he preserved include those which his son Edward wrote to him from Eton. One of these is headed simply '1878':

> Thanks very much for your letter. I shall know if I am in 5th form on Tuesday or Wednesday. I have gone into Tails as I am quite big enough . . . I have been skating, but the ice is nearly all gone . . . Can you please send me some money to pay for a football and one or two other things. How did the park shooting come off; were there many birds. What a pity poor old Plaid will not be able to do any more work.
>
> I hope I have got through Trials.
>
> Love to Mamma and all the others. Goodbye from your affectionately, Edward Pennant.

In February 1881, having learned from his sister of an addition to his stepmother's family, Edward wrote to his father as follows:

> I heard this morning from Alice that there is another Baby; I hope Mamma is going on all right. Do you mind Frank and I bringing home two young beagles for drag hunts etc. We will pay all expenses and promise to keep them away from foxes and covers[4].

George Douglas Pennant believed that the years from 1874 to 1886 were years of serious mismanagement at Penrhyn Quarry; and he attributed this management to the undue influence exercised by the trade unionists through their Committee. Figures for union membership suggest, at any rate, that the union's power reached its height during this period. The North Wales Quarrymen's Union had 2,808 members at Penrhyn in 1876, 2,956 in 1877, 3,043 in 1878, and 2,956 in 1879; but membership declined steadily in the 1880s, reaching 1,288 in 1885 and 292 in 1889. A revival in the 1890s produced figures of 2,522 in 1896 and 2,600 in 1897; but in the years 1900–1903 membership was falling again[5].

Some impression of conditions at Penrhyn Quarry between 1874 and 1886 can be gathered from the evidence presented during a bitterly-contested libel case in 1903. The Rev Thomas Parry, a curate at Llanddyfnan in Anglesey who was a quarryman from 1859 to 1889, said that a small body of about a hundred non-unionists, who did not come out on strike in 1874, formed the nucleus for a growing body of non-unionists in the 1880s. He claimed that Arthur Wyatt as chief manager and J. J. Evans as local manager favoured the unionists, not because they liked all that the unionists did but because they were afraid of the unionists' powerful Committee. Non-unionists could not represent their grievances to the management, because only complaints made by the Committee were taken seriously. Unionists were given the best bargains and openings, and were punished less severely for lateness. A unionist who was often absent 'owing to his drunken habits after pay day' was never punished, whereas a non-unionist who behaved similarly would have been dismissed. W. J. Parry 'carried on business largely as a money lender amongst the Quarrymen, which increased his hold and influence over them very much'; and he was also 'on very friendly terms with Mr Wyatt and Mr J. J. Evans', so that 'to make an enemy of Parry by anybody employed in the Quarry was a very dangerous thing to do'. Another witness, Ellen Williams of Llandegai, recalled an occasion in 1883 when her husband had been dismissed because of a misunderstanding with an official after he and others had received permission to go fishing on Lake Ogwen. When he put his case to the Committee, one of its members said to him, 'Well John we could come through your case like through butter but we won't do it because you refuse to pay the union.' Three weeks later, however, he had 'his work and bargain back from Mr Wyatt'[6].

Despite the buoyancy of the home market, the slate industry experienced some economic difficulties between 1876 and 1880 because of a decline in exports. This was attributed to a contraction in the German market, and to a stoppage in the Australian market from 1879 to 1880 during a financial crisis. Between November 1878 and November 1879 Dinorwic Quarry dismissed hundreds of workers and reduced wages by 20 per cent. The North Wales Quarrymen's Union encouraged emigration to the U.S.A. by lending members £3 for their first year's membership and £1 for every additional year; and in 1879 155 quarrymen emigrated at a cost to the union of £1,232[7].

The Penrhyn Quarry Committee, which was officially known as Lodge No 2 of the union, resolved on 2 December 1874 that no complaint should be received 'except from one who was a member of the Union.' They also decided to 'exhort regular and unfailing payment of the Union' and to 'obtain for the next Committee meeting the names of those who refused to pay'; the representative entrusted with this last task was urged to 'adopt the most secret method of doing so[8].' Despite the emphasis on secrecy, the Minute Book containing these resolutions came into the possession of Lord Penrhyn's solicitors, who had it translated into English for their client's benefit.

In 1880 a barrister named C. J. Watkin Williams stood as Liberal candidate for Caernarfonshire and defeated George Douglas Pennant by 3,303 votes to 2,206. The 1880 election, which almost extinguished the Tory party in Wales, was seen as the 'real turning point of landlord influence[9]', and the 1884 Reform Act enfranchised many agricultural workers and divided Caernarfonshire into the constituencies of Arfon in the north and Eifion in the south. In 1885 George Douglas Pennant took over the quarry; and on 31 March 1886 his father died at Penrhyn Castle.

The new Lord Penrhyn received letters of condolence from many sources. J. de Winton of Caernarfon paid tribute to his 'kind, good and noble hearted father', and Colonel Henry Platt regretted the loss of a 'true friend'. The Secretary of the Penmachno Constitutional Association spoke of the 'great interest his late Lordship took in the religious, charitable and educational objects in our parish'; and the Mayor of Caernarfon recalled how he had always been 'foremost in every good or charitable cause' connected with the town. The Royal Welsh Yacht Club, of which he had been Commodore, ordered 'that the flag be kept at half mast until after the funeral'. George's sister, Lady Caroline Hogg, referred to the problems facing the heir:

> I feel so much for you in all your heavy responsibilities. They must feel a *terrible* burden at first . . . I can hardly as yet realise Penrhyn without him.

On 14 September W. J. Parry wrote to 'Dowager Lady Penrhyn, Lord Penrhyn and all the family' on behalf of the General Committee of the Penrhyn Quarry Benefit Club. His letter spoke of the quarrymen's 'great and sincere sorrow' on the death of a 'considerate, benevolent, kindhearted and sympathetic Master . . . who always studied their wants, and never spared himself to make them happy in their work and in their homes[10]'. The dead man would no doubt have found it all 'rather amusing'.

The business which George Douglas Pennant took over in 1885 was unhealthy in both economic and organisational terms. On 1 December 1883 J. J. Evans had told Wyatt that Penrhyn Quarry paid 'higher wages than any other quarry in the County[11]'; but trade was declining, and it was difficult to establish the truth when complaints were made about setting. On 28 April

1885, when the new owner was beginning his investigation of the business, Wyatt indicated where he should place the blame:

> The worst part of it is the Union Committee has endeavoured to interfere with the bargain setting, which virtually means managing the quarry.

The facts which emerged from the investigation, however, prompted a search for someone other than Evans to take over Wyatt's job.

Of the eleven candidates for the post of chief manager, the strongest was J. S. Hughes, who was forty years old and a member of the Church of England. He claimed to be 'thoroughly acquainted with the Welsh language'; and his referee, R. M. Wynne, said that he was not only 'a good churchman and a staunch Conservative' but also a 'very clever civil engineer' with a sound knowledge of quarrying. He had been a partner for thirteen years with C. E. Spooner, and had prepared surveys and plans for the narrow-gauge line from the quarry to Port Penrhyn. Another applicant was J. Ernest A. Wyatt, a relative of the dismissed manager, who wanted his family's 'long connection' with the quarry ('I believe 102 years') to be taken into account. A third, W. A. Darbishire of Nantlle, could speak 'Welsh quarry language' a little, and saw the present state of Penrhyn Quarry as a 'magnificent opportunity'; but his belief that the men should be given 'participation in the profit' may not have recommended him. In the event the post was offered not to any of those who had applied but to E. A. Young, a Londoner of twenty-six with no experience of the slate industry[12].

Emilius Augustus Young (1860–1910) had few of the qualifications claimed by Hughes; but as a chartered accountant he had been instrumental in exposing the malaise which afflicted the quarry under Wyatt's management. He was the eldest son of Alexander Young of the firm of Turquand, Young and Co, which was given the task of auditing Wyatt's accounts for 1883–4; and their report of 31 January 1886 revealed gross inefficiency and financial mismanagement. Wyatt had prepared no balance sheet for several years, and 'his Account of Expenditure and Income arising from the Quarry, Mill and Port was incorrectly framed'. By valuing his stocks at their full selling price without allowance for transport, discount or breakages, he had overstated the value of quarry stocks at 1 January 1884 by 'about £10,953'. He had given excessive discount on slates, and had overpaid income tax by 'about £37,296'. The total profit for the year was only £16,873; and when the profit from the mill was deducted, that from the quarry and the port was shown to be only £7,449. On the basis of this report 'the Hon G. D. Pennant intimated his decision to terminate Mr Wyatt's Agency[13]'; but no publicity was given to that decision, and it was generally understood that Wyatt had resigned. A 'generous' pension was paid to him; and in 1887, when Young reported that he had died 'from Heart Disease aggravated by Dropsy', this pension was transferred to his widow[14].

Young's duties as Wyatt's successor were defined in an agreement dated 24 February 1886. He was to carry on the agency business at Port Penrhyn, receive remittances for slates, and 'proceed every four weeks to the Quarries' to superintend the payment of wages. On 9 March he told his employer that he feared 'a deal of mischief' was being done at the quarry, and a letter of 14 May shows that he had not finally decided to accept the post:

> I fully appreciate your speaking first to my father with reference to your Lordship's offer to confirm my appointment here and hope I may take time to consider such an important step with him[15].

Young knew that he was taking on a difficult role; and the spirit in which he approached it may be judged from his later comment, 'Our family motto "Press Through" is my watchword[16].' As an outsider who spoke no Welsh and knew little about the technical processes of quarrying, he brought the skills acquired in a London accountancy practice to the task of re-organising a run-down business. He was eminently successful as Lord Penrhyn's investment manager; and he formed a close relationship with his employer, often directing his policy but always deferring to his judgment. On 1 November 1887, writing to Lord

Penrhyn about his impending marriage, he proposed a change in the name of the manager's official residence:

> I shall feel extremely obliged by your favourably considering my request that Tanybryn may in future be called Glenrosa. I may add that I am joined by another in this desire, whom I hope to bring to Bangor to brighten my home, in the early part of next year.

Lord Penrhyn's defence of the Welsh name has not survived, but its cogency was immediately recognised. On 25 November Young replied that 'with regard to the name of the house' he had 'no wish to press any further for its alteration'; and he assured Lord Penrhyn that he would always take pleasure in showing his 'esteem and affection' for the Pennant family[17].

It was already clear in 1885 that the labour force at Penrhyn Quarry would have to be cut; and it was equally clear that the people of Bethesda were no longer as servile as W. J. Parry had considered them in 1868[18]. The radicalism of the Welsh Liberal Party was now a force to be reckoned with, and in 1884 650 quarrymen had joined the Liberal Association of Bethesda[19]. A factor which stimulated the new militancy was the introduction of stricter rules in the quarry. This was part of a general pattern in British industrial relations at this time, when employers were reacting to low prices and increased competition[20]; but in Bethesda it came to be seen as the inhuman action of a tyrannical aristocrat and his English henchman. While the management sought to increase efficiency in the face of economic difficulties, the men's leaders were resolved to end the old quasi-feudal relationship between the quarry-owner and his employees.

On 27 April 1885, when dismissals and reductions in wages were being contemplated, the Penrhyn estate agent Colonel W. E. Sackville West wrote to George Douglas Pennant about the anxieties felt by some of the quarrymen:

> There is considerable alarm among the non-union portion of the Quarry as to the mode of discharging the 100 men. It will be fatal to leave any power of selection in Mr Evans' hands.
>
> A strict rule should be observed as to those last taken on and then

nothing can be said against it.

Your instructions were only delivered yesterday, and in consequence have been misrepresented or misunderstood in transmission to the men.

Would it not be better to give them in writing? W. J. Parry is urging the men to ask for short time but they won't strike.

Pray stick to the mode of discharging or the Union will make the Non-Unionists feel it[21].

On 4 May 1885, as a consequence of Sackville West's letter, a notice signed by George Douglas Pennant was posted in Penrhyn Quarry. This notice marked the beginning of a new era in the quarry's history.

The earlier part of the notice was concerned with the procedures for setting bargains and calculating wages:

> The basis for setting the bargains at the Penrhyn Quarry will be more in accordance with the rate of wages paid at the other quarries in the county.
>
> All settings to be re-set at the beginning of every quarry month, unless a contract has been entered into for a longer period.
>
> Wages to be calculated on actual days.
>
> Termination at the end of the present quarry month of what was called 'Mr Pennant Lloyd's agreement'.

Having thus curtly repudiated an agreement which had been in operation for eleven years, Douglas Pennant went on to lay down new procedures for his dealings with the workforce:

> I decline altogether to sanction the interference of anybody (corporate or individual) between employer and employed in the working of the Quarry, and in order to ensure fairness for all parties, no deputation or memorial professing to speak for the general body of quarrymen will be received or considered, unless it equitably represents the views of both non-Union as well as Union men; but in the event of questions arising which may lead to discussion between employer and employed, I should always be ready to treat with a deputation composed of quarrymen, equally in number representing the non-Union as well as the Union Men.

Having acknowledged the 'good feeling' which had so far characterised the men's 'receipt of the news of the proposed alteration in wages', the notice ended by expressing the belief that the new arrangements would place their interests 'upon a sounder footing than of late'[22].

The immediate response to this forthright proclamation was a letter dated 11 May 1885. Its origins are obscure, but it was signed by three unionists named Richard Evan Jones, John Williams and Griffith Edwards and three non-unionists named David Thomas, William Roberts and Richard Owen Jones. In asking for an interview with George Douglas Pennant, they referred ominously to the popularity of his father:

> Your right honourable father made himself endeared by all his workmen beyond any other master in North Wales, and his name will be handed down by us to our children.

They attributed Lord Penrhyn's popularity to the fact that he made direct contact with his workmen and did not rely on 'self seeking or ambitious persons' who had 'no sympathy whatever with the working classes'. They appealed for the restoration of the Pennant Lloyd agreement, declaring this to be the wish of both unionists and non-unionists; and they assured their employer that 'those who were not Unionists never had any cause for complaint about the presentation of grievances'.

Giving evidence in the 1903 libel case, the Rev Thomas Parry said that this letter had been 'concocted' by the Committee and was generally attributed to W. J. Parry. His statement that the non-unionists did not know what they were signing is partly confirmed by the evidence given in the same libel case by Richard Owen Jones. Jones said that he joined the union in 1874 but had left when it became a 'political body'. Like Thomas Parry he gave an unfavourable account of the Committee's role in the quarry's affairs:

> The Quarry Committee refused to take up any complaint except from Members of the Union . . . The only remedy of the Non-Unionist was to rely on the mercy of the Setter . . . I personally believe that the Stewards were afraid of doing anything against the Committee, and by that way the management came very much into the hands of the Committee.

Jones admitted that he had signed the letter, but explained that he knew little English and that the text had not been translated to him. Both he and David Thomas had later repudiated the document; and although William Roberts had stood firm, Thomas Parry alleged that this was because his real sympathies were with the union.

1,842 unionists gave their signatures at the quarry to a petition stating that the letter of 11 May expressed all the men's views. 683 non-unionists signed a petition repudiating the letter; but they signed this at the National School, 'because they dared not do it in the Quarry'. The letter was answered on 20 May by George Douglas Pennant, who declared that the Pennant Lloyd agreement had created a 'disastrous state of affairs' and would 'under no circumstances' be restored. He argued that a guaranteed minimum wage would put a premium on idleness, and re-iterated that any deputation professing to speak for the whole workforce must represent non-union as well as union views. He also accused the authors of the letter of misrepresenting the agreement which they were defending. He pointed out that Rule 7 of that agreement referred not only to the Benefit Club but also to the appointment of a Quarry Committee; and he said that Rule 18 defined the procedures on minimum wages more precisely than they suggested.

According to W. J. Parry the three unionists who had signed the letter were dismissed in May 1885, and although re-instated in June 1886 continued to be regarded as marked men. David Prichard, who was sub-manager at the time, denied in his evidence during the libel case that they had ever been dismissed at all. He claimed that one had worked at the quarry until the dispute of 1900–1903 and another until his death, and that the third had left the quarry about 1890 of his own accord[23]. It is not clear what procedure Wyatt followed in choosing the hundred men who were dismissed in June 1885; but his dismissal of ten Churchmen and ninety Nonconformists suggests that he did not 'leave any power of selection in Mr Evans' hands'.

Around 1885–6 industrial relations were even worse at Dinorwic than at Penrhyn. In 1881 Assheton Smith had forced his employees to contract out of the 1880 Employer's Liability Act; and although this decision was revoked in 1885, it was still resented. The Dinorwic men had suffered reductions in numbers and cuts in wages; and they had no confidence in their chief manager the Hon. Walter W. Vivian or in their manager John Davies. On 12 October 1885 they held a mass meeting during working hours; and as a consequence of this they were locked out from 31 October 1885 to 1 March 1886. On 15 December 1885 Colonel Sackville West wrote to George Douglas Pennant about the Dinorwic lockout:

> I do hope Assheton Smith will hold out. It is now purely a question whether the owner or the men are to choose their managers and if there is a weakness shown at Llanberis, the consequences to the Penrhyn Quarry may be disastrous. On the other hand if he holds out, the opportunity is a great one for putting both quarries on a proper footing.

The terms for a settlement were negotiated by John Robinson, the owner of Talysarn Quarry in Nantlle. As part of the settlement an undertaking was given that men's religious and political principles would not influence decisions about employment; and the management also promised that no-one would be denied employment because he was a member of the Quarry Committee[24]. In fact, some of the men's leaders were victimised; but labour relations at Dinorwic became in general less acrimonious. Vivian, who had attributed the dispute to interference by 'Agitators, Government Officials and the Press', declared after the settlement that 'right and justice' had triumphed[25].

Wyatt's contracts as shipping agent and quarry manager were terminated on 2 February 1886 and his salary ceased to be paid on 1 July[26]. On 25 February 1886 Young wrote to Douglas Pennant from his temporary home at 15 Menai View in Upper Bangor, reporting 'serious revelations' about overpayments at the quarry. He also asked his employer to obtain a copy of the Dinorwic rules, since he could find no 'trace of any rules' at Penrhyn. When he received the rules from Llanberis, he was prompted to insist that all Penrhyn workmen should leave at closing time so as to prevent 'any tampering with the slates'. Informing Douglas Pennant of this decision, he commented:

> At the Port I have made myself popular but I am told that it is not the same at the Quarry which I can easily understand[27].

In June 1886 Young had a brief meeting with John Menzies, the owner of Alexandra Quarry in Nantlle, who was also chairman of the employers' association. It says something about conditions in the industry at this date that they discussed the relative advantages of dismissals and short-time working.

Also in June 1886 Young had a visit from W. J. Parry, who was seeking orders for oils and explosives. Young told him that his prices for these items were too high, and that 'the Oil he had been supplying was complained of'; and when Parry said he 'was not up in the qualities of Oils', Young concluded that he did not 'attend much to his Business'. A statement of prices dated 17 December 1886 shows that Parry charged 4s 2½d per gallon for machine oil, whereas Young could get superior oil at 3s 3d; that Parry charged 2s per gallon for naphtha, whereas Young could get equally good naphtha for 11d; and that Parry charged £35 per ton for powder, whereas Young could get it for £34 per ton and Vivian got it direct from the makers for £28[28]. Parry responded to this evidence by reducing his price for powder from £35 to £34, and Young 'acknowledged the reduction with thanks'; but in due course all Parry's contracts with the quarry were terminated.

In September 1886 Young suggested to Lord Penrhyn that he should pay a third of the cost of a trip to London for the quarrymen and their families. This excursion took place on 15 October, with a special ticket costing 7s 6d instead of 18s; and Young reported that the men had appreciated the gesture, and that their orderly behaviour had been praised by officials at Euston. Discussions between Penrhyn and Dinorwic in November 1886 produced agreement on prices, but trade remained slack. Young recommended that 200 to 300 men should be dismissed, and that the others should be placed on a five-day week; and this action was taken in February 1887, the men dismissed being those most recently recruited.

In May 1887 there was some correspondence about the allocation of seats on the workmen's train between Port Penrhyn and the quarry. An extension of the line had brought requests for seats from residents of Craig y Pandy, Waen y Pandy and Sling; and on 24 May Young wrote to Lord Penrhyn offering to ensure that the available seats were 'allocated fairly'. In order to protect J. J. Evans from charges of favouritism, Young asked him for a list of men over 55 in the relevant districts; and he devised a procedure which involved a 'ballot' for 24 seats, or for a smaller number if there were 'any cripples' who deserved prior attention[29]. Young was suffering at this time from 'anxiety' and from too many journeys in search of orders, and he asked for a few days' holiday combined with business. He reported that he had allowed the port and the quarry to be closed for Ascension Day; but he expressed the hope that this would not happen again, since it was 'not done elsewhere' and had proved 'extremely inconvenient[30]. Many of the men, however, believed that Ascension Day was unlucky and that accidents would occur if the traditional holiday was not observed.

Thomas Parry maintained that labour conditions at Penrhyn Quarry were 'very good' under Young's management[31]; and in June 1887 Young himself wrote that a 4 per cent reduction in wages had not been 'attended with any difficulty whatever' since the wages remained above 'the standard[32]'. On 2 November 1887, however, *Y Faner* reported the resignation of J. J. Evans. The newspaper interpreted this as a triumph for the 'Plaid Fain', the minority or Conservative party; and it argued that such a triumph meant 'the Destruction of the District of Bethesda'. According to *Y Faner*, Evans was 'not Tory and Churchman' enough to satisfy those who had 'determined to do their part in trying to "boycott" and root up Nonconformity and Liberalism out of the district'. In December 1887 W. J. Parry resigned as Secretary of the Benefit Club; and his place was taken by E. A. Young.

One of Young's most unpopular actions in this period was his withdrawal in 1888 of the holiday known as the *trannoeth*. The men had traditionally enjoyed two holidays in each four-week period, the day the old bargains were given up and the day the new bargains were set. Thomas Parry argued that it was not unreasonable to replace this arrangement with a single holiday on Quarry Pay Saturday; but even he acknowledged that the men resented the manner in which the change was made[33]. On 18 January 1886 *Y Faner* had spoken of the *trannoeth* as a monthly holiday which the quarrymen had enjoyed 'from time immemorial'. The 'young man from London' was attacking a long-established tradition of the quarry community; and it is hardly surprising that he was made to feel he was 'not at home at Port Penrhyn'.

The Local Government Act of 1888 reduced the power of the land-owning class by transferring most non-judicial functions from the Justices of the Peace to elected County Councils. In January 1889, however, Lord Penrhyn became a member for the Llandegai district on Caernarfonshire County Council; and despite Liberal successes in other districts Llandegai re-elected him unopposed at regular intervals thereafter. He continued to play an active and controversial role in local government affairs until his death in 1907.

3
The New Management: 1888–1896

On 12 June 1888 Young wrote to Lord Penrhyn about the admission of boys to the quarry. He said that he had taken in about 50 orphan boys, but that he had applications from another 300 boys and could with advantage take in 200 of them. He asked for guidance:

> For instance am I to take into consideration at all 'Church and Politics' or shall I do my best to ascertain the most deserving cases . . . If I were to take in those who are in families of 6 and upwards . . . that would admit 40. Again am I to limit the admission to boys not over 16?

Young had presumably received answers to these questions by 18 June, when he wrote:

> As to the boys – they should all be under 17 (if not 16) and must have fathers in the quarry.

At the same time Young was trying to establish order in the Quarry Hospital. On 13 December, having attended a 'troublesome' Hospital Committee meeting at the quarry, he wrote:

> Their last move is to elect WJP as Auditor and that must not be allowed. The Matron must also be got rid of – she really is most objectionable.

The matron having gone, Young inspected the Hospital on the morning of Sunday 3 February 1889, 'whilst the quarrymen were all in Chapel etc.':

> The general condition of nearly everything was filthy. One room at least had not been scoured for nine months . . . Under one bed the dust was thick and looked ancient.

Young hoped to engage a Mr and Mrs Jones, who had promised not to allow either 'Church or Politics' to be introduced into the Hospital.

On 9 February 1890 Young reported to Lord Penrhyn about divisions among the unionists. He claimed that the 'old union' was not prospering, and that most of the men were subscribing to a 'new one' confined to Penrhyn Quarry. The new union had been set up to provide support for the Committee while they were negotiating on behalf of the men, but Young said that they were trying to 'buy' the assistance of the big unions and of the labour leader John Burns (1858–1943). Young expected the Committee to demand a return to full-time working and an increase from 24s to 27s 6d a week. He said that he could not increase wages. On 22 March 1890 there were rumours of a strike; but the men were dissuaded by the level of quarry stocks and the opposition of local tradesmen.

In 1890 the death of the Conservative M.P. Edmund Swetenham caused a by-election in the Caernarfon Boroughs constituency, which comprised the boroughs of Bangor, Caernarfon, Conwy, Criccieth, Nefin and Pwllheli. There was a stiff contest between the young David Lloyd George and a popular local landowner named H. J. Ellis-Nanney. Young, who had little interest in politics, expressed the hope that this election 'would pass off happily without that bitter spirit exhibited in the past', since a poll which was not 'carefully conducted' might 'increase the agitation in the Quarry[1].' On 11 April Lloyd George was returned, rather to his surprise, with a majority of eighteen votes.

An attempt was made within the N.W.Q.U. to reconcile the demands of unity with those of local independence. A minute-book of the Bethesda Lodge reports the men's commitment to a strong union for all North Wales[2]. On 19 February 1890 *Y Genedl Gymreig* reported that full-time working would be resumed on 27 March, and commented ironically:

> Thanks for the news, it will be an acquisition for the poor men who are almost half-starved . . . wages have come down, down for at least ten years.

In the following month Assheton Smith and Lord Penrhyn each bought £2,500 worth of shares in the *North Wales Chronicle*. It was hoped that the quarry-owners would gain inside information from reporters who attended quarrymen's meetings, and that the owners' views would be sympathetically treated in a paper whose directors included Lord Penrhyn, Lord Boston of Anglesey and Sir R. Williams-Bulkeley. These hopes were only partially realised, because the editor until 1904 was an ineffective man named D. Williams, who was often in financial difficulties. The *North Wales Chronicle* could not match the polemical eloquence of the Welsh press, as represented by an attack on Lord Penrhyn printed in *Y Werin* on 14 December 1889:

> Lord Penrhyn said at the time of his father's death that he was standing in his father's shoes, but the shoes of his generous and respected old father are too big for him . . . Ever since he came to possession and authority he has confined the liberties of the people; every ordinance of his is a turn of the screw, until his workmen are groaning for want of bread for their children. He has screwed them to such poverty and captivity during the last two years that its like has not happened during the life of any living men. The boy King has become a despot, and a terrible despot he is.

In April 1890 Young warned Lord Penrhyn that the 'Strike agitators' were increasingly active:

> In the town the old political tactics are going on, and I got very rough handling verbally, but having only done my duty it cannot be avoided – there is very little principle in politics here!

Reporting his meeting at the Trosyffordd office on 18 April with a six-man deputation, Young said he had rejected their request for an increase in wages because prices were lower than for many years and because wages at Penrhyn were 'very considerably above the standard'. He also explained that from 1 May quarrymen would be free 'as formerly' to choose partners to fill any vacancies other than 'those created by any dismissal or transfer of a partner from one bargain to another'. He could not allow all the bargains to be filled; but the *trannoeth* was to be suspended 'for the present', and work was to be allowed on Pay

Saturday. Until 1899, according to the local manager David Davies, the men continued to enjoy Bangor Fair holidays on 5 April, 25 June, 16 September and 24 October. In 1890, however, the 16 September holiday was cancelled when the quarry was being visited by a party including the Queen of Romania; and although the men were given holidays on two later days this break with tradition was resented.

In March 1891 Young told Lord Penrhyn that his readiness for a strike could not be maintained indefinitely because the merchants suspected him of using the strike threat to overload them with slates:

> I have done all I can think of to be thoroughly prepared for a Strike and it seems to me after anxious consideration that unless some steps are taken to show the men that we do not care for their union and thus morally induce the men to withdraw from it, we shall be compelled to be always in the same state of preparedness every spring.

Young therefore proposed to abolish work on Pay Saturday, to pay only badrockmen's wages to those for whom no bargains were available, and to keep poundages low. The first two proposals had already been adopted at Dinorwic, and the third was judged necessary because poundages had been rising. Young saw possible advantages even in the hostility which this policy would arouse:

> If it forced a trial of strength between Employer and men would not now be a better time for both? Short and decisive and with far less misery to the neighbourhood.

Young stressed the need for new investment in the quarry, where two new inclines and 'some miles of rails' were needed:

> All the locomotive engines but one require expensive overhauling – and worse of all many of the best bargains at the bottom of the quarry have got so inferior, that high poundages are given where it used to be *minus*.

In addition, the tall pillar of granite known as Talcen Mawr was becoming so dangerous that the local manager wanted to have it demolished[3].

The Welsh press continued its campaign against Lord Penrhyn, often alluding to his ownership of racehorses. On 13 May 1891 *Y Faner* contrasted the Welsh quarryman, who was 'a hot Dissenter, a severe moralist, a Radical and more often than otherwise a little republican', with Lord Penrhyn, who was 'a Tory, one of the Primrose Lords, a Churchman' and 'a great huntsman'. Lord Penrhyn, the paper concluded, was everything 'John Jones the quarryman' was not; and it took 'ten John Joneses . . . to support one racehorse.' On 3 June 1891 a Caernarfon solicitor named George Owen informed Lord Penrhyn that *Yr Herald Cymraeg* and the *Carnarvon and Denbigh Herald*, which had not printed 'vile abuse to the extent of the other Welsh Radical papers', had now decided 'to go in for it as much as possible'. According to Owen, Welsh Radical M.P.s like Samual Evans, T. E. Ellis and David Lloyd George intended to use against Lord Penrhyn 'the whole of their powers of invention and exaggeration[4]'. In the 1892 Lloyd George was in fact to be concerned in the formation of the Welsh National Press Company, which took over *Y Werin*, *Y Genedl Gymreig*, the *Observer* and the *North Wales Express;* the Company's directors were to include W. J. Parry, who had been editor of *Y Genedl Gymreig* since 1888[5].

The quarrymen's Committee had an unsuccessful meeting with Young on 1 August 1891, and on 20 August Lord Penrhyn met a deputation of eight men: the Committee's president Robert Davies, its secretary John Moses Jones, William H. Williams, W. Williams, H. H. Davies, John Williams, William Thomas and Lewis Jones. Lord Penrhyn challenged John Moses Jones on his statement, widely reported in the press, that he had not earned a pound the previous month. Jones admitted that he had been talking in a 'general way', since the 'month' in question had been only twelve days; and Lord Penrhyn commented:

> Well, a general way of talking must be put a stop to . . . people get the idea that I am a very bad master and now I must put a stop to that sort of thing[6].

In 1891 a Royal Commission on Labour was set up to enquire into the relations between employers and workmen. Young was called to give evidence, and confessed to Lord Penrhyn that it was 'a decided ordeal to look forward to', although he knew he must 'dumbfound the enemies of truth'. In his evidence he said that quarrying was as healthy as any outdoor work, and that he did not believe it to be excessively hard. A different impression was given by W. J. Williams, the secretary of the N.W.Q.U. In his evidence Williams referred to the coldness and danger of the work, and to the fact that those inside the sheds inhaled dust. He also mentioned the lack of an apprentice system, and the lack of proper supervision in open quarries[7]. On 10 February 1892 *Y Faner* renewed its attack on the quarry managers, describing them as 'strangers' who had 'no practical knowledge' of quarrying and made no attempt to learn Welsh. There was some justice in these charges; but many officials of the N.W.Q.U. also lacked practical knowledge, and the union was often more interested in attacking the Conservative and Anglican landowners than in improving the quarrymen's wages and conditions[8].

The celebration of Gŵyl Lafur or Labour Day was initiated in 1892, and the Conservative M.P. Sir John Gorst (1835–1916) agreed to speak at the first Labour Day meeting in Caernarfon. In a letter to Sir John Puleston (1829–1908), who had been nominated as Conservative candidate against Lloyd George, Young complained that Gorst's presence would give the union a 'fresh fillip' when it was 'practically discredited among the men'. Young would have attached 'no importance whatever' to an address by William Abraham (1842–1922), the Labour M.P. for Rhondda who was commonly known as Mabon, or to a speech by W. J. Parry 'or any other demagogue'; but though Gorst was strongly opposed to strikes Young felt that his visit, which Puleston had encouraged, would enable Mabon and Parry to 'throw a garb of respectibility over the Quarrymen's Union[9]'. By 1892 Young had terminated all Parry's contracts with Penrhyn Quarry, and was buying explosive powder at lower rates from a Mr Newton of Caernarfon[10].

The Liberals won the 1892 election; and Lloyd George, after what Puleston called 'desperate efforts', was returned for Caernarfon Boroughs by 196 votes.

On 17 May 1893 a strike began at Llechwedd Quarry in Blaenau Ffestiniog because of anger at the harshness of the rules and punishments. The tougher industrial discipline characteristic of this period was particularly resented in Blaenau Ffestiniog, which was Radical by tradition and had welcomed the Irish land reformer Michael Davitt in February 1886. Lord Penrhyn and others claimed that Davitt had on that occasion revealed a socialist plot to nationalise Penrhyn Quarry. In a letter from Dublin reported by the *Cambrian News* on 17 April 1903, Davitt dismissed this plot as a fantasy; but Lord Penrhyn's right to the ownership of the quarry was often challenged, especially by Lloyd George. Blaenau Ffestiniog was known as the 'city of slates', and its several quarries included the Oakeley Quarry, which employed about 1,600 men. Blaenau Ffestiniog quarrymen thus had much better opportunities than Bethesda or Llanberis quarrymen for finding work nearby during strikes and lockouts. The Greaves brothers who owned Llechwedd agreed to take the men back individually on 4 July 1893; but as they refused work to some of the leaders, the strike was renewed. With only 500 workers to support, the N.W.Q.U wanted to fight on the issue of harsh rules; but the Llechwedd men could not face a long strike, and in September 1893 they returned to work without their leaders[11].

Conflict at Penrhyn over the Labour Day holiday was averted in 1893 when Young agreed to close the quarry, the mill and the port. On 24 May Robert Davies and Owen Owens asked Lord Penrhyn to receive a deputation over their demand for a 'Standard' of 5s. Young told Lord Penrhyn that they did not 'in the least understand their own demand'; but he arranged for eight men to see Lord Penrhyn on 7 June. He explained to Lord Penrhyn that such deputations had for some years consisted 'exclusively of unionists', and that it would therefore be 'useless' to refuse this deputation a hearing:

By meeting the Deputation we do not in any way recognise the

> union and if any *non*-union men apply to be heard by your Lordship, you would see them at once, therefore they can feel no grievance – they have never expressed one.
>
> I fully admit that it is the self-seeking agitators who wish to air themselves by frequently asking for interviews, but the several rebuffs they have recently met with cannot have improved their position but rather the contrary.

The meeting proved yet another rebuff for the men.

That slate quarrying was a dangerous occupation could never be forgotten for long. On 29th September 1893 Young wrote to Lord Penrhyn:

> Yet another fatal accident – the poor fellow died at 3 a.m. this morning – I was with him a while yesterday afternoon and he recognised me but was sinking then.
>
> He was more or less buried by loose earth and rubbish and crushed very badly, but worst of all I think his spine must have been broken. Three doctors attended him but could do nothing.

T. H. Owen, the head clerk at the Pay Office, had been concerned in 1885 with the publication of *Y Faner*, and his journalistic activities may perhaps have affected his work. On 26 November 1893 Young told Lord Penrhyn that he no longer had any confidence in Owen, since he was 'constantly away from his post at all hours of the day'. Young decided to give him three months' notice, but on 9 December 1893 Owen resigned on grounds of ill-health[12]. On 12 January 1895 Owen asked Lord Penrhyn for 'a small pension', declaring that his 'faithful and blameless service of 25 years' had been ended by Young's 'unfair, unjust and cruel' treatment, which had destroyed his 'house and happiness' and 'contributed very materially' to his poor state of health. Owen received no pension, but Lord Penrhyn sent him £200 as compensation[13].

A ballot early in 1894 showed Penrhyn quarrymen supporting the union by 800 votes to 180, with the majority abstaining[14]. Later in the year the Prince and Princess of Wales visited Penrhyn Castle, and arrangements were made for them to watch the demolition of Talcen Mawr. In May Young supervised repairs to the roof and windows of Ogwen Bank, a house near the quarry which was used for shooting-parties, and saw to the refurbishing of a saloon carriage on the train by which the visitors were to travel. He was also involved in preparations for a concert by the Penrhyn Choir; and he suggested that policemen should be engaged to guard the quay, and that 'responsible and strong quarrymen' should be employed to keep order and protect the royal party from the crowds. On 17 June he commented on the plans being made in Bangor:

> The town people seem to be making a hash over the Bonfire and fireworks display and therefore I contemplate taking charge of the fireworks entirely and sending them from the Quay at about £100 cost . . . It will all reflect credit (at least I hope so) upon *Penrhyn* as I mean it to be such a display as was never seen in Bangor before.

After the visit Sir Francis Knollys wrote to Lord Penrhyn on behalf of the Prince and Princess of Wales to express their satisfaction. On 14 July Young declared that he was

> particularly glad for the sake of the 500 Quarrymen (who were selected by their fellow workmen to keep order) that their Royal Highnesses were so impressed with the excellent order that was maintained.

Acknowledging Lord Penrhyn's 'kind recognition' of the success of all the quarry arrangements. Young admitted to being 'overstrung', and continued:

> Even had you not written at all (tho' I knew you would for you have never failed to encourage our efforts) I should have known from our face how pleased you were – the blasting was the finest show the Princess has ever seen, I am sure, and tho' you remained almost silent I could see your face gleam with a happy pride and after seeing that I felt as light as a bird and the rest of the show and the run along the Quay came quite easy.
>
> Many thanks for doing me the honour of introducing me to the Prince and Princess.

The demolition of Talcen Mawr did not eliminate all sources of danger, and on 30 August 1894 Young had a serious accident to report:

> This afternoon just as I was arriving at the Quarry I met a man being carried into the Hospital after having fallen headlong 36 ft owing to his *not* using his rope. No bones were broken nor even his skull cracked but being of a very poor constitution he died in two hours from concussion of the brain.
>
> This is the first accident of the year and I cannot say how much I regret its occurrence.

In 1895 there were indications that the union was preparing for a fight over the employment of large contractors. In response to the claim that this introduced a 'sweating system' into the quarry, it was argued that the contractors were skilled workers, and that the men were paid not by the contractors but by the management; in addition, Lord Penrhyn pointed out that the contract procedure had been in existence for fourteen years.

In January 1896 David R. Daniel (1859–1931) was appointed full-time organiser of the N.W.Q.U., and thereafter union activity was intensified. On 1 May 1896, three days before the Labour Day meeting to be held at Blaenau Ffestiniog, Young wrote to Lord Penrhyn about the tense situation that was developing:

> The men's tactics on this occasion are very peculiar and I have come to the conclusion that at the instigation of Headquarters the Penrhyn men are ordered to try and pick a quarrel. And their ultimate view will be to establish the Union and the old Quarry Committee which is really at work now at the bottom of the present movement.
>
> As it takes two sides to make a quarrel I am still of the opinion that discretion is the better part of valour and that to take no notice of their abstention from work is the best policy under present awkward circumstances of no stock.
>
> By absenting themselves without leave they score the first point against themselves and that will be to our ultimate advantage.
>
> I have given instructions that everything is to be started on Monday morning as if nothing were happening, and if there are enough men to justify it, to keep open, but otherwise to close.
>
> I am sorry to say I do not feel so sanguine as Mr Prichard that after Monday it will all blow over – the whole plot seems to me more deep laid than that. Some new demands will probably be made and

then must come a pitched battle and apparently Penrhyn Quarry has been selected for the trial of strength.

By 3 May 1896, when he wrote to Lord Penrhyn again, Young had changed his mind:

> After all to *take no notice* seems to be rather equivalent to tempting the men to further insubordination which is hardly fair and above board; I shall therefore suspend all those who absent themselves without leave *two* days counting it as a first offence, warning each individual that any future similar act will be more severely punished . . .
> Two days suspension cannot possibly be considered vindictive. I had thought of putting up a printed notice about the two days suspension, but Mr Vivian, who came over here to ascertain what was going on, strongly recommended no notice but just suspension by the District Overlooker in each case in the ordinary way, so I am adopting that course.
>
> He tells me that nearly all his men have asked and been granted leave, and most of them have already gone away to Liverpool and Manchester. Some asked for two days and will be away both Monday and Tuesday but very few will attend the Festiniog meeting . . . he will act similarly towards any of his men who maybe absent without leave . . . I am furthermore directed towards this course of immediate action because I learn that the scheme is to try and re-establish the old 'Pennant Lloyd's Agreement'.
>
> By the way I should have said that it is clearly understood that leave would be given on application to the Overlookers and I am informed that several men on the Union Committees were averse to the men leaving work without leave, but the majority prevailed, apparently being bent on mischief.

Representatives of the Committee toured the quarry, persuading men neither to work on 4 May nor to seek leave of absence from the management. On 4 May Young informed Lord Penryn that about 130 had permission to be absent, and that the others, with the exception of one *rybelwr,* were absent without leave. Young declared his intention of suspending the absentees for two days, and commented:

> Then will come the crisis if they refuse to be suspended.

> But if it comes to a fight, it will, I am confident, be sharp, short and decisive. It is the new generation up there that require a lesson. W. J. Parry and J. J. Evans are at the bottom of it I believe[15].

Later events were to show that Young's confidence was misplaced.

On 31 May 1896 Young reported to Lord Penrhyn that 'the wirepullers in the quarry agitation' had 'decided to postpone action for three months'. One of the leaders of the union activity in the quarry, according to Young, was a 'churchman' who was 'hand in glove' with the former head clerk T. H. Owen; and Owen himself had recently visited the Pay Office. Union membership increased at the quarry, and on 2 July 1896 the Committee demanded a standard daily wage of 5s 6d for quarrymen, miners and sawyers, a minimum daily wage of 4s 6d, and poundage of 10s for apprentices. On 29 July Young rejected these demands; and on 7 August the men sent a statement of their grievances, which included the contract system and the fact that some men earned less than £1 a week[16]. On 11 August the Committee told Young that they received 'continuous complaints' about the lack of a minimum wage, the ill-treatment of *rybelwyr*, the reduction of wages at the mill, and the introduction of unskilled contractors. On 18 August Young told Lord Penrhyn that his assistant David Prichard had just phoned to report 'a deliberate attempt by some parties in the quarry to get the men out'; but at 1 p.m. on that day Young said that the men were settling down to work.

On 20 August 1896 *Y Cymro* acknowledged that the problems of the *rybelwyr* had been overstated and that the deputation's figures had been inaccurate 'in minor details', but continued:

> The haughty and autocratic manner in which his Lordship spoke to the Deputation cannot be justified, and it would be well for him to go for a few days to the cottage of some of his workmen to learn manners.

Y Cymro condemned Lord Penrhyn's habit of 'upbraiding and scolding' the men, and regretted his inability to address them in their own language. On 23 August Young's informant reported that the men's last meeting had been 'a very tame affair', that the 'agitators' evidently had no case to offer, and that '*no* motion to strike' appeared in the resolutions. Young told Lord Penrhyn that several hundred men had attended the meeting, and that he had received a detailed report naming all those who had spoken. On 26 August Robert Davies and others wrote to Lord Penrhyn, admitting that large contracts had been introduced into the quarry about 1882 but claiming that they had been 'almost discontinued . . . owing to the ill-feeling they aroused'. According to this letter, the contract system often meant 'an unskilled man employing a number of skilled Quarrymen as his subordinates', and this was resented as a 'practical injustice to skilled labour'. At the end of August Robert Owen and David Davies were accused of insubordination because they had carried out unauthorised measuring in the quarry on behalf of the Committee; and a deputation, considering of Robert Davies and six men 'formerly active as non-unionists', pleaded their case on the ground that the measuring had been done to ensure that the Committee got correct information. When Prichard informed Young that a strike was imminent, Young tried unsuccessfully to 'laugh him out of it'; but it is clear that Young himself was very anxious.

Young arranged to have Hugh Morris, a setter 'with a cool head', in charge of the quarry the next Monday morning. He still hoped that the trouble might 'blow over', since some of the 'older hands' were in favour of a secret ballot; they had been 'howled down', but in the event of a strike would be eager to return to work. In the meantime Young paid a visit to the Bethesda Flower Show:

> I attended . . . for two hours and I could see anxiety in many faces fearing a strike – well we cannot foretell, but I will not believe them such fools till I see it.

Lord Penrhyn's fifteen-year-old daughter Lilian, writing to her father from Felixstowe on 1 September, appeared unaware of the growing crisis:

> We are enjoying ourselves here very much. It poured this morn-

ing like anything – the rain ran in rivers down the road . . .

There are going to be heaps of blackberries but they aren't all ripe yet. Yesterday it was so baking hot, we did not know what to do. We are getting on with our swimming, we time it to see how long we can keep up without floating or landing.

In North Wales, however, the situation at Penrhyn Quarry was arousing widespread interest. On 2 September 1896 Miss L. Wynne of Bettws y Coed invited Lady Penrhyn to tea at six, and told her that according to the Rev Pierce Jones of Aber it was 'quite well known' that Prichard gave the best places to Nonconformists. Challenged by Lord Penrhyn, Pierce Jones became more specific and said on 5 September that 'the best places were given to Methodists'; but on 21 September Lord Penrhyn concluded that these 'false reports' were being directed against Prichard simply because he was a Dissenter[17].

On 14 September 1896 Hugh Morris informed Prichard that Robert Owen and David Davies had called on him at 12.30 p.m., saying that the Committee had 'told them not to go down to the Port Office, as there was a resolution passed for them not to go'. As a result the two men were suspended, and after twelve days dismissed. On 25 September Lord Penrhyn gave his reply to the representations he had received from Robert Davies and others. On the issue of 'Standard Wages' he said that 4s was the nominal standard wage but that average wages were about 5s 3d and some received over 6s. He declined to raise the standard wage, saying that the labour of many of the quarrymen was not worth more than 4s a day; and he refused to pay a minimum wage of 4s 6d a day, denying the men's claim that this was in force at Oakeley. He rejected the allegations which had been made about injustice to *rybelwyr;* some men had been moved because their places were temporary, others had been without places for only two days, and one of the incidents complained of had happened eighteen years earlier. He attributed the failure to attain standard wages to incompetence and drunkenness, and pointed out that men who received low pay had 'Lost Days' when they had not worked. He denied that there had been any reduction in mill wages, explaining that the one exception was caused by neglect of duty; and he re-iterated that contracts were not an innovation and that the contractors were not unskilled.

On 26 September 1896 the Committee responded to Lord Penrhyn's letter by passing the following resolution:

> That we as a Committee of the Penrhyn Quarries after serious consideration of our position in the face of Lord Penrhyn's unfavourable reply to our requests and complaints, are of the opinion that no good can result from continuing the negotiation on the same lines as hitherto, and we regard it as our duty as workmen to make it known that we shall strike in March next unless in the meantime we find that the chief points of our grievances in the various departments of the works have been conceded[18].

The Committee knew that many of the older quarrymen still hoped for concessions, and that the N.W.Q.U. lacked the resources for an immediate strike. In a second resolution they asked the Board of Trade to intervene under the new Conciliation Act of 1896; and in a third they demanded a strike ballot throughout North Wales.

On 27 September, when the weather was rough and Lord Penrhyn was staying at Glan Conway, Young gave his employer a detailed account of his plan of campaign. The Committee had sent in 148 bills from a 'Low Wage List'; and after Young had weeded out 73 of these as the bills not of quarrymen but of badrockmen and *rybelwyr*, the remainder had been published. He had been 'out and about till after Midnight' collecting evidence, and had decided to visit the quarry about 10.30 the following Monday morning. He would telephone Prichard or Hugh Morris in advance, and would ask them to invite all the partners of certain crews, whose bills had been published although they had earned high wages over the previous six months, to meet him at 11.40 ('dinner hour') in his Trosyffordd office. In the presence of the chief clerk William Gray and of a shorthand writer, he would ask these men if they had made any complaints to the Committee. If they said they had, he would ask them 'when and why'; and if they said that they had not, he would ensure they did not converse with the other men waiting to see him. Young and his employer had already decided to suspend but not dismiss seventy-one men who were connected with the Committee; and Young was confident that some of those he questioned would deny having made complaint, thus rendering the 'suspension of the Committee afterwards . . . still more defensible'. After these interviews he would send 'individually for each of the seventy-one men and personally hand them the note suspending them'; and by passing them 'quickly along thro' a second room' to receive a Welsh version of the note, he would ensure that 'no argument or question and answer or comment' was possible. Young continued:

> After that I should adjourn for tea at Ogwen Bank and remain there or at the Hospital till 7.30 that is until the Mass meeting is over and a reporter will come and give me a report of the meeting.
>
> I have really been evolving this all night long and it is the best plan of action I can think of – because I think it would be cowardly on my part to defer the suspension until after the Mass Meeting because it then would certainly be said I was doing all I could to force a strike – the way I suggest seems more honest and straightforward and therefore certain to succeed.
>
> Now please tell me when you will come over – I should then arrange about reporting to you my day's campaign at 5.0 or 6.0 by sending Mr Gray to the Castle and after the Mass Meeting I would undertake to come and report on that personally about 8.30 or so.
>
> If you like to defer coming over to the Castle till the evening please do so – I mean I shall not feel deserted by you in fact it is my turn to be in the forefront of the fight and meet these fellows face to face in the Quarry and your coming so early in the day might give them the false impression that you are anxious.
>
> 'Aequo Animo' and 'Press Through' are two good mottoes[19].

This last sentence referred to Lord Penrhyn's motto, 'With steadfast mind', and to the motto of the Young family.

On 28 September Young saw fifty-three men, all of whom 'denied that they had made any complaint whatever to the Committee' and said that they 'had simply sent in their bills after pay day' at the request of the *ponc* or gallery. As a result seventy-one men connected with the Committee were given notes which suspended them from 29 September 'until further notice'. On 1

October Lord Penrhyn received a letter of support from Assheton Smith:

> I must write a line to sympathise with you on the shameful behaviour of the men after all the trouble you have taken in the matter. I only hope that these fanatical agitators will get a lasting lesson this time. I think their cool cheek in stating that they were going to wait till March and strike then, certainly takes the cake[20].

The newspapers gave various accounts of the situation following the suspensions. The *Liverpool Mercury* of 29 September claimed that the men's complaints had been exposed as 'without foundation and empty'. *Y Werin* of 3 October said that a war had been declared in Bethesda. *Yr Herald Cymraeg* of 5 October reported that two recruiting officers from the 23rd regiment of the Welch Fusiliers had made a 'fruitless journey' to Bethesda; and the same issue described the proceedings and the atmosphere at a mass meeting:

> The workmen determined unanimously to refuse to take new bargains, until this injustice is righted. The workmen carried out their determination in a quiet manner, but with a silent and unswerving determination which suggests that the battle-time of freedom and justice to the men has arrived and that the Cae quarrymen have girded and armed themselves for the battle, and confidently look for victory. The most noble spirit was manifested in the great meeting on Wednesday morning. Nothing derogatory was said about Lord Penrhyn, or his officials; but the most worthy courage and valour were shown.

Young required those who had refused bargains to remove their tools from the quarry, and the dispute thus became both a strike and a lockout.

The only men at work during the mass meeting were some fitters, joiners and labourers, whom Young decided to employ on loading slates in the 'handiest part of the quarry'. On 5 October *Y Genedl Gymreig* announced a relief fund for the men, and described the scene in Bethesda as the exodus began:

> Today the streets were full of life and activity with crowds of people going to the station on their way to the country to look for

> work. The scene was a strange one, some were happy, and others dejected, and all who remained behind wished them well . . . The managers of the Welsh National Press have arranged to open the columns of *Y Genedl* and *Y Werin*, to acknowledge sums contributed to the relieving fund.

On 6 October *Yr Herald Cymraeg* provided fuller information about the men's destinations:

> Early after midnight large crowds of men met and they commenced their journey without anything but a bag of food with them. Scores walked to Aber, dozens went in brakes to Bettws y Coed. Scores of others crossed the mountains to Beddgelert and Llanberis while 108 went by train to Nantlle Vale . . . This morning a cheap train ran to Manchester, and some hundreds went with it, some to Liverpool, others to St Helens . . . The majority of them secured work in large warehouses . . . It is not necessary to state that there was an active appearance on the station.

On 10 October *Y Faner* described the new routine which had been established:

> By this time the lockout is a fact and the workmen have come to realise it. The workmen went to different places in the middle of the week to seek work, but by Saturday night they had all returned to their families, and on Monday morning hundreds will have turned out again to work.

Y Faner compared the men's solidarity on this occasion with the divisions of 1874:

> The difference of party and denomination is lost; the workmen have been in the severe furnace of tyranny for some time past, and they have been welded together . . . Twenty-two years ago there was a long list, whose names are kept up to the present, working.

The implied threat was confirmed by a reminder that the *cynffonwyr* or sycophants of 1874 had been 'disheartened' by 'the victory which followed honest workmen'.

On 12 October, affirming that he would not say 'a single word for the purpose of embittering feeling', Lord Penrhyn set out his reasons for suspending the seventy-one men. Under the heading of 'Misrepresentation', he said the Committee had falsely claimed that many competent quarrymen could not reach the quarry's recognised standard wage. Under the heading of 'Insubordination', he said that the Committee had incited the men to disobey instructions both on 4 May, when 2,500 absented themselves without leave, and on 14 September, when Robert Owen and David Davies failed to appear at the chief manager's office. Lord Penrhyn continued:

> I neither object to, nor attempt to oppose, any legitimate combination amongst my workmen; but the form of the combination against which I set my face, and shall continue to resist, is that which (as in the case of this Quarry Committee) forbids the workmen to obey the orders of his master, or those of his officials; which prohibits evidence being given, or an explanation being made to the management by the workmen, unless such evidence or explanation has previously been reported to the Committee, the effect of which would be, that in the event of an enquiry into an alleged grievance, the employer would be compelled to accept replies and assurances from a mouthpiece of the very same Committee which had prepared (or even possibly fabricated) the complaint, in lieu of independent testimony from persons who were not subject to the influence of that body; and I need hardly point out that under such circumstances it would be next to impossible for an employer to arrive at the actual truth concerning alleged grievances, moreover, under such a system, the management of the quarry would practically pass into the hands of a Committee.
>
> Events prior to 1885, at which date I refused to sanction the interference by a Committee in the management of the quarry, have taught me that it is no imaginary evil or risk of which I now speak, and to which an employer is exposed by the methods of such a Quarry Committee, and I am fairly resolved not to allow a body of that nature to assume the tone of supreme dictation either to master or men in the Penrhyn Quarry.

Lord Penrhyn received many letters of advice at this time, and kept even those which he did not answer. A letter written on 3 October 1896 by Isaac Williams of Bethesda began:

> The Lord God forbid that I should be too presumptious in sending your Lordship this letter . . . I am about 80 years old.

Williams suggested that Lord Penrhyn should address a mass meeting at the quarry the following Saturday; and Lord Penrhyn annotated his letter with the words 'Well meaning meddler'. Many correspondents were prompted by the dispute to make unrealistic offers for the purchase of the quarry; but Lord Penrhyn simply categorised their letters as 'Ridiculous proposals'. Among the letters containing statements of support for the men was one from the Composing Department of Southwood, Smith and Co, who expressed their sympathy

> with the lock-out quarrymen on Lord Penrhyn's estate; also their unqualified disgust with that nobleman's inhuman and unchristian-like action in endeavouring to ruin thousands of his fellow-creatures in order to satisfy a tyrannous and peevish disposition, the power to do so having been unfortunately invested in him through an accident of birth[21].

This letter too Lord Penrhyn chose to leave unanswered.

4
The First Dispute: 1896–1897

On 14 October 1896 Young informed Lord Penrhyn that a fire in W. J. Parry's yard had destroyed a warehouse, and that the explosions caused by the fire had broken windows in Station Terrace and near the Conservative Club. There was no loss of life, but the fire was financially ruinous to Parry[1]. On 3 November *Yr Herald Cymraeg* rejected, under the heading 'Another Libel', a report that quarrymen had tried to derail a train in which Young and others were travelling to Port Penrhyn. On 15 November *Y Faner* carried an account of Pay Saturday at the quarry:

> There were only tens of old people who work by the day, and the officers of the work receiving their pay for the last month. The chief road of the village was almost clear of workmen at midday, when it used to be full.

The N.W.Q.U. was unable to support the men; but funds were collected in other quarries, and the Penrhyn choirs made £2,400 by fund-raising tours. The *Daily Chronicle* took up the men's cause, thanks to Lloyd George's influence with the editor Henry Williams; and its readers contributed over £7,000. The total sum collected, according to Parry, was £19,161; and Bethesda was divided into twenty-two districts to facilitate the distribution of relief[2].

On 24 November 1896 notices were posted announcing the re-opening of the quarry; but no quarrymen went back to work, and so the strike continued after the end of the lockout. Mass meetings were held to keep up morale, and the proceedings were regularly reported to Young. On 29 November he wrote to Lord Penrhyn:

> There is but little to tell of last night's meeting except that the Committee shirked the responsibility of proposing any resolution but caught at a shout from some fellow 'Stand out' which he shouted in response to a suggestion that it was for them to decide what they would do in face of the notices. 'Stand out' was shouted to them. The chairman said, if that is seconded I will put it to the meeting – several seconders shouted and it was rushed through in a few minutes – The rest of the meeting was the usual rubbish but the usual speakers were away, some at the Board of Trade and others collecting funds.

Some of the older labourers had continued to work, but Young now suggested a complete closure of the quarry:

> I really do think it will be the greatest kindness to entirely close the quarry next Saturday and throw the old men upon the Union Fund. You will have kept them on nearly ten weeks by then.
>
> I merely suggest it for very anxious reflection, in view of it being the *greatest kindness* in the long run to the greatest number – if it were done because of the men's decision to decline work and in view of their decision to strike again on March 1 next, it would *appear reasonable* to all right minded persons.

The National Free Labour Association, founded in 1893 by William Collison, issued a monthly journal called *Free Labour*, which opposed the New Unionism represented by organisations like the N.W.Q.U. On 5 October 1896 *Free Labour* attacked the new unions for their adherence to the 'closed shop' principle, declaring that such 'liberty-loving agitators' were indifferent to the sufferings of strikers and their families. Vivian was a member of the Association's executive committee; and its fifth Annual Report gave its membership in January 1897 as 160,000. Its sympathies were with Lord Penrhyn from the first, and in October 1897 he and Young became members.

The men hoped for intervention by the Board of Trade under the Conciliation (Trades Disputes) Act of 1896; and in October 1896 Lord Penrhyn received a proposal from the Secretary of the Board, Sir Courtenay Boyle, that an official from the Board be present at a meeting of the two parties. On 5 December 1896 Young reported the men's views on this suggestion:

The following resolutions were passed at the Mass meeting of Quarrymen held at Bethesda this evening:

1. That this meeting of Penrhyn Quarrymen, understanding through the Board of Trade that Lord Penrhyn is prepared to have an interview with a deputation representing the Quarrymen, hereby appoints Mr W. H. Williams, Glanrafon, Mr Henry Edwards, Bryntirion, and Robert Jones, Carneddi Rd., as our representatives to wait upon Lord Penrhyn with a view to discuss a basis for the settlement of the present dispute.
2. That this meeting expresses its earnest and strong desire that one or more of the representatives of the Board of Trade should if possible be present at the first interview, believing that the adoption of this course would greatly facilitate the opening up of the negotiations.
3. That this meeting is of opinion that the deputation should be accompanied by its own interpreter and shorthand note-taker, if any notes of the proceedings are to be taken.
4. That a copy of these resolutions be forwarded to the Board of Trade[3].

On 9 December Lord Penrhyn wrote to Boyle rejecting the plan for a meeting in the presence of a Board of Trade official; and he also objected to the men bringing their own interpreter and shorthand writer. A mass meeting held in Bethesda on 26 December expressed gratitude to the Board of Trade, and regretted that Lord Penrhyn and his advisers had 'flouted the Conciliation Trades Disputes Act of 1896' by seeking to impose conditions on the plan for a conference[4].

In December 1896 Young decided to close the quarry again and to dismiss about a third of the men. 'It must be done', he told Lord Penrhyn, 'but my heart is very heavy and I have a very bad headache'. In the same month Young received a letter from Lord Penrhyn's legal adviser J. E. Vincent, who wrote:

> My advice to Lord Penrhyn is to keep silently and resolutely on the course he has laid down and to make no advances of any kind; for all such advances are construed into a sign of weakness. Victory, which has got to come some day, will then come all the sooner.

On 29 December Vincent wrote in similar terms to Lord Penrhyn himself:

> You must be prepared, I fear, for a good deal of misrepresentation, for the correspondence as published yesterday, and particularly the letter from Daniel to the Board of Trade, was distinctly circulated to give a false impression. But I counsel you most earnestly to take no notice of misrepresentation. You are, I take it, determined to win and never concede the main points; and I opine (this is treading on delicate but unavoidable grounds) that you have the staying power for a long fight. I opine, also, that you desire to win sooner rather than later.
>
> In these circumstances the attitude I venture to advise is the following: I would not answer any charges except charges embodying plain lies; I would not argue at all; I would make no advances save perhaps to open an offer of work on the old terms to the men once a month. This firm demonstration of your firm resolve will I am sure be successful sooner than a Demonstration of a desire to make friends which will be construed into an admission of weakness. Such was the invariable construction placed upon James Thompson's . . . manifesto to the men during the Scotch Railway strike.

Also on 29 December Young wrote to Lord Penrhyn about inaccurate reports in the press:

> The only troublesome newspaper today is the London *Daily Chronicle* . . . but I *very very* earnestly wish we had nothing to do with the paper as no possible good can come from such a correspondence . . . substantial misrepresentation to charge me with having 'dismissed' seventy-one men when I did not do so[5].

As London's chief Liberal newspaper, the *Daily Chronicle* made as much political capital out of the dispute as it could.

Lord Penrhyn had friends and admirers, however, as well as enemies. On 1 January 1897 Harold Williams wrote to him from Temple House in Great Marlow:

> My dear George,
>
> As one of your very oldest friends I write a line to congratulate you most heartily on the firm and decided line I see by the papers you have taken with regard to your quarries. As to the exact dispute I am ignorant, but I feel quite convinced that you have been fair and just throughout and I cannot help thinking that in the strong course you have just adopted you will prove the pioneer of the pol-

> icy that all large employers of labour must adopt for the salvation not only of themselves but of the Country. The Tyranny of the trades unions is a source of real danger and (as the electorate is now constituted) so impossible to legislate against, that Capitalists must combine against them and refuse to employ any man belonging to a Union other than one to afford relief for sickness or old age.
>
> A strike . . . is easily got up by the unions even against the wishes of the men themselves . . . and brings ruin both to Employers and Employed. Contracts cannot be made, and the old good feeling between Employers and their work people is at an end. Conciliation boards are humbug.

After strenuous efforts, the Board of Trade finally told Lord Penrhyn that it was 'useless for them to continue' with their attempt to resolve the dispute; and on 2 January 1897 Lord Stanley wrote to congratulate him on 'having had the best of it with the Board of Trade' and its 'very objectionable' President C. T. Ritchie. On 4 January 1897 the Rev M. Roberts wrote to Lord Penrhyn from Penmachno Rectory in Bettws y Coed:

> In my opinion there is very little sympathy with the men anywhere. In this parish, although a quarry district, the sympathy is very low. Several of these quarrymen have told me that your lordship's men were much better off in every respect than *they* are here . . . Your lordship's honour is as high as ever in the County. The strike cannot injure the honoured name of the noble family of Penrhyn Castle.

On 9 January A. Peel of Broxbourne in Hertfordshire wrote to Lord Penrhyn reporting a conversation with his friend the Archbishop of Canterbury. Peel had suggested that 'it would be a good opportunity for the Church to intervene', and the Archbishop had 'seemed not to disagree'. The Archbishop had told Peel that Lord Penrhyn was in the right, but that although he had 'the hand of steel' he lacked 'the glove of velour'[6].

On 11 January the *Daily Chronicle* reported a speech made by Lloyd George at a farmers' conference in Carmarthen, where he was appealing for funds for the quarrymen:

> The owners of the soil of Wales, he said, were in many instances the descendants of successful robbers. (Laughter) Let them con-

> sider, for instance, the case of a man whose name had been unpleasantly prominent of late – Lord Penrhyn. (Hisses) Yes, let them hiss; but he trusted the hisses would turn to honest pennies to help the quarrymen. ('Half-crowns') The history of Lord Penrhyn's family and its connection with Wales was brief and inglorious. One of his forebears was a Scotchman who came to live in Bangor. Not far off there dwelt a simple, innocent, honest community of small cotters, farmers and shepherds. He said they were honest, and he had the best possible proof of their honesty – they forbore to steal the common land. (Laughter and cheers) The mountain at whose foot they lived was not enclosed, for they looked upon it as belonging to the community. But the stranger thought otherwise. Today the mountain had been turned into a vast quarry, and the common land had become the source of one man's overgrown wealth – ('Shame') – and for this successful negotiation the Scotch family was ennobled. (Laughter) The free mountain had become Lord Penrhyn's quarry. Three thousand Welshmen, the descendants many of them of the simple people who knew not how to rob in legal fashion, had become his hewers of wood and drawers of water. They had been refused the right of free men – the right of combination. Several of their lives were sacrificed annually on the altar of Lord Penrhyn's wealth, [but] because they had claimed the privilege of union, they were debarred by his lordship from the means of sustaining themselves and their families. ('Shame') . . . He trusted the farmers of South Wales would be united among themselves, and would band themselves, not merely as farmers, but as Welshmen, to resist the forces of oppression and tyranny. (Cheers)

Though enjoyed by its immediate audience, this speech was not universally approved. On 15 January W. Davies wrote to Lord Penrhyn from London, enclosing a report of the speech from the *South Wales Daily News*, and commenting:

> I consider such language from a member of Parliament most mischievous and contemptible. I think Lloyd George and the paper ought to be prosecuted for a gross libel on your family and yourself.

Though Davies was 'simply a working man from Carnarvonshire', he claimed to represent a substantial body of opinion:

> We London Welshmen read and hear a great deal about this Penrhyn Quarry dispute. Notwithstanding the libellous articles in the radical papers, the British public on the whole is on the side of Lord Penrhyn.

Collections on behalf of the Penrhyn quarrymen were organised, however, not only in Carmarthen but also in Llandeilo, Llandovery, Swansea, Cardiff, Merthyr, Aberdare and other places in South Wales.

On 14 January 1897, just before the opening of Parliament, Young put another notice offering work. Once again there were no applicants, and on 31 January Young described the men as 'poor deluded fools'; but he hoped that the offer would make a favourable impression on M.P.s, who were shortly to hold a debate on the dispute. On 15 January a young Welshman named D. Roberts, who had 'greatly benefited' from Lord Penrhyn's generosity, placed on record his 'emphatic protest' against the 'mean and villainous attacks' delivered by 'the base and rabble'. He referred in particular to the 'many-headed Lloyd George' and to the supporters of William Jones, the Liberal M.P. for Arfon; in Roberts' judgement, such men were 'not worthy to black Lord Penrhyn's boots'. Another committed supporter of Lord Penrhyn was George Assheton Smith, who wrote on 18 January:

> I cannot tell you how sorry I am for you at having all this worry and trouble and press abuse. You deserve the thanks and support of every employer of labour in the country. The only mistake made seems to me to offer these devils their work back instead of their coming to you[7].

A debate took place in the House of Commons on 28 January 1897 on the motion by William Jones, which referred to

> the loss and privation arising from the dispute between employer and employed in the Penrhyn quarries, and the failure of the efforts under the Conciliation Act to terminate the dispute.

Attributing the dispute to dissatisfaction over terms and conditions of service, Jones declared the Penrhyn quarrymen to be among the 'most intelligent workmen in the whole British

Empire'. They had built and maintained three schools, had built twenty chapels, and had contributed £1,500 towards the University College at Bangor. Bethesda, he claimed, was an almost crimeless district; and at the last mass meeting, when the men had sung hymns and passed resolutions, 'not a word of denunciation was uttered against Lord Penrhyn himself'. It was not surprising, Jones concluded, that money was 'flowing fast into the funds'. The member for Eifion, Bryn Roberts, said that the question was whether the quarrymen had the right to combine to secure their joint interests; he stressed that the strike had involved no riot or disturbance, and declared that it had not occasioned even a single charge of poaching.

The next speech came from Lord Penrhyn's son, Edward Sholto Douglas Pennant, who represented southern Northamptonshire. He corrected some of the statements which had been made about the average daily wage, the reasons for the May Day suspensions, and the nature of the Quarry Committee before 1885. He said that the men had proclaimed a general strike; and he argued that Lord Penrhyn's wish for an interpreter from the quarry could easily have been met, since the local manager David Davies could have undertaken that role. He said that the men's leaders included not only the members of the Committee but also such able men as W. H. Williams, the 'quarrymen's Gladstone'. With reference to the conciliation procedure, he reminded the House that the Act contained no compulsory principle; and he said that his father believed the Board of Trade to be decidedly partial to the men. The Leicester M.P. Henry Broadhurst took the opposite view, saying that the House of Commons 'had not yet become the slave of Lord Penrhyn'. He had attended the May Day celebrations, which had concluded with 'sacred songs of the most elevating and impressive character'. He believed that the men should have the right to celebrate May Day, and he hoped that the 'great landowner' would not use his wealth to 'crush out by starvation and tyranny the spirit of independence of his workpeople'. It was necessary to limit an employer's rights, he contended, when they were used in a 'cruel and vindictive manner'.

William Bromley Davenport, the member for Macclesfield, questioned the notion that the Penrhyn quarrymen were simple people unable to express themselves in English. Members of the Committee, at any rate, had written 'very able' letters to the *Times;* if they had employed a translator, the translator was to be congratulated. He doubted the impartiality of George Rowley, the Board of Trade's labour correspondent for North Wales, who owed his position to the recommendations of Welsh-speaking Radical M.P.s. Bromley Davenport declared his own friendship for Lord Penrhyn, who had been denounced in newspapers and even in sermons. A preacher had compared Lord Penrhyn to the pharaoh who would not let a people go; but the preacher had forgotten that the people in the present case went of their own accord. Lord Penrhyn was no hard-hearted pharaoh but an 'honourable, fair-minded English gentleman, and wholly incapable of any mean, paltry, or dishonourable action.' The men had good wages and comfortable houses; and their relative affluence was shown by the fact that they could build twenty chapels, subscribe £1,500 to the university fund, and spend £1,000 on a cricket ground. The four hundred men who had remained at work were kept for thirteen weeks; and when they were dismissed, those over sixty-five were given £1 a month for life and those under sixty-five £1 each to help them find work elsewhere.

C. T. Ritchie, the President of the Board of Trade, rejected the charges of partiality which had been brought against him. He said that the Board had not relied solely on George Rowley, but had also sent Lord Dudley to Bethesda to gather information. Sir William Harcourt, the member for West Monmouthshire, condemned Lord Penrhyn for rejecting the good offices of the Board of Trade, and interpreted his action as a declaration of war on the trade unions. John Burns, the member for Battersea, said that there was an 'industrial calamity in Bethesda', and that he questioned not Lord Penrhyn's heart but his head. He denied the plutocrat's right to coerce men by the power of his wealth: 'Was he omnipotent in the kingdom of Wales, this lord who talked in so lofty a strain?' Burns was less impressed than other speakers by the men's piety. He felt that they were too 'conciliatory and peaceable', and that they had been 'singing hymns instead of learning how to box'. He suspected that even Lord Penrhyn's purse might soon be exhausted; but he appealed for an end to the quarrel, which was driving the creators of Lord Penrhyn's wealth 'away from their native place'. Burns's speech was an impressive one; but like other speakers he seems not to have realised how a hymn like *O Arglwydd Dduw rhagluniaeth* ('O Lord God of providence') could be used by the quarrymen as a *Marseillaise* or rallying cry.

Writing to his wife on 29 January, Lloyd George said that he had never made a more effective speech than that in which he 'roasted Penrhyn' during this debate. His account of Lord Penrhyn shouting about 'these monoglot Welshmen' does not ring true, however; and even he acknowledged that the men blamed the quarry agents more than they blamed the owner. He was on stronger ground when he argued that the *Times* was not impartial in the dispute, since its correspondent J. E. Vincent was Lord Penrhyn's counsel and a brother of his solicitor. The last speaker was Hugh Ellis, the member for Anglesey. Ellis argued that Lord Penrhyn had been unwilling to use the Conciliation Act because he knew he was in the wrong; but he hoped that the debate would encourage the men to continue on their law-abiding course, and that they would triumph in the end. The debate concluded without a division[8]; and on 3 February the *Journal of Gas Lighting* declared that it had vindicated Lord Penrhyn, and that the 'wretched labourers' were being used as 'pawns in the political game'.

On the same day Lord Halifax wrote sympathetically to Lord Penrhyn, enclosing a cutting about the Penrhyn choirs:

> The talk of Lord Penrhyn as having taken a high hand is simply 'balderdash'. It is all very well to send up to London a troupe of musicians selected from the quarrymen to sing songs in a language nobody understands outside Wales. This will not unbutton John Bull's pocket. John Bull is very well aware that when labourers are paid high wages and are well-treated they have only themselves to

> blame if they elect to starve by going on strike, and to needlessly entail sufferings on themselves and their families.

On 7 February Young noted that the *Daily Chronicle* was successfully redirecting against Lord Penrhyn the hostility once aimed at Prichard; and on 8 February he reported rumours that 500-700 Conservatives 'would go in at the next invitation'. Young had told Vincent that the seventy-one suspended quarrymen would be re-accepted, unless he had 'some other very good reason against anyone of them totally unconnected with the strike'. Notices announcing the re-opening, which were posted on 8 February, said that men had to apply individually for re-engagement, but that all applications including those of the suspended men would be considered impartially. On 9 February H. Lloyd Carter, a member of the legal firm of Carter, Vincent and Jones, wrote to Lord Penrhyn in somewhat discouraging terms:

> I believe the first signs of any wavering among the men is most likely to emanate from the ranks of the Conservatives and the *older* Methodists. Now that the Notices are out I confess I am not so sanguine the Men will give way as when I last wrote.

On 14 February Young advised Lord Penrhyn to go away 'to Algiers or elsewhere' for his asthma:

> I know you would trust me not to give your position away in your absence . . . Shut up Penrhyn Castle etc – that will bring some to their senses[9].

The following day Young wrote again:

> No one applied for work. Only time will unravel the situation but I can see that a large section of the men want to return to work but they are so deficient in moral courage that I fear it will take some time yet to split them up unless their money fails.
>
> Lloyd Carter is very keen that the Board of Trade should at once be influenced through Mr Balfour or someone to advise the men to send the Deputation or any other deputation (outside the seventy-one) to you at once . . .
>
> Evidently the game is to force the appointment of a conciliator

> and try and put you in the wrong when you decline to meet him and turn the tide of sympathy. It would be better to meet a deputation from a tactical point of view, that is *if* they apply direct to you – not through the Board of Trade[10].

Lord Penrhyn agreed to meet a deputation; but *Y Cymro* reported on 25 February that the meeting had been a failure, although 'the parties acted in a gentlemanly manner except Mr Young who lost his temper and his gentlemanliness.'

Lloyd Carter was the secretary of the Arfon Conservative Association; and on 18 February 1897 *Y Cymro* reported, under the headline 'Whitewashing the Master', his speech to the 'bit of a Tory Club' in Bethesda. Carter celebrated the 'liberality and munificent benevolence' of the Pennant family, and described Lord Penrhyn as 'the Soul of honour'; but *Y Cymro*, affirming that the dispute was not about Lord Penrhyn's virtues but about 'his right to act towards his workmen as inferior beings', challenged the *cynffonwyr* to demonstrate that the men had ever shown Lord Penrhyn anything other than respect. After Lord Penrhyn had received another deputation on 18 March, one of the men's representatives was reported by the *North Wales Chronicle* of 27 March as saying that he had proved himself 'a gentleman to the core'; but he still refused to accept interference or dictation from a committee, and the meeting produced no agreement.

On 2 April Young made another unsuccessful attempt to re-open the quarry; and on 4 April he wrote to Lord Penrhyn about the need for retrenchment on the estate. One of the economies suggested was the closure of Penrhyn Castle for twelve to eighteen months; this, he argued, would 'let the neighbourhood feel the fullest significance' of the family's absence, and remind people of 'the enormous benefits that were always carried about with it.' Young also proposed that Lord Penrhyn should cut the workforce on the estate, 'only retaining the requisite number of men in the garden and a few foresters', and that he should 'reduce the building department (where the money runs like water) to simply the size absolutely needed for repairs'. Young believed that the 'game department could be reduced by say £2,000 a year easily', that economies could be made in the farm department, and that all the house servants could be discharged. He said that the decisions taken at the previous day's mass meeting gave Lord Penrhyn the opportunity to tell Sackville West he would not return to the castle for an indefinite period. He also proposed a curtailment of all subscriptions, arguing that Lord Penrhyn was 'far and away too generous'; and he suggested that tenants should be made to pay all taxes and should lose the customary 15 per cent rent abatement, since Lord Penrhyn got 'very little credit' for all his 'generous deeds'. He even raised the possibility that Lord Penrhyn might absent himself from Britain in order to visit his estates in Jamaica. Young enforced his advice by saying that the dispute had now become 'a battle of money'; but Lord Penrhyn did not take up any of his proposals.

On 7 April 1897 Young wrote to Colonel A. A. Ruck, the Chief Constable of Caernarfonshire, to ask for extra police and in particular for 'two or three mounted policemen'. At the Bethesda mass meeting his name had evoked shouts of 'shoot him' and 'kill him', which came from 'irresponsible youth' but had a 'a mischievous effect'; and there had been an attempt to ambush him near Ogwen Bank on one of his cycling expeditions, which had failed only because he returned by a different route. Because of rumours that he was the obstacle to negotiations Young was rapidly becoming a focus of hostility; but in writing to Lord Penrhyn on 8 April he took an optimistic view:

> Such lies are of course very annoying but . . . all indicate a growing feeling that the men are beaten and disheartened and failing argument are reduced to rioting.

On 9 April Young told Lord Penrhyn that Ruck thought more police 'inadvisable' and had warned him '*not* to visit Bethesda or go far *alone*'. Young obeyed the order reluctantly, saying that although the men were becoming 'more sullen' he had 'no fear at present[11].'

Lord Penrhyn continued to receive letters of support, some of them from strangers and others from childhood friends. On 2

April 1897 J. Robbins wrote to him from the vicarage at Clumpen Hill:

> You will wonder why I write to you, as we have not met since our Eton and Ch. Ch. Days, for the work of my life keeps me away from society. I once knew you very well as Douglas Pennant. Now why I write is this. The Radical parsons condemn your conduct, while as a church dignitary and a great friend of working men (so called as *we* are working men also) I admire your dignified judgment and pluck. I am sure you are in the right and your money enables you to hold firm.

Lord Penrhyn answered this letter on 3 June:

> My dear Robbins,
>
> Many thanks for your note and word of encouragement in the line I have taken and which seems to be regarded as 'Anathema' and 'Cussedness' by certain church dignitaries (in a small way) by their hostility towards myself and prejudgment of a matter on which they were not in a position to pronounce an impartial opinion. If Canon Eyton, Dean Stubbs and a few more would truly live up to the precept, 'Judge not, that you be not judged', I am sure that the chances of harmony between employers and employed would be greatly advanced.

In July 1897, when the strike was nearing its end, Lord Penrhyn received what he called a 'very kind letter' from his closest ally in the quarrying world, George Assheton Smith:

> When in town I called on you as you will remember to say how sorry I was that you were having all this trouble at your quarries . . . Now what I am coming to is this – You are not only fighting your own battle but those of other owners of quarries – probably of *all other* employers of labour and it is a damned shame. Of course 'Penrhyn' etc cannot be kept up for nothing and I ask you if I can be of any assistance at this time of worry. I mean (and I feel sure you will not take offence) you having a large family, and I but one child, that you might allow me to offer you a loan, of course without any interest, which you could repay when things settle again – Perhaps you will say, 'Confound Assheton Smith, does he suppose I am hard up'. I can't help it if you do, but I want to show my sympathy and appreciation of your pluck in more than empty words.

Lord Penrhyn replied on 6 July:

> I really do not know how to thank you enough for your most kind offer of help in this strike. Your words have done much to bring home to me a feeling of thankfulness that I have been able to make a fight for the freedom of employers and employed.

He felt confident, however, that he would not have to avail himself of Assheton Smith's 'most generous offer', since he expected to 'wear them down before long anyhow'[12].

On 8 April 1897 the *Daily Chronicle* made a number of statements which Lord Penrhyn regarded as 'malicious libels': that he denied individual freedom to his workmen and treated them as serfs, that he refused to allow them to combine for their own protection, and that he had kept three thousand men out of the quarry for seven months. Young argued that a libel action would be worthwhile only if large damages could be claimed, and that even then its effect on the 'future run of the strike' had to be considered. On 10 April Young told Lord Penrhyn that a visit to Bethesda by Colonel Ruck had done some good, and that Prichard reported 'everything very quiet again now'. He went on:

> I further learn that ere long many of the tradespeople will be ruined . . . and there is far more distress than anyone thinks, as the better class hide it as much as they can.

The relief payments, he said, were 12s 6d a fortnight for men not at work, while pensioners received a 3s order for goods.

On 13 April 1897 *Y Genedl Gymreig* used the term 'Penrhynism', said to have been coined by Sydney Webb, and defined as the

> absolute denial of the right of anyone whomsoever to interfere between master and workman, or landlord and tenant, when the latter contends that the former does injustice to him.

The opposite of Penrhynism was often called 'Tillettism' after Ben Tillett, who had led the successful dockers' strike of 1889. Also on 13 April *Yr Herald Cymraeg* announced that a large English labour union had asked its five hundred branches to provide £125 a week for the Bethesda men for the duration of the strike. On 21 April *Y Faner* appeared confident of victory:

> A large body of the quarrymen have already secured work in other places. Others are leaving so that they may get work. The trade has never been more brisk than it is at present.

A boom in the building trade at this time increased the demand both for slate and for quarrymen; but there was also a great rise in slate imports, mainly from the United States but also from Belgium, France and Portugal.

On 5 May 1897 W. H. Williams wrote to Young to arrange a meeting, but nothing came of their discussions. Reporting the Labour Day festival at Caernarfon, *Y Cymro* on 6 May observed that 'though the sun smiled . . . the circumstances of one class of quarrymen' were 'dark and depressing'. *Y Werin* reported the same event on 8 May, naming among those present John Burns, William Jones and David Lloyd George. Lloyd George was given 'a princely reception', and told the meeting that Lord Penrhyn's title to his quarry was to be challenged in the House of Commons. On 11 May Vincent sent Young a cutting whose enigmatic wording confirmed this prediction:

> We understand that the Welsh members when they raise a discussion on the Penrhyn quarry dispute next Tuesday evening will press for a Select Committee of inquiry into the whole history and origin of the quarrel. The debate is to be raised on a motion of Mr Herbert Roberts calling attention to the administration of Crown lands in Wales.

W. J. Parry, who was keenly interested in the public ownership of land, had been presented with plans and pamphlets relating to the Penrhyn estate by Arthur Wyatt at the time of Wyatt's dismissal in 1886. These documents were concerned with charges made by Dr O. O. Roberts of Bangor, who in 1849 had questioned the Pennants' right to the land occupied by the quarry, maintaining that waste and common land which had been enclosed belonged to the Crown. The matter was given much publicity on 10 August 1849 by the *Times,* which was then a Radical newspaper; but Dr Roberts made no headway with his claim. Having reprinted the plans under the title *Crown Lands in North Wales,* Parry was chosen to represent Caernarfonshire on the Parliamentary Committee; and the issue was kept alive until after the First World War, when land reform ceased to be part of the Liberal Party's programme[13].

In May 1897 Young reported to Lord Penrhyn the terms he had offered to a deputation from the men. He had proposed that any deputation should consist of not more than six employees chosen from the 'class of person or persons aggrieved'; that as far as practicable all former employees who re-applied would be 'readily admitted in a body'; that 'suitable rybelwyr' would be given monthly bargains 'from time to time' at the management's discretion; and that the size and letting of contracts was to remain in the management's hands. The men objected to the proposed method of re-engagement; but Lord Penrhyn told Young on 15 May that it was ridiculous for the men to pretend that there was 'anything degrading' about an application 'made in due form at the proper office'. If the men were 'foolish enough to keep on strike for the same of this pretence', the world would perceive that there was 'no little humbug' about the whole exercise. At a mass meeting held in the open air on 29 May the men rejected Young's terms, declaring that they would go back all together or not at all. About five hundred of the men staged a demonstration at Young's home; and on 31 May Lord Penrhyn told Young that they 'ought to be ashamed of themselves for going down in that cowardly manner to do their best to frighten a lady and her children'. Young took the 'mobbing of Tanybryn' quite calmly, pointing out that his wife was unharmed and that no damage was done; but he felt that he could have done without the presence of Lloyd Carter, who helped to 'cool the mob' but was 'very fussy'. On 25 June Young advised Lord Penrhyn to take a holiday, saying that his 'continued presence' enticed attack[14].

Early in June 1897 the N.W.Q.U. Secretary W. J. Williams, acting on his own initiative and without consultation, took the first step towards a settlement of the dispute. On 6 July Lloyd Carter reported that he had received a letter from W. J. Williams, who wanted him to act as 'a sort of conduit pipe'. The letter was supposed to be confidential; but Carter observed that something was 'sure to leak out', however 'cautious and circumspect' they might be. On 10 July Carter told Lord Penrhyn that he should not hesitate to turn off the taps if the conduit pipe conveyed 'dirty water[15]'. On 18 July Young informed Lord Penrhyn of two recent deaths:

> Another of the seventy-one has been killed at Dorothea and a late blacksmith committed suicide and another man I hear wished to, but was prevented – these items must influence the Committee.

In the same letter Young referred to Lord Penrhyn's financial situation:

> As to your Banker's account, I would go on overdrawing until after your Norway trip and then reconsider the position[16].

Carter gave Lord Penrhyn a full account of the developing negotiations. W. J. Williams went to see W. J. Parry, who was an old friend and a fellow Congregationalist; and Parry undertook to contact W. H. Williams, whom Carter described as 'the men's leader'. Two weeks later, after Young had asked what was happening, he and Carter met at Criccieth; and Carter reported that W. H. Williams had had talks with Parry but had said he could 'make nothing of him'. Though Parry was 'anxious . . . to assist in a settlement of the strike', Carter felt that he no longer had 'very much influence with the Penrhyn Quarrymen'. Carter had met Parry, who 'certainly appeared very much annoyed at the reticence of W. H. Williams'; and Williams had told Carter privately that he 'did not desire to be mixed up with W. J. Parry'.

Parry, who was accustomed to writing letters for other people, set out in the first person the terms on which Lord Penrhyn was prepared to settle:

> I have all along stated that I am not prepared to acknowledge a committee in my quarry to interfere with the management and to stand between me and my workmen and I have also stated distinctly that I am prepared to receive at any time a deputation of my

workmen on behalf of a Body of them or on behalf of an individual complaint by whoever appointed provided an aggrieved party forms one of such deputation and the number does not exceed four and the complaint is presented in writing.

The other suggested terms included an end to the subletting of contracts, and an agreement that if all the workers could not be re-admitted those left out would be those most recently recruited.

Carter received a visit in Caernarfon from D. R. Daniel, W. H. Williams, Robert Davies and Henry Jones; and they agreed to meet again on 30 July at the Erskine Arms Hotel in Conwy. Before then, however, Carter received another visit from W. H. Williams. W. H. Williams wanted to know how the negotiations had been re-started; and when he was told of W. J. Williams' letter he expressed astonishment that such a letter should have been written without authority from the other strike leaders. When he heard the contents of the letter, he agreed that there was no harm it it; but he indicated that he would report the matter to D. R. Daniel, Robert Davies and Henry Jones. This incident was later used to oust W. J. Williams from his position as Secretary of the N.W.Q.U.

Carter learned that D. R. Daniel was to have a meeting on 27 July with the T.U.C. in the presence of the Liberal Chief Whip T. E. Ellis; and he suggested that W. J. Williams write to Ellis, urging him to advise D. R. Daniel and W. H. Williams that nothing was to be gained by continuing the strike. On 3 August, having discussed the proposed terms with Young, Lord Penrhyn sailed for Norway; the men's representatives, while expressing disappointment at the news, agreed to go on with the negotiations in his absence. While Young was entertaining Carter on board his launch in the Menai Straits, they exchanged greetings with Walter Vivian as he passed in his yacht; and on 9 August Carter gave Vivian an account of the negotiations to date. Three days later Carter had a meeting at the British Hotel in Bangor with Ben Pickard M.P., who was accompanied by the Secretary and the Treasurer of the Miners' Federation. Carter gave Pickard a full history of the strike, going into some detail about the quarrymen's pay and conditions; and Pickard, whom Carter described as 'very agreeable and of the plain rough John Bull type', looked hard at his two colleagues and said, 'I begin to see daylight here'. According to Carter, Pickard expressed sympathy with Lord Penrhyn 'quite as much as with the men'; and he indicated that if the terms offered to the men in May had provided for 'the cause of one man being the cause of all', the major unions 'would have ceased to contribute to the Strike Fund'. At the end of the meeting Pickard shook Carter warmly by the hand, saying, 'Mr Carter, I am for peace, and I shall advise these men to settle this strike'. He then went to Bethesda, where he met the Committee in the Bethania Chapel.

There was no immediate settlement, because there was still disagreement about contracts and about re-admission. Even when Young, Carter and Vivian had worked on the terms again, those relating to contracts and re-admission did not satisfy W. J. Williams; but after private discussions between W. J. Williams and Vivian at the Sportsman Hotel in Caernarfon the terms on contracts were settled. On 15 August, finding that he was staying near D. R. Daniel's home, Carter took the opportunity of calling there. He found Mrs Daniel 'a kind hearted sort of person'; and he explained to the Daniels

> how very hard it was for innocent persons to suffer and the slate trade to be perhaps permanently dislocated owing to the continuation of the strike.

He also suggested, somewhat misleadingly, that 'of all the parties concerned Lord Penrhyn would suffer least as he could afford to hold out for any length of time.' On 16 August Carter had a further meeting in Caernarfon with D. R. Daniel, W. J. Williams, W. H. Williams and Robert Davies. Carter asked W. J. Williams to explain the outstanding problem of re-admission; and 'in the confusion of tongues' W. J. Williams

> unintentionally led the men to think that all that was required was for their names to be printed and that then they would resume work.

No reference was made to the need for a 'permit'.

When he heard of this incident from Carter, Vivian insisted that the misunderstanding about re-admission must be cleared up. After meeting Young at Port Dinorwic on 18 August, Carter went with W. J. Williams to see the deputation in Bethesda. The clarification caused 'a great hubbub', and when Carter called at Tanybryn he was despondent:

> When Mr Vivian came in his evening dress (he had left his dinner table) he found both Young and myself in the dumps and we both had given up all hope of the strike being settled for at least a time. However Mr Vivian cheered us both up and when I told him that the committee were still sitting, he jocularly told me to cheer up and go back to Bethesda.

Carter rejoined the Committee around midnight, and found the proceedings 'at times somewhat excited and uproarious'. When the meeting re-convened at 8 a.m. on 19 August, it was said that the Committee dared not face the men with the proposed terms. Asked if there would be a black list, Carter replied that he was prepared to say publicly that he had not heard of any; and in response to a question from the chairman William Evans, Carter said that he would be willing to speak at a mass meeting. It was decided by majority vote that a communication should be sent to Young; and when Carter and Henry Jones left with this in the carriage, a crowd cheered them off. Young agreed to meet the deputation at 12.30 p.m.; and when Carter telephoned him at about 2 p.m. he reported that W. H. Williams, Robert Davies and Henry Jones had just left after signing the terms of settlement. Carter exclaimed, 'Thank God', and Young replied, 'Amen[17]'. In view of this intricate sequence of events, it is hardly surprising that the agreement was later said to have been reached in 'mysterious circumstances[18]'.

Carter wrote to Robert Jones, a Conservative quarryman whom he considered thoroughly reliable, and urged him to persuade 'as many Conservatives as possible' to attend the mass meeting 'so as to assist in carrying the terms of settlement'. On 20 August Robert Jones replied as follows:

> There is general rejoicing expressed on all hands at the termina-

> tion of the strike and declarations that there will not be another strike in the Penrhyn Quarries as long as they live.
>
> The men seem very grateful to you for bringing things to a close as you will observe no doubt at the meeting on Saturday. I have made it a point to see as many as possible to carry out your instructions and I feel pretty sure now that the terms will be accepted, although I believe there will be some hot ones against Mr Prichard but as I mentioned before I say nothing against Mr Prichard although he is a methodist and Radical as it is our duty as Conservatives to always respect those who are put over us.

On 21 August the Bethesda Market Hall was 'densely packed' for the mass meeting. At Carter's suggestion, English trade unionists were not allowed to speak, and the meeting was addressed only by W. H. Williams and by Carter. The terms of settlement were not announced 'until the very last moment'; and Carter commented afterwards that if the men had had 'an opportunity of digesting the terms earlier' the meeting might not have been 'so unanimous as it was in accepting them'.

On the same day Carter wrote to Lord Penrhyn, who had been informed of the settlement by telegram when he landed from the S. S. *Angelo* at Hull. Explaining that he was 'somewhat knocked up with all the excitement' he had been through, Carter warned Lord Penrhyn not to assume that the men were 'completely smashed'. In reality there was 'plenty of fight still left in them'; and the 'quarrymen proper' were all 'comfortably off', so that they could 'hold out for a long time' if they chose to do so. Carter compared the men to 'mountain sheep', saying that they had to be 'led not driven'; and he described how they had been rushed into a vote about the terms which had not been announced until the last moment. Understandably, Carter asked that this letter be destroyed[19].

Young was not entirely happy about the way in which the settlement had been achieved. On 24 August he told Lord Penrhyn that he had not authorised or approved Carter's attendance at the mass meeting, and that some of Carter's statements to that meeting had been 'incorrect'. Young accepted, however, that W. H. Williams could not have carried the meeting without

Carter, and that the strike might have dragged on for many months. He did not anticipate any action from the Committee for the present, as they had 'had quite enough of it'; and although problems would continue so long as the press was 'badly worked', the men's knowledge that Lord Penrhyn had been victorious offered 'the best safeguard against any further trouble[20]'.

Carter had implied that there would be no black list, but Young examined the applications thoroughly and excluded twenty-five men. On 27 August he told Lord Penrhyn that he had completed this task, and that the final list was in the printer's hands. On 28 August he reported that everything was going 'like clockwork . . . without any hostile demonstrations', and that W. H. Williams and other leaders had applied for work. On 29 August he wrote:

> About a hundred more men applied yesterday and no doubt a good many more will do so tomorrow. . . . I went to the Bethesda Show at 2 p.m. and spent one and quarter hours in the crowd without the least sign of a 'booh', and afterwards cycled to Ogwen Lake and after tea cycled back through a great crowd in Bethesda where I heard only a very feeble boo on the doorstep of a public house.

On 1 September Young thanked Lord Penrhyn for three brace of grouse, which he described as a 'most welcome diversion from quarry matters'. On 23 September he reported the death of Ben Pickard, describing him as 'valuable and respected'; and on the same date he confessed that his own heart had been 'strained' by the strike. Young was now faced with an 'agitation in favour of the men *not* re-admitted'; but he reported that the unionists were divided, and expressed his confidence that the matter would 'Blow over'[21].

The terms of the 1897 settlement were as follows:-

> I a) The grievance of any employee, crew, or class shall be submitted by him, or them in the first instance to the local manager. If dissatisied with the decision of the local manager, then the said grievances shall be submitted to the chief manager either personally or by deputation appointed in such manner as the workmen may

deem advisable, but to consist of not more than five employees selected from the same class as the person or persons aggrieved who must be included in the deputation.
b) Grievances in which the employees generally are interested or which they may adopt on behalf of an employee, crew, or class who have submitted their grievances under the preceding clause and are dissatisfied can again be submitted to the chief manager by a deputation consisting of not more than six employees appointed in such manner as the workmen may deem advisable.
c) Finally in a similar manner in all cases of importance an appeal may be made to Lord Penrhyn either by the individual or by a deputation, against the decision of the chief manager; the grounds of such appeal shall in all cases be first submitted to his lordship in writing.
II Suitable rybelwyr will be given monthly bargains without delay as soon as the management find it practicable.
III The letting of contracts to be left in the hands of the management who engage all persons employed thereon and see that each employee receives his just ratio of wages.
IV Previous to the cessation of work the average wage paid to the quarrymen was 5s 6d per day, other piece work classes being in proportion, (viz: Badrockmen 4s 7d and labourers 3s 7d); when work is resumed this same basis will be continued so long as trade permits.
V All the late employees who desire work in Penrhyn Quarry will be readmitted in a body as far as it is practicable and the remainder as soon as work can be arranged for them. Reasonable time being allowed to those who may now be employed at a distance.

Even if the last clause had been scrupulously observed, this settlement would clearly have been a defeat for the union.

Lord Penrhyn's postbag at this time contained many letters of congratulation. On 22 August there was an exultant letter from his son Edward:

> No question of the right of a committee to interfere, or dictate to you in any way. . . . I congratulate you on a great victory; whatever the men may put in the papers about you having given way, your terms are the same as you placed before them 12 months ago, and which poor deluded and misguided creatures they were not allowed to accept.

What a relief this will be to you after all the strain and worry of the past year, but it is a great triumph.

On the same day J. Menzies of Caernarfon declared that 'employers of labour generally and Welsh quarry proprietors in particular', were under 'a deep debt of gratitude' to Lord Penrhyn for the 'justly determined attitude' he had maintained 'at so much self-sacrifice'. On 23 August Thomas Lewis of Bangor wrote of the relief felt by thousands who had been 'in greatest anxiety as to facing the hardships of the coming winter'. On the same day H. A. Duff wrote that Lord Penrhyn had 'certainly been badgered and baited in some quarters in the most disgraceful way', and that he had 'rendered a great service' to the 'trade' of the country. On 26 August George Livesey of the Southern Metropolitan Gas Co wrote that the unionists were engaged in a struggle 'not for the benefit of the workmen but for their own power'. On the 27 August the Rev M. Roberts of Penmachno Rectory in Bettws y Coed sent the congratulations of 'an old Llandegai boy', praising Lord Penrhyn for his stand against Radical bigotry and tradeunionism tyranny'. On 28 August the Duke of Grafton congratulated him on ending a dispute which had been caused by 'outside agitators'.

On 30 August 1897 the Rev Samuel Jones of Llandrygan vicarage paid a more eloquent tribute:

During the twenty years' clerical work which I carried on in the Bethesda neighbourhood whilst curate of St Ann's, on your Lordship's Estate, from 1876 up to July 1896, (than where I was never happier) I always regarded the Penrhyn quarrymen as the best treated, the best cared for, and the most comfortably quartered class of workmen anyone could ever meet with.

With their good habitations, and surrounded as they were with such comforts, blessings and privileges, they owed your Lordship a lasting debt of gratitude. I have, always, unswervingly, upheld the quarry proprictor and management, and have in my public and private teaching . . . inculcated truthfulness, honesty, loyalty to the throne, wth due and respectful submission to all in authority, as primary and fundamental duties incumbent upon all.

When I heard of the strike at Penrhyn Quarry no one deplored the men's ill-advised and most uncalled for action more than I did, and I sincerely trust, that by the sufferings which they have brought on themselves and others they have learnt a lesson for good, never to be forgotten[22].

A literary man might have recognised here the voice of Jane Austen's Mr Collins; but Lord Penrhyn was never much of a reader.

After the initial jubilation, the men began to ask themselves what had been achieved. On 31 August 1897 *Y Genedl Gymreig* offered a bitter answer:

> We must confess that we cannot see how the men have won anything. . . . The men . . . are very disappointed. They have lost over £100,000. . . . There are strange rumours about the country amongst the people as to the termination of the strike. . . . It is also suggested that the committee did not know anything of the means taken to terminate the dispute until things had gone too far. If the story is true the old curse of Welshmen follows us still. Treachery conquers us when the force of arms fails.

A principal target for this attack was W. J. Williams, the Secretary of the N.W.Q.U.

W. J. Williams was a native of Tregarth, a quarryman's son, and a chartered accountant. He was 'in no sense an agitator', and 'invariably spoke of the Penrhyn family in terms of great respect'. In July 1897 Lord Penrhyn observed privately that he had tried to prevent the strike, and that 'having regard to his position' he was doing everything possible to end it. Lord Penrhyn regretted only that he was 'somewhat timid', and that he did not 'control sufficiently the actions of the union'. On 18 September W. J. Williams circulated from 'Caebraichycafn Lodge No 2' a printed letter, in which he sought to defend himself against the charge that he had betrayed his colleagues by writing privately to Carter. He said that he had written because:

> funds were dwindling, the demands were increasing, while the workmen and all who contributed were enquiring what was being done to effect an understanding.

Despite these arguments W. J. Williams was removed from

office by a change in the union's rules: his responsibilities as General Secretary were taken over by D. R. Daniel as Organiser, and in December 1897 W. H. Williams was elected to the new post of Financial Secretary[23]. The union moved to new headquarters at 1 Turf Square, Caernarfon; and W. J. Williams died soon afterwards[24]. Another prominent figure whose standing with the union was endangered by his role in the negotiations was W. J. Parry. Parry had hoped to regain the contract for supplying explosives to Penrhyn Quarry; and on 21 August 1897 he actually wrote to T. J. Shand of Nobel's in Glasgow, saying that Lord Penrhyn's solicitor had promised to try to restore that contract in return for his help in ending the strike[25]. Carter had no authority to restore Parry's contract, however, and Young predictably showed no inclination to do so.

Lord Penrhyn wrote several letters to people who had been helpful during the strike, and one of these was addressed to the Prince of Wales. In July representatives of the strikers had asked the Prince to invite Lord Penrhyn to nominate an arbitrator from a list consisting of the Duke of Devonshire, Lord Rosebery, Lord Peel, Lord Reichel, Lord James and Arthur Balfour; they said they had a 'very kind feeling towards Lord Penrhyn', and were prepared to abide by the arbitrator's decision. On 27 July Lord Penrhyn had written to the Prince from Goodwood, saying that the men's advisers had already approached Balfour without consulting himself or agreeing terms of reference, and that arbitration in these circumstances was out of the question. On 24 August Lord Penrhyn wrote from Mortimer House to the Prince of Wales, who was taking his annual cure at the Bohemian spa of Marienbad. In this letter Lord Penrhyn said that the Prince's 'attitude of impartial neutrality' at a 'critical moment' had 'materially forwarded the settlement', and that the settlement itself was 'in every way satisfactory'; although the *Daily Chronicle* claimed a victory for the men, they were in fact returning to work on the terms they had rejected in May[26].

Lord Penrhyn also wrote to John Gibson, the editor of the

Liberal *Cambrian News*, to thank him for the 'very able and thoroughly impartial manner' in which he had dealt with the strike. Lord Penrhyn said that he had read Gibson's articles with 'deep interest', and had been pleased to find such a 'fair-minded spirit' and such a grasp of the situation in one who was 'generally speaking' a political opponent. After this date the *Cambrian News* gave Lord Penrhyn considerable support. On 4 September 1897 William Gray, the chief clerk at the quarry, wrote to thank Lord Penrhyn for the £100 cheque he had received for 'extra work in the past year'[27]. On 9 September the 'Old Workmen Class', who had worked during the early part of the strike, wrote to thank Lord Penrhyn for the pensions of £1 a month which had been paid to them.

On 25 September W. H. Williams, Robert Davies and Henry Jones wrote to Young asking why some men had been refused work. On 29 September Young told Lord Penrhyn that this was 'not a very formidable letter'; but he recognised the implication that the management had promised there would be no black list. The position he adopted was that no-one had been refused work in connection with the strike; and he attributed the various rejections to drunkenness, incompetence, defective eyesight, defective hearing, physical disability, and 'other reasons' which made re-employment impracticable. Having received this explanation, the men's leaders said that they were dissatisfied, since the settlement terms provided for the re-admission of all former employees. When they raised the matter with Lord Penrhyn, however, he replied that no-one had been refused re-employment because of any action connected with the strike, and that he should not be expected to take back workmen who were unsuitable or of 'bad character'. Robert Davies and Henry Jones also approached Lloyd Carter about the question of re-admittance, but he said that he could not interfere. In a letter to Lord Penrhyn, he commented:

> It will never do for these men to come trotting over to Carnarvon to see me as if I was some little Court of Appeal every time anything occurs at the Quarries[28].

Sixty-seven of the seventy-one men were re-admitted; and it was claimed that the only one refused re-employment was Azariah Roberts, a Conservative and churchman who was said to be an 'inferior workman, lazy and discontented, and . . . frequently absent'.

Lord Penrhyn's victory in the dispute of 1896–7 led to a slump in trade union membership in North Wales, the figure dropping by 1899 to a mere 822. The right of combination and the principle of collective bargaining had suffered a serious blow; and most employees were reluctant to be seen as rebels, since the union appeared unable to defend them. Lord Penrhyn's counterattack against trade unionism had for the present been successful; and he had shown the weakness not only of the union but also of the Government, which despite the Conciliation Act was unable to intervene effectively[29]. Lord Penrhyn himself was convinced that he was fighting for individual freedom against the impersonal demands of a New Unionism which mistakenly supposed the days of the master were over.

5
An Uneasy Truce: 1897–1900

The settlement of 1897 was followed by attempts to impose stricter discipline, and in November Young appointed Thomas Ellis as 'private Inspector (or detective) in the Quarry'. On 5 January 1898 Young wrote to Lord Penrhyn suggesting that Ellis might be accommodated in a house known as Penrhiw, which was just above Ogwen Bank and overlooked the quarry exit. This would necessitate the eviction of the present occupant, the widow of a former quarry official; Young argued that it would become increasingly difficult to find accommodation for employees if the system of letting widows keep possession were maintained. One of Ellis' duties was to enforce Home Office regulations about explosives; and when he gave evidence in the 1903 libel case he said that his aims were firstly to look after the men's safety and secondly to prevent action against Lord Penrhyn by the Inspector of Mines.

On his first visit to the quarry Ellis merely cautioned the men; but on his second he reported 'four or five men' to Prichard for breaking the rules, and these men were suspended for three days. On 18 February Richard Hughes was observed smoking while carrying powder, and this led to his being suspended for a week. On 12 March there was a visit by G. J. Williams, the Assistant Inspector of Mines, who said that the hinges of all explosives boxes should be on the outside. Ellis ordered the men to remove all inside hinges from explosives boxes; and on 19 April, when only a box belonging to John Williams and Peter Roberts remained unchanged, these two men were reported and dismissed. During the libel case W. J. Parry said that they were both noted for their union activities, John Williams being one of the men's principal speakers and

Peter Roberts a 'very prominent man always with the union'. Giving evidence in the same case, John Williams said that he had worked in the quarry for thirty-eight years, was on the Committee in 1897, and was dismissed in May 1898 after only one warning; but he also said that Peter Roberts, who had worked in the quarry since 1850, was not a member of the Committee and did not play any large role in the 1896–7 dispute. Both men appealed against the dismissal notice, but Young insisted that the rules had to be enforced. On 9 December 1898 Young answered Lord Penrhyn's questions about this episode:

> The man Peter Roberts and his partner John Williams of Ynys were dismissed for deliberately disobeying the Home Office special rules *after* they were cautioned and specially ordered to conform to those rules. All the men in their gallery except these two men obeyed at once, but these two men continued to *disobey* quite deliberately for three weeks.
>
> The very fact of their having been employed by you (and your father) for fifty years surely should have induced them to set a *good* example, as you say, and curiously enough that is the very reply I gave them at the time I dismissed them[1].

Young added that the two men were not 'amongst the *faithful* 300 who worked during the strike', and that he regarded them as 'agitators'.

In September 1898 a dispute arose between the local manager David Prichard and William R. Evans, who was chairman of the Committee and had been treasurer of the union lodge since 1882. Although he had already lost six days and the usual maximum was a week, Evans asked for another four days' leave on the ground that he never lost time 'except to attend a funeral now and again'. In the subsequent quarrel Prichard accused Evans of being 'the head of those who challenged Lord Penrhyn'; and Evans replied that he had 'done nothing personally', and that the Committee 'meant no harm to anyone' but was simply 'trying to get places for rybelwyr'. Evans was given not four days' leave but two; and when he subsequently received a bargain of poor-quality slate, he allegedly accused Prichard of punishing him for his role in the strike. When he refused to withdraw this accusation, the matter was brought to Young's attention and Evans was dismissed. On 9 December Young wrote uneasily to Lord Penrhyn:

> No doubt you will have an appeal from William Evans soon and in his case although I feel exactly certain I am acting rightly it would be next to impossible to justify this dismissal in black and white.

Evans did indeed appeal to Lord Penrhyn, but on 4 February 1899 he was sent a curt rejection:

> I am instructed by Lord Penrhyn to say that after due consideration, he regrets he cannot see his way to finding you further employment in the quarry.

Young had convinced himself that the men were heartily tired of the Committee, and that these dismissals would help to break its 'tyranny'; but in fact the dismissal of W. R. Evans aroused great indignation, and contributed to the process which led to the confrontation at the end of 1900[2].

At the end of 1898 Young wished Lord Penrhyn a 'cloudless New Year', and on 30 January 1899 he reported the success of his investment policy:

> You will, I fear, scarcely believe it, but nevertheless it is true that your investment a/c is now worth nearly £30,000 more than it was on the 14th inst.

Having given this encouraging news, Young sought permission to enlarge Tanybryn by adding two bedrooms and 'a large schoolroom suitable for billiards as well'. The house had only six bedrooms, and Young's household consisted of 'two parents, four sons, one governess, two nurses and four servants'. A 'further increase in the family' was expected at this time, though in the event there was a miscarriage. Lord Penrhyn gave his permission for the proposed extension to be built.

Prichard's health was poor, and in March 1899 his doctor told him that indigestion was the 'root of all the trouble'. He was advised to take plenty of food and exercise, drink less tea, have two glasses of port a day, and go on a sea voyage. Young had initiated a generally unpopular efficiency drive; and he resolved to have Prichard pensioned off, declaring on 29 May that he was a 'perpetual hindrance' because he was 'so antagonistic to new methods'. As replacement for Prichard Young urged Lord Penrhyn to accept an engineer named H. P. Meares, who had worked in India and later became Young's brother-in-law; this was to prove a disastrous appointment, but in 1899 Young was enthusiastic about Meares' role in his reform plans. Young considered that Prichard had not been 'strong enough', and that in consequence the other officials had become 'dreadfully slack' and had failed 'to report men or punish them adequately'. In his struggle against the general laxity Young had been supported only by his 'detective' Thomas Ellis, who had no relations locally and acted promptly and decisively.

Young wanted to replace most of the officials, not by handing out pensions as Lord Penrhyn would have preferred, but by catching them 'at fault' and then dismissing them 'with no pension for the sake of example to others'. He dismissed the 'head marker' John Jones for 'absolute refusal to do his duty towards his employer', and commented:

> He would rather let the men come late than catch them and become unpopular and then made it worse by trying to excuse himself because it was not in his district – I told him his duty to his employer never ceased in any part of the quarry . . . but it seemed useless talking to him. It was a painful duty for me to dismiss him after 54 years in the quarry but I feel he deserved his punishment.

John Jones had been 'insolent' to Ellis, and his son the Rev W. J. Jones later made 'a very cheeky appeal'; but Young paid him for an extra month to prevent him from alleging wrongful dismissal. Two quarrymen who had cheated their partner of £1 a month were dismissed and faced police prosecution; the case had been brought by Ellis, the victim having received no help from the marker Evan Jones, who boasted that he had £3,000 invested at 4 per cent and would soon be pensioned off. Young said he was convinced that there was bribery in the quarry, and observed regretfully that Evan Jones was 'another Churchman'.

On 2 June 1899 Young told Lord Penrhyn that he needed a 'better class' of men for the posts on the weighing machines. He explained:

> It is all very well to be charitable and fill them with the most deserving invalids but it is not business. . . . In winter sometimes as many as six at a time are away ill, therefore I propose as vacancies occur, putting in sound good men for the future.

Prichard having been given a pension of almost £3 a week, Young wrote re-assuringly on 2 June about the appointment of Meares as chief engineer. Young said he would be careful to avoid any action which would allow 'a practical quarryman to say that he objected to being under the management of an incompetent foreigner', and continued:

> I hope that Mr Mears will learn enough Welsh, but meanwhile I will take care to guard against the danger that you have called my attention to. Mr Meares will have to move very slowly at first but I am hoping that he will obtain the loyal support of all the new officials at any rate – but the old ones are beyond altering and must go when a chance comes.

In the same letter Young reported that three *rybelwyr* had been caught at 4.50 a.m. stealing a total of 430 slates; they were dismissed, but a prosecution before the Bangor magistrates on 20 June proved unsuccessful. In another attempt to improve discipline, Young appointed as setter a former Nantlle quarry-manager named Hugh Pennant Roberts, who spoke English well and was described by Young on 20 June as 'a *strong* man of the sort I want *badly*'. These rapid changes caused much resentment, and in November 1900 Ellis, Meares and Pennant Roberts all became targets for violent attacks.

On 2 June 1899 Young informed Lord Penrhyn of yet another decisive step:

> I am ceasing to employ Robert Davies the 'King' after Tuesday – he has been involved in a very discreditable chapel money affair.

Robert Davies, a long-serving member of the N.W.Q.U., had been president in 1897 and was one of the signatories to the terms of settlement. On 13 June Young sent Lord Penrhyn a report on Robert Davies, which has not survived. In a separate letter, he commented that the material in the report could not be used to justify the dismissal:

> They all lie so terribly and screen one another that we should be landed very awkwardly.

A mass meeting on Pay Saturday with W. R. Evans in the chair was to be addressed by the 'two agitators' D. R. Daniel and W. H. Williams; but Young insisted that dismissals were a matter for the management alone, and that he would not discuss the matter with any deputation[3].

D. R. Daniel (1859–1931) had no practical experience of quarrying. He was the son of a Merionethshire tenant farmer, a supporter of the temperance movement, a member of Caernarfonshire County Council, and a friend of the Liberal M.P.s T. E. Ellis and David Lloyd George. As a leader of the quarrymen he was not ultimately a success; but he enjoyed considerable popularity, and his speeches at mass meetings stiffened their determination. W. H. Williams (1848–1917), who was born at Llwybrmain near Bethesda, worked in Penrhyn Quarry and was known for his deep religious convictions and his links with the Calvinistic Methodist chapels. He served as vice-president of the N.W.Q.U. in 1889, declined to give evidence before the Royal Commission on Labour in 1891, and was involved in meetings with Young and Lord Penrhyn during the dispute of 1896–7. His disapproval of the 1897 settlement brought him into greater prominence, and his powerful speeches made him a dominant figure thereafter[4].

On 16 June 1899 Young told Lord Penrhyn that the union officials were trying to use 'the dethronement of the King R. Davies to give a fillip to the union'; the reason for this dismissal was 'very generally known', however, and there was 'little sympathy with him amongst the best men'. Two days later Young reported that the mass meeting on this issue had been 'one of the tamest ever held', with only 250 to 300 men present; the names of Young and Lord Penrhyn had not been mentioned, and instead of proposing a pension for Robert Davies the men had simply collected £6 to 'set him up in business'. Young had warned Colonel Ruck that there might be another attack on Tanybryn, but in fact he encountered no hostility:

> The threatened mob never came nor was I attacked on the road as was hinted to me might happen, but it was quite the reverse – I cycled after pay through a lot of them in Bethesda and they were all cheerful and respectful. I got off and chatted with several on the way up the New Road (a stiff hill) – it was intensely hot and I chaffed one or two for wearing such heavy black felt hats and so on.
>
> I collapsed after lunch but had nearly three hours sound sleep and woke up quite fresh again. I can't help feeling the strain but now that the meeting was such a failure I feel I have won a great victory towards discipline.

Press reports of the mass meeting spoke not of a 'fiasco' but of 'intense excitement'; but Young was convinced that 'the only excitement was in the papers'.

Young decided not to appoint a new local manager for the present; but on 8 July 1899 he told Lord Penrhyn that he was spending half his time in the quarry, where he was learning more and keeping 'everything going straight'. He also reported that trade was 'not so good'; and in fact the boom which had reached its height in 1898 was to be followed, because of depression in the building trade and reduced foreign demand, by a steady decline in slate production, in the numbers employed, and in the value of slate per ton. On 24 July Young asked Lord Penrhyn to send a subscription of £2 2s to the newly formed Bethesda Sports Club; the quarry doctor Mills Roberts, who wanted to encourage sport among the quarrymen, said that 'stirring them up with football, cricket etc' would not 'do any harm'. Commenting on Meares' arrival, Young reported that things were 'all quiet' so far; and he said that he had found Meares helpful when he was 'pegging away at the officials . . . to try and make them . . . more strict with the men'. A setter named Benjamin Thomas had been building a house with 'free labour of quarrymen who were helping to build it in the lunch-hour', and the men had been carrying slates to the site from the mill. Young put Benjamin Thomas on half-pay, and intended to dismiss him if a replacement could be found[5].

In his campaign for stricter discipline, Young was supported by Ellis and Meares. On 31 May 1899 John Jones and Griffith Parry were dismissed for 'illegal fishing on Lord Penrhyn's estate'; and on 10 July Ellis wrote about the problems of organising an industrial concern in a rural setting. Many of the men had smallholdings with one or two cows and a few sheep, and leave was often granted for sheep-shearing, hay-making and harvest. The consequent difficulties may be deduced from Meares' account:

> Hitherto six days a year was the limit of leave given to each man, not including funerals, but leave was granted for haymaking in excess of this, but as sparing as possible.

Meares believed that leave was increasing in some districts of the quarry, and was anxious to establish a regular procedure for dealing with requests. There were also attempts to enforce stricter time-keeping, officials being told on 13 July that

> the minimum punishment for coming late was to be two days, and for going away before time in the afternoon, a week's suspension.

An extract from the Discipline Book indicates how the rules were enforced:

> 26 May 1900 Thomas Price found sneaking away from his work at 4.30 p.m. on 25 May by J. R. Pritchard, Marker, and suspended for six days. He did not come back to the quarry.
>
> His previous character was good and he was a handy man[6].

Even pensioners were affected by Young's economy drive. On 3 August 1899 he told Lord Penrhyn that he would continue to pay 7s 6d a week to those already on the list, but that new pensioners would be paid 5s a week as at Dinorwic. Young said that 'none but necessitous men of good character' would be granted pensions; and he rejected an application from Joseph C. Hughes, after learning that Hughes received 10s a week from two clubs and had not worked during the 1896–7 strike.

Young was a keen gardener, and in August 1899 his black Hamburg grapes won a first prize in the 'great show at Shrewsbury – open to all Great Britain'; he attributed his success to Lord Penrhyn's generosity, presumably in providing a vine from the Penrhyn Castle gardens. On 17 October 1899 Lord Penrhyn received a letter in Welsh from John Griffith, who wrote on behalf of the quarrymen in connection with the forthcoming marriage between Lord Penrhyn's daughter Gwyneth Pennant and Sir William Eley Cuthbert Quilter. Young described Griffith as a 'harmless sort of man', but explained that the present the men wished to give would be financed chiefly by those who 'led to the strike in the autumn of 1896', and would be presented by the Bethesda Lodge secretary Griffith Edwards, a 'well-known agitator' who had organised the mob descent on Tanybryn. On 2 November Lord Penrhyn wrote to John Griffith declining the gift:

> I beg to thank you, and those on whose behalf you have written, for the kind thoughts you have expressed concerning a gift to my daughter on the occasion of her marriage . . . with regard to which I hope I may not be misunderstood when I say that without any actual gift, I and my family are quite contented to know that my daughter has the good wishes of some of the Penrhyn quarrymen for her future happiness.

On 23 November, five days after the wedding, Young commented that 'no doubt some of the loyal men in the quarry felt aggrieved at having their subscription returned', but that it would 'surely . . . teach them' that when they wished to show their loyalty 'it must be done through some other channel than the quarry union officials'[7].

Applying his financial skill to his own investments as well as Lord Penrhyn's, Young became steadily wealthier; by 1899 he owned one-third and Lord Penrhyn two-thirds of a sailing-ship named *Mary B. Mitchell* and of four steamers named *Pennant, Penrhyn, Bangor* and *Harrier*[8]. Although his health was affected by the strains of his job, Young persisted relentlessly with his reform programme; and on 29 November he outlined to Meares his plans for new blasting procedures and a change in holiday arrangements. Having been struck by the 'tremendous waste of time caused by our blasting in the Quarry so frequently', he proposed to introduce new hours for blasting. Blasting would take place at 9 a.m., 11 a.m., 12 noon, 12.55 p.m. and 3 p.m.; and when the bell for stopping work was to ring at 5 p.m., blasting would also be allowed at 4 p.m. He proposed to abolish the holidays known as the 'Bangor Fair Days', replacing them with holidays on Good Friday, Easter Saturday, Easter Monday, Whit Monday, Ascension Day and Christmas Day; and he was prepared to add a holiday called Harvest Thanksgiving, which was already in force at Dinorwic. These new rules were to be posted in the quarry on 1 December 1899, and were to come into force at Dinorwic and Penrhyn simultaneously on 1 January 1900. That Young expected opposition is apparent from his warning to Meares:

> Please keep the contents of this letter very particularly private and do not even let a suspicion of what I intend doing leak out to a single soul.

In December 1899 an overlooker was dismissed for failing to keep the galleries under his charge at an angle that provided for the men's safety. The Assistant Inspector of Mines had reported an unsafe gallery in March, and found it even worse in May; but Young had heard about this and put the work in hand, so that a surprise visit by the Inspector found it safe. Young knew that he could have been prosecuted if the gallery had not been dealt with; and this incident strengthened his concern about safety and about discipline[9].

The South African War was opposed by Radical papers like *Y Faner, Yr Herald Cymraeg, Y Genedl Gymreig, Y Cymro* and *Y Tyst;* and at a later date striking quarrymen were to identify with another persecuted community by calling themselves 'Boers'. There was also much British patriotism among the quarrymen, however, and on 4 January 1900 Young wrote enthusiastically about the two 'patriotic concerts' for the benefit of the troops over which he had presided in the Bethesda Market

Hall. Seven choirs 'representing various Chapels and Churches' were seated on the platform, and they 'worked heartily together'. Everyone stood up for 'Rule Britannia' and 'God Save the Queen', and 'what with all the Choirs and all the audience, the Chorus was a terribly rousing and inspiring performance'. Young was 'astounded at the hearty reception' he was given; and he told the audience that Lord Penrhyn would make an allowance to the dependants of every man who volunteered. Lord Penrhyn, whose son Charles was to serve in the war, was sent a programme and a 'one shilling book of words'. Young knew 'only too well' that the 'extreme enthusiasm' shown at these concerts would not last, but he believed that 'full advantage' should be taken of it while it lasted. That he remained critical of his workforce is clear from his reply on 24 January to a Bristol firm who wanted a 'working foreman'; he professed to need a foreman himself, but said that he had found 'Welshmen, when promoted, very poor foremen indeed'. In February Lord Penrhyn was sent a ticket for a concert at which Young hoped he would preside; and in March a cheque for £60 8s 9d, the proceeds of the last two concerts, was sent to Lord Penrhyn as a contribution to the County Fund. On 7 April 1900 Young exclaimed:

> What with Patriotic Concerts, Nurses' Institute and one thing and another, I shall be heartily glad to start on my holidays on Monday.

Young's holiday was to be a cycling tour in France.

On 11 April a meeting in Bangor was addressed by two Liberal M.P.s, Bryn Roberts and David Lloyd George, who argued that the South African War was being fought for the benefit of capitalists with interests in gold and diamonds. There was a noisy demonstration outside, and stones were thrown at the windows; but the meeting continued according to plan, and after it the speakers succeeded in evading the mob. On 19 April the *Aberystwyth Observer and Merionethshire News* deplored this 'rowdyism', arguing that its only effect would be to make Lloyd George 'a hero in the estimation of many people'.

At this stage Young professed to be very pleased wth Meares. On 5 January 1900 he had told Lord Penrhyn that Meares' salary of £600, which was £200 less than he had received in India, should be gradually increased in view of the change he had wrought in the quarry. Praising Meares' organising power and his untiring energy, Young said that any increase in his salary would be more than repaid in 'improving and economising the methods in the quarry'. On 7 April, just before he left for France, Young told Lord Penrhyn of his sister Adeline's formal engagement to Mears; the couple had known each other for some time, and Lord Penrhyn had been told of their relationship before Mears was appointed. The wedding was to take place in the summer, and Young was confident that his sister would be 'a useful addition to Bethesda'; he hoped that the couple would be able to live in Brynderwen when it had been repaired[10]. While Young was in France, however, Meares was informed that 'the union men were forcing men against their will to join and subscribe towards union funds'; and he reacted to this news by prohibiting the collection of union subscriptions in the quarry. On 24 April *Yr Herald Cymraeg* prepared for Labour Day by printing a letter signed 'The Spirit of Talcen Mawr', which declared that 'the oldest inhabitant in Bethesda' could not 'remember a time when so little money was paid for labour as at the present time.' On 1 May, having returned from France, Young was writing cheerfully to James Townley:

> There is nothing whatever in the rubbish in the papers but the usual May agitation, preliminary to what they call Labour-day. We have that sort of thing regularly every year.

On the following day, however, Meares confessed to Young that he regretted the 'mistake' he had made in 'stopping union money being collected at the Quarry'[11]. Young confirmed the decision which had been taken in his absence, and never publicly revealed that Meares was responsible; but the position Meares had adopted was to become a very serious grievance.

On 9 May 1900 Young gave Lord Penrhyn a reassuring account of the Labour Day meeting:

> As far as I can gather the Union demonstration at Carnarvon was a very feeble affair and I cannot trace any reference to their supposed grievance against being managed by monoglot Englishmen, nor do they appear to have made any mention of their not being allowed to collect money *inside* the Quarry. The same rule exists at Dinorwic. The meeting seemed to be more like a wail that the men had dropped off very considerably.

Referring to 'increasing evidence of the falling off of trade', Young said that when a reduction of wages became necessary Dinorwic Quarry would be quick to follow Penrhyn's example; and he ended by wishing Lord Penrhyn good luck with his horses at Chester[12]. Young's view of the situation was to some extent confirmed by a report in the *Manchester Guardian* of 12 May, which said that the two largest quarries in Wales were being 'governed with an iron hand' and that the men felt they had been 'crushed'. The apparent weakness of the N.W.Q.U., which at this date had only 369 members in Penrhyn Quarry, was to some extent offset, however, by its connection with the General Federation of Trade Unions. Being affiliated to the G.F.T.U., the union could expect support in a long dispute which exhausted its own funds; and this fact was to be of great practical and psychological importance over the next three years.

6
The Closure of the Quarry: 1900–1901

The year 1900 had begun quietly enough for the Pennants, the family letters received at Penrhyn Castle after Christmas including one from Lord Penrhyn's grandson Jevon Mostyn. Jevon was the son of Pamela Georgina Pennant, whose wedding in 1883 to Henry Mostyn of Llandudno had caused the quarrymen to rejoice that 'one of the Pearls of Penrhyn' was marrying a member of the 'honoured house of Mostyn'. On 4 January 1900 Jevon wrote to his 'grandpapa':

> Many thanks indeed for that nice little gold compass you sent me, it is truly superb and please could you thank Granny for those two books she so kindly sent to me. I have had some stories read to me by mother, they are really excellent.

Jevon, who was at Eton, apologised for not visiting Penrhyn Castle at Christmas: being ill at school, he had concealed the fact for fear of not being allowed to travel, with the result that he was very ill after arriving home. On 21 January he wrote again, expressing sympathy for a fellow-invalid:

> I was very sorry indeed to hear that you had sprained your back, and later to hear that you have got Influenza but I sincerely hope that you have almost recovered.

In the same letter he reported his own activities and those of his brother:

> I went hunting on the thirteenth of this month, we had only one jump, and Bay, after he had jumped, fell off in some inexplicable way but did not hurt himself.

Lord Penrhyn's son Charles was with the army in South Africa, and on 18 July a friend named Wilfred Seymour wrote to the anxious father:

> Dear George,
>
> You must have been pleased at the way Charlie has been already mentioned in dispatches for his coolness under as heavy a fire I imagine as troops have ever been subject to for so long a period[1].

Before the end of the year, however, the Pennant family was to have no less alarming news from much nearer home.

During the first half of 1900 the minutes of the N.W.Q.U. reflected a desire for economy, especially in connection with Labour Day. There was a proposal that fewer bands should be present, and it was said that Labour Day should be the concern of all quarrymen and not merely of union members. There were few signs of militancy, though it was argued that quarrymen were too quiet, and that the lively state of the slate trade offered the chance to win a fair price for fair work. It was agreed that no support should be given to an M.P. who ignored the labour question; but there was no reference to the ban on collecting union subscriptions during the dinner-hour, although this grievance was soon to push up union membership in Bethesda to 1,959[2]. On 1 August 1900 Young wrote to Lord Penrhyn:

> All quiet here on the surface at any rate and I hear no rumours – slates still *all* selling as fast as made but short by £12,000 compared with last year to date owing to decrease in output[3].

Returns had been high in 1899, both on the investment account and on the quarry account. In the first four months of 1899 the investment account had made a profit of £95,000, and in April 1899 its value was £358,214. The total profit on the quarry account for 1899 was £119,912, and Young's commission was £3,595; the total profit for 1900, despite the closure in November, was £92,120, and Young's commission was £2,206[4].

The crisis which began in October 1900 was later interpreted by the Liberal M.P. William Jones as the inevitable result of men being 'sworn at, abused, punished for trivial offences, and subjected to a system of espionage' under a sub-manager 'who had been accustomed to dealing with coolies in India, and who knew nothing about quarrying'. Young saw it as a terrifying outbreak of violence and riot; but Asquith, speaking in the House of Commons, presented it as a conflict over the right of combination. Historians have described it as a series of confusing incidents through which a 'smouldering conflict' developed into an 'open battle'[5]. The immediate context for this crisis was an intense resentment against individual contractors and officials, which led to a rebellion against managerial control and to the establishment of mob rule. Dissatisfaction with the contract system flared up suddenly in a gallery known as Ffridd, where there had been earlier disciplinary problems. There were two separate outbreaks, a week apart, involving about 500 men from the total workforce of 2,612. No grievances about contracts or anything else had been presented; and Young, who was about to go on holiday again, was taken by surprise.

The trouble started in a group of fourteen badrockmen who worked 'in Ffridd gallery near the top of the right side'. After conflict with the management, one man was suspended for six days and some others for three; and the rest of the fourteen did no work until the suspended men returned. Because he wasn't sure whether this was 'wilful' or due to the rain, Young punished only the 'ringleader', who apologised and admitted to having a 'rather quick tongue'; but the other men, on hearing that the ringleader had been suspended for another six days, stopped work again. They resumed work when threatened with suspension; but because of their 'mutinous spirit' they were told at the end of the quarry month that they could no longer work in Ffridd gallery but would be given bargains elsewhere. On hearing this, they said they would rather leave the quarry than be transferred to other galleries; and they were therefore told that they would be 'paid in a day or two'.

On the following day, 24 October 1900, Edward Williams, who was a partner in a big contract, was sent up to Ffridd gallery with four or five men. Despite warnings that it could be dangerous, he went up to Ffridd; and he there encountered some of the fourteen men who were putting away their tools. Although they told him to go away, he started work on the gallery; and soon afterwards some of the young men in the gallery above began to stone him and his assistants, shouting 'Hurrah'. Being compelled to run for his life, Williams made his way down the slate incline with fifty or sixty men at his heels, and sought shelter in the weighing-machine building. Because it was setting day, there were many young men standing around waiting for their bargains; and the crowd soon increased to between 300 and 500. The door of the weighing-machine building was broken down, and Williams, having been struck across the cheek with a piece of slate, tried to hide in the head marker's office. Having been dragged out and driven down towards the slab mill, he found shelter in a house; and when the men had gone back to work he was taken by cab to his home in Pentir, where the quarry doctor visited him at once.

On 26 October 1900 Young informed Lord Penrhyn that there had been 'a serious riot . . . in Ffridd gallery', and also gave a somewhat belated account of the events which had preceded it. He asked Meares to produce evidence for the identification of the rioters, since he hoped to prosecute 'a few of the offenders'; but he declined to give any information to the newspapers, wishing to keep 'absolutely quiet in the matter lest the men should start a campaign against the contract procedure which they 'so stupidly' called the 'sweating system'. He told Meares that he should not send anyone to work on the bargains in question, and that he should avoid 'irritating' the men for the next few weeks. Young did not anticipate any difficulty in finding another contractor for Ffridd if Williams was unable to go there; but though he claimed that the general body of quarrymen had very little sympathy for the 'rioters', he decided to stay out of the quarry himself so that things could 'cool down'[6].

Reporting the riot on 26 October 1900, the *Liverpool Echo* quoted Edward Williams' partner Richard Hughes as saying that 'one of the best workmen and kindest men in the quarry' had been attacked by a group of 'loafers'; but at the trial on 13 November Hughes denied using the term 'loafers', which had aroused some anger. Also on 26 October the *Carvarvon and Denbigh Herald* said that the ban on collecting subscriptions during the dinner-hour was seen by the men as a manifestation of hostility to the principle of combination, but that the men's leaders had 'wisely counselled patience' in this matter. On 28 October Young told Lord Penrhyn that 'nothing but quiet' reigned in the quarry, and that 'scores of men' had 'protested to police sergeant Owen against the riot'. He expressed the hope that Edward Williams would have 'the pluck to come back', and said that if 'nothing unexpected' happened he would go ahead with his trip to Great Yarmouth[7]. On 30 October Young told Meares not to accept any collective application for work from the fourteen men previously employed on the Ffridd gallery, but to allow them to submit individual applications for work in other parts of the quarry[8]. On 31 October the *Liverpool Daily Post* reported that 'large gangs' were assembling in various galleries during the dinner-hour.

The second outbreak of violence took place on 1 November 1900, and was reported in the *Carnarvon and Denbigh Herald* the following day. Although the police in Bangor and Bethesda warned him not to go near the quarry Richard Hughes insisted on returning to work. His two sons tried to protect him; but he was dragged out of a hut on the gallery, and 600 'stalwart youths' formed a procession to escort all three men off the premises. Hughes and his sons were bareheaded and terrified; and their faces were 'smeared with blood, which also dripped on to their garments'. Half of the crowd returned to the quarry to look for Thomas Pierce, the overlooker or understeward who had given the contract to Williams and Hughes. In marching Pierce back to his house, they went through the grounds of Brynderwen, the home of the chief engineer, and Meares himself came to the door. When he saw how Pierce was being treated, he 'raised up his hands in horror' and tried to speak; but the men 'pelted him in the face' with mud and gravel 'in a most unmerciful manner', and he 'hurriedly beat a retreat'. Accompanied by Sergeant Owen and two constables, the procession then resumed its journey to the village; according to the *Carnarvon and Denbigh Herald* they were marching 'quietly', but according to Sergeant Owen as quoted in the *Liverpool Courier* of 22 November they were singing 'Soldiers of the Queen'. Once

Pierce was in his house there were shouts of 'Now for Ellis'; but though 'search parties scoured the mountains and searched the grounds of Brynderwen', Ellis remained in hiding. According to the account which Hugh Vincent gave to the *North Wales Chronicle*, the crowd visited Ellis' house and tried 'to make his wife go down upon her knees to swear that her husband was not there'; when they eventually left, they told her they would murder Ellis if they caught him. At this stage, according to Vincent, 'the quarry was entirely in the hands of the mob, and a reign of terror existed'. In the meantime Pennant Roberts, realising that he would be the next target, 'jumped on a locomotive and was taken to Bangor before the crowd could secure him'. There was much support for the rioters among the women of Bethesda, one of whom told a reporter that 'anything' was better than a mode of working by which they were being 'slowly starved to death'. The police were 'utterly helpless' throughout the day, but there was no attack on the police or on men under their protection. At midnight, when the crowd had dispersed, Ellis and his family left their house and were driven to Bangor.

On 2 November the *Carnarvon and Denbigh Herald*, reporting that Young had visited the quarry, warned that terrible consequences would follow if the men were treated harshly. The *Daily Mail* of 2 November said that there was anger at the appointment of monoglot English officials, and that an attempt was being made to re-establish pre-1896 conditions; and the *Daily Express* of the same date said that the men were very determined. On 3 November extra police were sent to the Bethesda district; and the *Liverpool Courier* reported that, although 'responsible persons in Bethesda' said the local police could maintain order, the Bangor magistrates believed military aid to be needed. Hugh Vincent arranged to apply for warrants, and Colonel Ruck asked him to call a meeting of the magistrates so that he could ask for military assistance. The magistrates gave Colonel Ruck permission to call in the army, and warrants were granted against nine people. Two of the magistrates later urged Vincent to issue summonses instead, explaining that they feared a riot in Bethesda; but Vincent rejected this argument, professing to share the magistrates' view that the quarrymen were 'an essentially peace loving and law abiding people'. On 4 November, according to the *Liverpool Echo* of the following day, the military depot at Chester Castle received a telegram asking that men of the Cheshire Regiment should be dispatched to Bethesda; and about 9 p.m. that evening a detachment of about forty arrived in Bangor and was quartered at the National Schools on Garth Road. The intention was that they should proceed to Bethesda the next morning and be billeted in the Quarry Hospital and Ogwen Bank; but there was 'great indignation' at the decision to call them in, and for the present they remained in Bangor.

The quarrymen, whose mood at this stage was buoyant, claimed to have gained more in a fornight than in twelve years of appeals and agitations. Press reports, which Young called 'the usual lies', attributed the second riot to the fact that one of the men could not afford breakfast; and there were rumours that the Dinorwic men were about to cross the mountain to Bethesda in a protest against the military presence. Young had posted notices saying that the quarry would be closed if there were further disturbances; but he begged Lord Penrhyn to keep away from Bethesda, so as to give the men no opportunity for calling him 'vindictive etc.' There were many reports, including one in the *Manchester Guardian* for 8 November, that Lord Penrhyn had visited Bethesda; but in fact he seems to have followed Young's advice. Young kept in touch with Hugh Vincent, who reported that he hoped to get twenty-two warrants in all[9].

In the meantime troops poured into the area. 180 men of the Lincolnshire Regiment under Captain Thorold arrived by special train and were quartered in the Garth Board School, which had been built as a British School on land given in 1848 by Colonel Edward Douglas Pennant. The streets of Bangor were brightened by the lance-bearing troops of the reserve Dragoons, who arrived from York under the command of Major O'Connor; and General Thynne sent a telegram to Lord Penrhyn, requesting 'kindness' towards the officers and men. On 5

November the *Liverpool Echo* described the calling-in of these troops as 'a totally unnecessary insult to the Bethesda quarrymen, noted throughout Wales as a law-abiding body of men'; but on the same day Young informed Colonel Ruck that the troops' presence was having a beneficial effect. In the same letter Young asked Ruck to provide protection for those officials who still remained in their homes, pointing out that they feared assault and had received death threats. The first name on his list of eight was that of Thomas Pierce, who anticipated a further attack because he had provided information leading to a number of arrests. Colonel Ruck replied that he could not guarantee the officials' safety.

On 5 November, the day on which work was resumed, the wife of the Bishop of Bangor called on Young, accompanied by Canon Thomas and one of his daughters; but he declined to see any of them. Intimidation against the contractors continued, and most of them were forced to leave the quarry[10]. At a mass meeting in the Bethesda Market Hall, W. H. Williams urged the men to respect the law, but said that he was glad they had rebelled against the contract system; and according to the *Liverpool Echo* of 6 November the meeting expressed its resentment at the presence of the army in the area. The Mayor of Bangor agreed to prevent troops and police from going to Bethesda to serve the warrants, providing the men would place themselves in the charge of Sergeant Owen and go with him to Bangor to stand trial; and on behalf of the men W. H. Williams and George Brymer agreed to this[11]. On 7 November the *Daily Telegraph* declared that Sergeant Owen was probably the 'most popular men . . . in the whole of the North Wales quarry district', because he had early on the previous day arrested the alleged ringleaders single-handedly and brought them into Bangor by train. Young, however, believed that Sergeant Owen was wholeheartedly on the side of the men; and he was confirmed in that belief when it appeared that in one instance the wrong man had been arrested.

On 6 November the men entered the quarry in defiant mood, and shouts of 'Hurrah' rang out from gallery to gallery; in a short time only a few old men and labourers remained at work. The others went home, changed out of their working clothes, and marched in procession to Bangor in order to show (as Young put it) 'their sympathy with those who had committeed the brutal assaults'[12]. According to the *Daily Telegraph* of 7 November, the men cheered as they passed the 'open and unguarded gates of Penrhyn Castle'; and according to the *Daily Chronicle* they were subsequently joined by a hundred students from the University College of North Wales, which was at that time housed in a former hotel near Port Penrhyn. At the Magistrates' Court in Bangor the prosecution was conducted by Hugh Vincent and the defence by William George, the brother of David Lloyd George. Three of the seventeen men who appeared in court were discharged, having demonstrated that they were not the persons named on the warrants; and the others were bound over in the sum of £10 to appear the following week[13]. That evening Young posted up notices throughout the quarry, suspending for fourteen days those quarrymen who had absented themselves without leave; and when the men learned of this on their return to Bethesda they began to chant, 'Yn wyneb pob caledi / Y sydd neu eto ddaw' (In the face of every hardship / That is or is to come).

On 7 November Young reported to Lord Penrhyn that many quarrymen had come into the quarry, read the notices, and gone home quietly. The loaders, however, asked to be allowed to work, saying that they were unaffected by the contract system and had joined the crowd only because they were 'afraid of them'; on being permitted to resume work, they sent back a message thanking Young for his decision. Young told Lord Penrhyn that he intended to follow the same policy with any fitters, blacksmiths, joiners or sawyers who might apply for work in the fitting shops or the slab mills; there was 'plenty of work' to be done in the way of repairs, and he wanted to bring down 'a valuable lot of slates'[14]. At a mass meeting reported in the *Liverpool Daily Post* of 9 November, William Jones M.P. said he was trying to bring about the early departure of the troops; and in the same issue the newspaper reported that 140 of the 180 infantry had already received orders to leave.

When the trial resumed on 13 November, twenty-six defendants faced charges under the Conspiracy and Protection of Property Act of 1875; and once again the Penrhyn quarrymen marched in procession from Bethesda to Bangor. Estimating the crowd at 500, Young told Lord Penrhyn that they were 'perfectly quiet' and took 'only two and three-quarter minutes' to pass his house[15]. The prosecution was conducted by the London barrister Charles Matthews, instructed by Carter, Vincent and Jones; and the counsel for the defence was David Lloyd George. Matthews tried unsuccessfully to persuade two of the magistrates to withdraw, on the ground that one was a suspended quarrymen and another the brother-in-law of one of the accused. On this occasion Lloyd George argued that a suspended quarryman was particularly well-qualified to try the case, but at the final hearing on 21 November he acknowledged that Matthews had been right. One of the defendants, William Thomas Jones, was released when it became clear that he had been mistaken for another William Jones. One charge of intimidation against George Owen was postponed for a month because Edward Williams was unable to give evidence. After prosecution witnesses had described the attack on Richard Hughes and his sons, the trial was adjourned for a week[16].

Colonel Ruck's relations with local politicians had never been easy, and as early as 26 August 1899 he had written to Lord Penrhyn expressing his desire to find other employment[17]. His decision to seek outside assistance came under attack on 14 November 1900, when a special meeting of the Standing Joint Police Committee was held to consider 'the importation of troops and extra police into the County'. Those present included Lord Penrhyn and W. J. Parry, and the meeting expressed strong disapproval of the decision to invoke military aid without the committee's authority. According to the *Times* of 15 November, Lord Penrhyn was joined in opposition to this motion by Henry Kneeshaw, Sir Henry Ellis-Nanney and Colonel Wynn Finch. Similar resolutions were passed by Caernarfon Town Council, Bangor City Council and Bethesda Urban

District Council.

The contractors told Young that they would have to give up their contracts because they were afraid to go to work. According to the *Liverpool Courier* of 19 November, the men welcomed the contractors' decision; but Young insisted that he had no intention of abandoning the contract system[18]. On 19 November Young issued the following notice:

> Subject to the reservation of the right on my part to close the Quarry at any time in case of a further disturbance or intimidation, I hereby give notice that the Setters have my instructions to commence 'setting' as usual TODAY, MONDAY at 10 o'clock a.m., to all classes except Rybelwyr, Boys and Daymen, who will be allowed to return on Tuesday at 7.30 a.m.
>
> I shall be at the New Quarry Office all day, and tomorrow, Tuesday, and if any workman has any cause for complaints, I shall be glad to listen to him, and give such complaint my full consideration.

Apart from the twenty-six who were being tried, the men returned to work; and the only disturbances were 'an occasional hoot or boo at Pennant Roberts and one feeble attempt by probably only one man' against Meares and Young. Young reported to Lord Penrhyn:

> Their faces showed unmistakably that they very much resented having been punished with fourteen days suspension. This, however, will die out in a few days if we only get to work.

That evening there was another mass meeting in the Bethesda Market Hall, and W. H. Williams urged the men to consult 'their reason rather than their feelings'. On 20 November there were threats of violence against Pennant Roberts, and Young recalled him from the quarry 'for safety'. During the morning the men gathered in groups all over the quarry; and at one o'clock they 'crowded into the Overlookers' Offices' to request leave for the day of the trial. Apart from the relatives of the defendants, they were refused; and at three o'clock they 'quietly began to leave the Quarry', so that by four 'no one was left except the loaders and daymen'[19].

The trial of the twenty-six Penrhyn quarrymen was concluded on Wednesday 21 November; and the proceedings were reported in the *Daily News*, the *Times*, the *Manchester Guardian*, the *Scotsman* and other newspapers. The men were defended by David Lloyd George and his brother William; and the *Carnarvon and Denbigh Herald* reported that the M.P. wore a white chrysanthemum in his button-hole. The *Observer and Express* found touches of comedy in the event; and the *North Wales Chronicle* observed that the Bangor magistrates were as Radical and Nonconformist a group as the George brothers could have wished. In his speech to the bench Lloyd George made much of the confusion surrounding the attacks, suggesting that witnesses were trying to 'have it both ways' when they claimed both to be badly injured and to have positively identified their assailants. Lloyd George poured scorn on the arrest of William Thomas Jones, saying that he always avoided trouble and had never left his gallery; and he claimed the benefit of the doubt for all those who had been implicated by the evidence of the Hughes family. Despite this plea the magistrates found three men guilty in connection with the attack on Richard Hughes. Holland Williams was found guilty of violence and fined £5 and costs; and William Holland Williams and George Owen were found guilty of intimidation and fined £5 with costs and £2 with costs respectively. On Lloyd George's application, a month was allowed for the payment of these fines. In connection with the attacks on Pierce and Pennant Roberts, three men were found guilty of intimidation: Hugh Jones was fined £4 with costs, William Parry £2 with costs, and Daniel Jones £1 with costs. In the case of John David Williams, whom William George undertook to defend when his brother left to catch the London train, the magistrates ruled that there was no case to answer.

In connection with the case which had been postponed, William George applied for an order to have Edward Williams independently examined by a medical man; but Matthews said that a specialist from Chester had been to see Williams, and had warned that he should not be disturbed, as 'his future, in great measure, depended upon his being kept very quiet for a time[20].' Young did not attend the trial, but was informed of the verdicts by telephone. From 11.15 to 5 he was busy interviewing 'about 101' contractors, all of whom said 'that they would be perfectly willing to return to the Quarry as soon as they felt their doing so would not interfere with the peace'. He told Lord Penrhyn that he believed many of the contractors would resume the following day[21]. Immediately after the trial Assheton Smith wrote to Lord Penrhyn, deploring the 'absurdly inadequate' fines imposed and predicting that the troubles would continue[22].

On 23 November 1900 the *Carnarvon and Denbigh Herald* commented scornfully that the trial had reduced to its proper dimensions that

> alleged riot at Bethesda, which required the issue of warrants; and as a consequence the introduction of 'foreign' police, and of cavalry (furnished with Dum-Dum expanding bullets).

The magistrates, by releasing the defendants without bail during the adjournments, had 'practically confessed that they had been ill-advised in issuing warrants'; and in the 'pitiful and absurd' anticlimax brought about by Lloyd George's 'searching cross-examination' and 'highly effective speech', a few men had been summarily convicted of common assault and very properly fined. Recognising that the 'tempers of both parties to the dispute' were now high, the article concluded with a prophecy of victory for the men:

> Lord Penrhyn can afford to keep the quarry closed for an indefinite period. He and the magistrates who support him can no doubt get some more regiments, if they are not more urgently wanted for the purpose of burning farms and fighting women and children in the Transvaal. He will be probably supported by the Property Defence Association . . . . But in the long run, his lordship is bound to fail ignominously, for he is struggling with a modern and enlightened democracy. Radical land reformers and opponents of hereditary landlordism ought to be very thankful for such an embodiment of the feudal spirit as Lord Penrhyn.

With the exception of the six men who had been found guilty, the men returned to the quarry on 22 November; but although

David Davies and H. Morris informed Meares that the men had arrived at 7.30 a.m., they did not start work until 8 a.m. At 8.30 a.m. workers on the lower galleries stopped work because of the 'threatening attitude of the young men who had collected in Ponc Clari'; and at 9 a.m. work stopped in the dressing sheds on the Red Lion gallery. All over the quarry the men gathered in small groups; and about 10 a.m. Young instructed the overlookers and markers to go round telling the men 'quietly' that they must either leave the quarry or start work. On hearing this the men began to leave the quarry in a 'very quiet manner', and by 1 p.m. they had all gone except the 'loaders, engine-drivers, roadmen, balance men and other classes of daymen'[23]. Professing himself 'very disappointed', Young told Lord Penrhyn that this walkout left him no choice but to close the quarry, and immediately put up a notice to that effect:

> Notwithstanding my Notices of November 3rd and 19th, there has been further disturbance at the Penrhyn Quarry, and the employés have again ceased work without permission. I therefore give Notice in accordance with the reservation named in my Notice of November 19th, that the Quarries are now closed.
>
> All tools, materials, and other effects belonging to those lately employed must be removed before 12 o'clock noon, Saturday November 24th.
>
> The next Pay Day will be as usual on Saturday December 1st, at 11.30 a.m.

The *Daily Telegraph* of 23 November, describing this 'general lock-out' as a 'grave crisis', explained that many parts of the galleries had not been let and that the men had been coming together to discuss this. To that account the *Manchester Guardian* of the same date added a description of the subsequent meeting in the Market Hall, where the men sang hymns, greeted their leaders with cheers, and hooted at the name of Young. It was also reported that the cavalry was under orders to entrain for York.

These events placed the N.W.Q.U. in a dilemma; but it was decided that, since some of the workers had been locked out and the others were expressing sympathy with them, all would be eligible for strike pay[24]. No one now expected an early end to the struggle; and on 26 November the *Liverpool Mercury*, reporting the exodus from Bethesda in search of work, said that 'gloom' had begun to settle on an 'erstwhile cheerful and busy hive of industry'. On the same day Lord Penrhyn wrote to the Blaenau Ffestiniog quarry-owner Richard Greaves, who at his request had tried to discover what the 'man in the street' believed to be the causes of the trouble at Penrhyn Quarry. Greaves had listed three factors: the contract or 'sweating' system, the managers' lack of practical and technical knowledge, and nostalgia for the 'halcyon days' when quarry discipline was slack. Thanking Greaves for this insight into public opinion, Lord Penrhyn commented that the phrase 'sweating system' had been taken up because it had 'a catch penny sound about it'; there had been no attempt to substantiate or even formulate complaints about the system, because the union leaders knew that investigation would show such complaints to be groundless.

The newspapers which sent special correspondents to Bethesda included the *Daily Chronicle*, the *Daily News*, the *Liverpool Echo* and the *Manchester Guardian*. On 26 November the *Manchester Guardian* reporter gave his impression of the setting:

> From the station you move by a pleasant pathway which runs along the banks of the Ogwen, a river which pours itself into the Menai Straits at Port Penrhyn. It is a noisy stream. The shallow waters break themselves on a stony bed and go fuming and fretting in their passage between great boulders. On the banks we have bushes . . . rich from the colouring of the red berry, and . . . we come to enormous heaps of slate, the refuse of the quarries . . . . These mighty wounds do something to spoil the fair scene, but cannot spoil it altogether.

On 27 November the *Daily News* reporter described the groups of 'disconsolate-looking men' and 'tearful women' he had observed in the streets, and added:

> The women especially and the spick and span cottages saddened me beyond adequate expression.

Writing to Lord Penrhyn on 27 November, Young commented:

> It appears that the newspapers are quite as anxious to make capital out of the workmen's troubles as the agitators always are[25].

Young was 'besieged' by reporters, and on 28 November he gave an interview to the *Manchester Guardian*. He said that the men could be union members or not, just as they pleased; and when asked why he had prohibited the collecting of subscriptions during the dinner-hour, he replied that he did not think the men had any right to 'transact private business inside the quarry'. He maintained that the use of contracts, on which only 180 men out of 2,500 were engaged, had cut the cost of removing bad rock from 2s 6¼d to 10d per ton, and thus made it possible to pay higher wages to the quarrymen and the badrockmen. A contractor provided a horse, paid for his own powder, made no more money than a quarryman, and had no power to engage or dismiss labour; and the introduction of contractors did not displace other workmen. Young said that he was 'practically ready to open the quarry on the old terms of settlement', provided the men agreed 'to allow the contractors and their workmen to work in peace' and undertook 'not to hurt any officials out of the quarry'. Pointing out that the discipline had been 'very slack' under the old régime, Young claimed that it had improved 'continuously'; and he asked why men were 'continually applying for work' at Penrhyn Quarry if conditions there were so bad.

On 29 November the *Sheffield and Rotherham Independent* described the struggle as

> a conflict between a man who possesses absolutely feudal notions of his rights over his employees, and a number of men who resist him stubbornly but without method.

The writer admitted that the origins of the dispute were 'obscure', but commented blandly:

> It seems to be of the kind that could be settled in a few hours by a conference between reasonable employers and properly qualified Trade Union delegates.

On 30 November the *Liverpool Mercury* rejected Young's statement that the contractors earned no more than the men, and defended the men's preference for a system of bargains or 'co-partnership'. On the same day an *Evening News* reporter, depressed by 'pitiless squalls of rain', deplored the emptiness of the 'long, straggling, climbing village street'; prompted no doubt by a recollection of men in white corduroy trousers, he lamented the disappearance of the 'white moleskinned quarrymen'. Less poetically but no less absurdly, the *Daily News* of the same date observed that the 'decision to close the Penrhyn quarries for a whole year' illustrated 'the vengeful side of the Welsh nature'.

Young spent a good deal of time with journalists, trying with little success to clear up 'some of the many misconceptions' that had been formed. On 28 November he complained to Thomas Naylor of the *Daily Chronicle* that the *Daily News* reporter, after spending two hours with him, had 'simply made use of perhaps two or three statements'. He gave Naylor a forty-five-minute interview, but told J. F. Doyle of Liverpool that he was not hopeful about the results:

> These Welshmen are so ignorant and so childish that there is no arguing with them at all[26].

On 29 November the *Daily Chronicle* printed Naylor's report from Bethesda:

> The trouble here seems to be inexplicable to an outsider. I am in a position to state that the management of the quarry is willing to meet a deputation from any of the grades of men who are working there.

Naylor said that although Robert Davies and W. R. Evans had formed part of a deputation, that was not why they had been dismissed; and he cited the case of Griffith Edwards, who was secretary of the Bethesda Lodge and had worked in the quarry 'uninterruptedly since 1853'. Writing on 30 November to Lord Penrhyn's son Edward Douglas Pennant, Young referred with approval to this 'decent leading article', and observed that their 'old enemy' the *Daily Chronicle* seemed to have 'completely turned round'. In the course of a long walk 'up and down the Quay' with Young, Naylor had admitted that he could get 'no truth whatever, or the basis of any grievance, out of W. H. Williams or any other quarrymen's leader'; he said, in fact, that he did not know what he was doing there since the dispute was not 'a public question at all'.

In the same letter Young reported that because trade was slack the men were finding it difficult to get work at other slate quarries; and he added that their case would not bring in 'sufficient sympathy to pay them to be idle', especially as the Boer War funds were making it hard to raise money for other purposes. Young told Edward Douglas Pennant, however, that the *Daily News* was still mounting a 'most violent personal attack' on himself, and would like to bring Lord Penrhyn into the fray as 'bigger game to shoot at'. He also explained that he hoped to re-open the quarry; and on 1 December 1900 a notice in Welsh and English was duly posted offering work to the former employees. In this notice Young said that bargains would be set on 5 December, but reserved the right to close the quarry in the event of violence. He continued:

> I therefore appeal to you all to assist in preventing any such occurrence for your own sakes, and for the sake of avoiding the misfortune which would otherwise fall upon the neighbourhood.

Re-iterating his willingness to meet a deputation, he expressed the hope that 'instead of adhering to an attitude of unprofitable silence' they would lay any grievances before him so that they could be discussed and, 'if practicable, remedied. He concluded by saying that members of a deputation need have no fear 'as to their future welfare in the Quarry', provided they conformed to the rules and maintained 'a good character'.

Through his conversations with Herbert Jones of the *Daily News* and Thomas Naylor of the *Daily Chronicle*, Young learned that the men had dropped their opposition to contracts and were concentrating on their demand that W. R. Evans should be re-instated; he relayed this information to Lord Penrhyn on 3 December. Young considered Naylor to be a 'very sensible man', but observed that Jones had no 'influence with his editor'. Jones admitted that he had been given a 'book' before coming to Bethesda; and Young took this to mean that he had been sent down to produce reports in accordance with a predetermined viewpoint. The general verdict on Young's notice was that it was more 'amiably expressed' and used more 'conciliatory language' than his earlier statements. On 3 December, however, the *Daily News* correspondent reported that, when the re-opening was discussed in the numerous chapels of the district, the quarrymen showed 'no desire whatever' either to return to work or to 'discuss their grievances with Mr Young'. In the event no one turned up for work on 5 December, perhaps because the men were pinning their hopes on intervention by the Board of Trade.

On 7 December the *Liverpool Mercury* reported that a relief committee had been formed with W. J. Parry as chairman and Daniel Lloyd as treasurer; and it was also announced that two choirs were to set off on a fund-raising tour. The *Carnarvon and Denbigh Herald* of the same date reflected on the conflict which had arisen between two groups with incompatible ideals, the Penrhyn quarrymen who were industrious and highly intelligent, and the owner and chief manager who in their private capacities were 'estimable and honourable'. The consequences of this conflict were starkly defined:

> Bethesda is ruined. Bangor is badly hit and the whole countryside feels the evil effects of the dispute.

The newspaper added that the men were not prepared to abandon those who had been found guilty by the magistrates.

On 10 December Young told the quarry officials that they should remain at their posts until 31 December in case any of the late employees applied for work; if there was no favourable response by 31 December, however, the officials were to be dismissed. At this stage Young was in correspondence with F. W. Webb, manager of the L.N.W.R. at Crewe, about rules, punishments and the presentation of grievances. On 11 December he explained to Webb that the piecework system made it impracticable to deduct fines from the men's wages, and added:

> As the smallest thing seems to irritate these Welshmen, I am afraid that such an innovation here would not be conducive to peace.

Young went on to explain some of the special problems involved in the management of a large quarry:

> One of my great difficulties in enforcing discipline, particularly punctual attendance . . . is caused by the fact that the Quarry is a large open hole right up in the mountain, open on all sides, without any gates of entry whatever, and in years gone by the discipline was so terribly lax that the men practically came and went at all hours of the day without let or hindrance, and now the more I try to introduce business principles the more they rebel . . . . One of the real grievances against the Contractors but which they never dare to utter is the fact that the Contractors work far harder than the other men in the Quarry[27].

On 12 December the *Liverpool Mercury* reported that the outstanding case against George Owen had been withdrawn, on the ground that Edward Williams was still not fit to attend.

By 14 December Young had a 'rough idea' of the grievances which the men were preparing to submit. The key questions were the minimum wage, the contract system, the rules of discipline, the membership of deputations, and the reinstatement of those leaders who had been dismissed. Young did not know what was to be proposed on the question of discipline; but he envisaged a settlement under which men would be expected to be in their places at 'bell-ring', but would not be suspended for lateness of less than fifteen minutes unless the offence was repeated. It is clear from Young's comments that he did not propose to make any signficant concessions; but he agreed to attend a meeting at the Salisbury Hotel in London on 19 December, and Clement Edwards of the *Daily News* persuaded the men's leaders to attend as well[28].

The men's representatives at this meeting were Henry Jones, William Williams, Richard D. Pritchard and Robert J. Jones. All four were quarry employees, and they were accompanied by an interpreter. Despite press assertions to the contrary, neither D. R. Daniel nor W. H. Williams was present. In a letter of 22

December Young summarised the terms he had put to the meeting. There would be no re-instatement of the seven men dismissed in the previous three years, or of the six men found guilty by the magistrates; but the twenty men who had been acquitted would be allowed to re-apply. The fourteen badrockmen from Ffridd gallery would be taken back if they agreed to work on the basis of a collective bargain. The ban on collecting money during the dinner-hour would be maintained. The proposed minimum wage of 4s 4d would not be introduced, since it would mean the dismissal of about 200 old or incompetent men who could not be paid that amount. The contract system would be maintained, but collective bargains would be tried. If any 'well authenticated case of unjustifiable language or conduct' on the part of officials, contractors or workmen was brought to Young's attention, it would be 'promptly dealt with'. Half a day's wage would be deducted for lateness of up to fifteen minutes, and a whole day's wage for lateness of more than fifteen minutes; and the deductions would be made on pay day and given to the Quarry Benefit Club. There would be no change in the existing system of representation.

The press showed little enthusiasm for Young's proposals. On 25 December the *Liverpool Daily Post* argued that the quarrymen would never agree to lose half a day's pay for being fifteen minutes late; and Clement Edwards of the *Daily News* noted that these were the 'relaxed' rules and commented, 'Heaven save our worst enemy from the infliction of the originals!' On 27 December, however, the *South Wales Daily News* published an anonymous letter from an ex-quarrymen contending that the 'hundreds of men' who had come south to work in the coalmines would 'never find a better master' than the one they had left. The writer recalled that in Bethesda houses had been provided at £3 per annum, and old men had been paid from 10s to 15s a week for 'almost simply doing nothing but walking back and fore to the quarry'. He acknowledged that there might have been changes since his departure in 1868, but said that the men themselves had brought those changes about.

Many journalists saw parallels between the 'battle at

Bethesda' and the South African War. On 28 December, for example, the *Railway Review* argued that the 'the Welshman' resembled the 'much reviled Boer in his mental attitude': 'upright, sober and chaste,' devoted to his chapel, 'stubborn as a mule and conscientious as a judge', he would leave his 'native homestead' only under 'a deep sense of wrong'. That the dispute was already causing deep suffering was shown on 30 December by the suicide of one of the older quarrymen, who had not wanted to come out on strike. According to his wife Margaret, John Jeremiah Williams had been unwell for six years; and 'after leaving work he broke his heart', complaining constantly that 'he and many others had been compelled to leave the Quarry against their will'[29].

Copies of the proposed terms were sent to the men, along with ballot papers allowing them to vote for or against acceptance; but Young was by no means pleased with the way in which the ballot was organised. On 28 December he told the *Times* that the voting papers were worthless, since the employees were required to give their names and addresses, 'thus providing a black list'. According to the *Times* of 31 December, the men resented Young's criticism; they contended that the papers had to be signed as proof that they were being completed by those to whom they were sent.

The votes were counted in the presence of J. Jones Morris, Chairman of the Caernarfonshire County Council, Charles A. Jones, Registrar and High Bailiff of the County Court, and Clement Edwards of the *Daily News;* and the result was announced in the *Daily News* on 4 January 1901. The 1,873 votes recorded consisted of 77 for the terms, 1,707 against the terms, and 89 spoilt papers; and the *Carnarvon and Denbigh Herald* reported 'general satisfaction' with this result. On 5 January the *Daily News* commented that while Young was an 'attractive gentleman' with a reputation for being 'shrewd and clear-visioned', his way of dealing with men suggested an 'iron hand' encased 'in mail and not in velvet'. The same report described the burning of the ballot papers after the count:

> What a scene it was! Kept back by a crowd of police, a great

> crowd, chiefly of pale-faced women and awe-struck children, stood watching the weird bonfire . . . . It was a strange and memorable incident.

The *Daily News* made no reference to the fact that about 800 quarrymen had failed to vote; but the *North Wales Chronicle* of 5 January assumed that those who abstained were treating 'the whole thing with contempt'. On 7 January the *Manchester Guardian* deplored the 'incessant strife' at Bethesda, arguing that the Penrhyn quarrymen were 'spoilt children' whose 'turbulence' was 'bred in the bone'. The *Daily News* of 8 January presented them as a 'quick, nervous people', whose love of home amounted to a passion; the trouble arose, it argued, from their 'racial clash' with an *uitlander* management 'blind to the local peculiarities'.

The closure of the quarry was now virtually complete. On 14 January 1901 the *Liverpool Mercury* reported the dismissal of a large number of loaders at Port Penrhyn, adding that the whole district was suffering acutely. At the same time Young was planning to re-open the quarry as soon as possible; and quarrymen were being encouraged to dissociate themselves from the rioters and declare their willingness to resume work. It was hard to ensure the safety of anyone who wished to return, however, especially as the earlier decision to bring in troops was still a cause of resentment. On 16 January Young told Hugh Vincent that W. J. Parry intended, when the Standing Joint Police Committee met on 24 January, to move the following resolution:

> That this Committee hereby records their approval of the conduct of Police Sergeant Owen for the manner in which he performed his duties during the disturbance at the Penrhyn Quarry and for his undertaking to execute the warrants without the aid of the military.

Young reminded Vincent that Sergeant Owen had not identified the accused, and had in one case arrested the wrong man; and he asked Vincent to give Lord Penrhyn any information about Sergeant Owen that he could find. On 21 January Young informed Colonel Ruck that the quarry was to be re-opened, and asked him 'to give ample protection to each individual workman both at his home and on his way to and from work'[30]. When the Standing Joint Police Committee held its quarterly meeting under the chairmanship of C. H. Darbishire, Young's letter was treated with derision. It was said that police could not be provided to 'chaperone' the men; and it was resolved that before bringing in extra police the Chief Constable should consult with the chairman and the four ex-chairmen, one of whom was W. J. Parry. After Colonel Ruck had praised his 'great tact and discretion' and W. J. Parry had observed that they 'could not say how much the county had been saved by him', the motion commending Sergeant Owen was passed unanimously[31].

On 1 February Young asked Joseph Millar of the Labour Protection Association if they could provide special constables. He was offered twenty, but replied on 5 February that this number would be inadequate because the district was so extensive[32]. The *Daily News*, now owned by George Cadbury and David Lloyd George, increased its efforts in support of the men. On 8 February the *South Wales Daily News* reported the appeal which had just been issued by the committee appointed to supervise the Relief Fund. This appeal was signed by W. J. Parry as chairman, by G. Roberts J.P. as vice-chairman, by Daniel Lloyd as treasurer, and by the Rev W. W. Lloyd as secretary; and it declared that Lord Penrhyn had promoted conflict between unionists and non-unionists and destroyed the 'good feeling' that had existed 'between his late noble father and his workmen'. On the other hand the *Cambrian News* declared on 15 February that there was little hostility to Lord Penrhyn, even among those who felt bound to oppose him because he was a peer, a Churchman, and a Conservative; everyone would be 'quite satisfied for the present' if Young could be 'offered up as a sacrifice', although Young had of course 'committed no fault that would justify' such an action. Hundreds of men had indicated their desire to resume work; and on 11 February the *Liverpool Mercury* reported that they had been sent a 'conciliatory circular', which replaced Young's system of fines for lateness with a less rigorous system of suspensions.

While the management was thus planning to re-open the quarry, the organisers of the Penrhyn Relief Fund were gathering widespread support. Meeting in London to consider the men's 'fight for the principle of free representation', the committee of the General Federation of Trade Unions heard an address by D. R. Daniel and urged all trade unionists to support the strike[33]. Relief came in surprising forms, such as the 2¾ tons of plum pudding sent by John Hill and Son of Ashton-under-Lyne[34]. In *Y Faner* of 5 October 1984 Ernest Roberts remembered singing in a school playground, long after the end of the dispute:

> Wele cawson ym Methesda
>   Bwdin gora fu erioed.
> Chlywodd Young nac Arglwydd Penrhyn
>   Ddim andano cyn ei ddod.
> Pwdin yw, du ei liw,
> Gora brofodd neb sy'n fyw.
> (We had in Bethesda
>   The best pudding that ever was.
> Neither Young nor Lord Penrhyn
>   Knew of it before it came.
> It was a black-coloured pudding,
> The best any living being has tasted.)

Contemporary newspapers, however, carried many reports of the distress which the dispute was causing in Bethesda. Several papers recounted how a doctor found a house still locked at 11.30 a.m., because the mother had stayed in bed with her children 'in order to save a meal'; and on 28 February 1901 the *Morning Leader* quoted an infant-school teacher who said that most children were now coming to school 'without the customary slice of bread and butter to be eaten during the play-hour'.

In reporting Lord Penrhyn's speech at the Bangor St David's Day dinner, the *North Wales Chronicle* of 9 March took the opportunity to celebrate his interest in the 'welfare and progress of the Welsh nation' and his support for local institutions like the Carnarvonshire and Anglesey Infirmary. It also told its readers that the toast to Lord Penrhyn had been 'drunk with enthusiasm', and that the singing of 'For he's a jolly good fellow' had been followed by 'ringing cheers for Lord and Lady Penrhyn'. Also on 9 March Lord Penrhyn's daughter Hilda wrote to him from Naples, expressing the hope that 'quarry matters' were looking more promising and that the audience had enjoyed his fishing stories. She also told him that she had met a Miss Hunt who had taken one of his cottages at Wicken and was 'charmed' with it:

> She seemed so very nice – she said she thought she had got amongst a terribly pious set of people at first for when she asked about something or other which wanted doing she was told, 'Oh! it will be all right – the Lord will provide it' – until she discovered that *you* were the Lord – the omnipotent power in Wicken![35]

By March 1901 Robert Blatchford's weekly paper the *Clarion* was receiving reports about Bethesda from Alex M. Thompson, who used the pen-name 'Dangle'. Thompson wrote that 'wealthy Bethesda' was now on 'the brink of starvation'; but he welcomed the management's attempt to ban dinner-hour collections, since this 'blunder' had 'saved the union'. The *Clarion* invited 'every socialist' to contribute to its 'Bethesda Relief Fund' as a means of fighting the 'capitalistic tyranny' represented by the 'bully of Penrhyn Castle'; and on 23 March it reminded its readers of Dickens' description of Lord Penrhyn's father as the 'Arch-magnate, the well-known Col. Slater', in *All the Year Round*.

The newspapers continued to print articles under such headings as 'Desolate Bethesda'. On 29 March 1901 the *North Wales Observer and Express* described the 'meagre display of commodities' in the shops, and reported that 'everybody complained' and 'everybody looked depressed'. Mothers and children were on a diet of 'dry bread and tea', and one tradesman declared that there was a curse on the town; but the women were determined not to give in. W. J. Parry had organised the reopening of the old Pantdreiniog Quarry on the Cefnfaes estate, and was providing work there on co-operative principles for fifty men. The *Daily Express* of 9 April reported that Ben Tillett, speaking at the Easter Monday mass meeting in Bethesda, had

Plate 1 George Sholto Gordon Douglas Pennant, second Baron Penrhyn of Llandegai, 1836–1907

Plate 2 Penrhyn Quarry: the north west corner and the main dressing floor

Plate 3 Port Penrhyn: the harbour for Penrhyn Quarry on the eastern outskirts of Bangor

Plate 4 Penrhyn Castle from the air

Plate 5 The Jerusalem Chapel in the town of Bethesda

Plate 7 The Penrhyn Quarry Committee. The standing figures from left to right are Richard Pritchard, Owen Griffith, Lewis Griffith and John Roberts. The seated figures from left to right are William Williams, the chairman Henry Jones, the secretary Griffith Edwards, and R. J. Jones

Plate 6 A group portrait taken at Penrhyn Castle in July 1894. The central figure is the Princess of Wales. The Prince of Wales is standing by her left shoulder, Lady Penrhyn seated on her right with an umbrella. Lord Penrhyn is the inconspicuous bearded figure in the doorway behind the Princess

Plate 8 Bethesda High Street at the beginning of the twentieth century.
Plate 9 Working quarrymen being escorted through Bethesda by police, with Hussars looking on. The lower picture shows a view over Bethesda with a banner in Welsh reading 'Be faithful to your fellow-workers'

Plate 10 A Conservative cartoon of April 1903, representing the Liberal leader Sir Henry Campbell-Bannerman as the 'catspaw' of the Socialists

Plate 11 A Liberal cartoon of April 1903, based on Sir John Tenniel's illustration to Humpty Dumpty's poem in *Through the Looking Glass*. The egg-shaped Herbert Asquith and the bearded William Jones attempt to communicate with Lord Penrhyn, while Sir Edward Clarke comments, 'He wouldn't listen to me!' The black kettle is from Tenniel, but is labelled 'Bethesda'

THE CAT'S-PAW.

VERY STIFF AND PROUD.

(WITH APOLOGIES TO SIR JOHN TENNIEL.)

SIR EDWARD CLARKE: "He wouldn't listen to me!"

They said to him, they said it plain,
"Then you must take them back again!"

They said it very loud and clear;
They went and shouted in his ear.

But he was very stiff and proud;
He said, "You needn't shout so loud!"

And he was very proud and stiff;
He said, "I'd interview them, if——"

(The vote of censure in connection with the Penrhyn labour troubles, which will probably come on in the House of Commons next Monday, will be moved by Mr. Asquith and seconded by Mr. William Jones. Whether it will have any more effect on Lord Penrhyn than Sir Edward Clarke's efforts remains to be seen.)

Plate 12 Bethesda Station at the end of a holiday, with striking quarrymen returning to the mines of South Wales

blamed all the suffering on Lord Penrhyn, 'who was a cross between Pharaoh and Nero, and had evinced savage brutality in ignoring human rights'. The *Daily Mail* of 10 April gave a fuller version of this 'characteristic speech,' in which Tillett accused Lord Penrhyn of regarding the quarrymen as 'mere chattels, serfs, to be exploited without scruple'. Urging the men to have 'a little more devil in them,' he told them not to blame Young, who was 'only Lord Penrhyn's jackal in this matter'; and he reversed the South African analogy of the *Daily News* by referring to 'old Kruger Penrhyn' and speaking of the quarrymen as 'economic Outlanders'. Although he spoke in English, a language 'strange' to most of his hearers, his comments were greeted with laughter and applause. On 12 April the *Manchester Guardian* contrasted the 'pretty hamlets' around Bethesda with the 'silence of the quarry', and reported W. H. Williams' call for an independent inquiry into the dispute. On the same day the *Cambrian News* condemned the 'vulgarisms' and 'bullying spirit' of Ben Tillett, whom it accused of treating the quarrymen as if they were 'London riff-raff'.

The possibility of intervention by the Board of Trade was unexpectedly raised in the House of Commons in April; but Gerald Balfour said that the Board had received no application from the parties to the dispute, and had no reason to believe that an inquiry would lead to any useful result[36]. In the meantime the Relief Fund continued to receive generous support, the choir of ninety singers under the direction of Evan Parry being eagerly welcomed in the large cities. Fourteen committees distributed vouchers for food to families in Bethesda and the surrounding district. There were 234 families on the books in Caellwyngrydd, 175 in Tregarth, 164 in Carneddi, 97 in Gerlan, 66 in Braichmelyn, 55 in Rhiwlas, 19 in Nant Ffrancon, 11 in Bangor, and 5 in Talybont. The Relief Fund provided support for the old men, women and children, while union members received union pay and support from the General Federation of Trade Unions[37]. In May the Bethesda Lodge of the N.W.Q.U. passed a motion thanking union members throughout Britain for their gifts; and at the same time they expressed their concern about the proposed re-opening of the quarry on 11 June[38].

On 10 May Lord Penrhyn informed Colonel Ruck that the officials and others who wished to return were likely to face 'interference or violence' from the strikers; and he asked that the police should ensure their safety[39]. When the quarry was partially re-opened on 15 May the police were on duty; and *Y Werin* on 16 May reported that eighteen officials had gone back to work under the protection of Sergeant Owen and two constables, watched only by a few women. The *Daily Chronicle* added that three former officials had not been invited to return, and that the women had expressed their disapproval by beating on tin cans. On 20 May Young put up a notice announcing that the quarry would be re-opened on 11 June to 'all the late employés' who had applied for work and been accepted. The notice indicated that Young was prepared to receive further applications from 'late employés', and that each applicant should give his full name and address, his former quarry number, and the name of the gallery in which he had worked. The men were told that Colonel Ruck had promised that the law in respect of violence and intimidation would be enforced through the provision of 'efficient police protection'. The notice also explained the new rules, under which all penalties would take the form of suspensions or dismissals. Lateness would be punished by a caution for the first offence, quarter of a day's suspension for the second, and half a day's suspension for the third; but 'persistent offenders' would be punished more severely, or dismissed. There would be a holiday of half a day at the end of every quarry month, when accounts had been settled and new bargains agreed[40].

In this period and for the rest of the dispute the management was very anxious to distinguish between 'loyal' and 'disloyal' quarrymen; and the problems of making that distinction led sometimes to confusion and embarrassment. Because she had found his daughter 'a highly superior and respectable servant', Miss Hughes of Bryn Menai recommended Thomas Owen to Lord Penrhyn's estate agent R. C. Trench for the tenancy of a new cottage in Tregarth; and when the tenancy had been granted to him it was discovered that Owen was a 'firebrand' who had supported Ben Tillett in his denunciation of Lord Penrhyn at the Bethesda mass meeting. On 16 May 1901 Miss Hughes explained to Lord Penrhyn that she had had no idea Owen was 'fighting against the Right'; she was 'greatly disturbed' and 'distressed beyond words' to think that despite her 'true and deep sympathy' with Lord Penrhyn she had 'unknowingly . . . introduced a Traitor' as his tenant and thus injured his cause. Replying to this letter on 22 May, Lord Penrhyn told Miss Hughes not to trouble herself any more about her recommendation of Owen. He said he wished that Owen had been 'as good a sort' as his daughter appeared to be; and he added that Miss Hughes' recommendations had no doubt been prompted by her own 'good natured belief' and her consequent failure to appreciate the 'duplicity' of others[41].

On 30 May 1901 R. C. Trench, who had succeeded Colonel Sackville West as estate agent in 1898, wrote to Lord Penrhyn about the letting of cottages to quarrymen. When the troubles had begun in Penrhyn Quarry, Young and Trench had agreed that a list of those applying for the new cottages at Tregarth should be sent to Young's office at Port Penrhyn so that he could examine it. The list had come back with several applicants marked with a 'D' for disloyal; and this placed Trench in a dilemma, since some of the applicants thus marked were living in poor conditions and had been applying for cottages for a long time. When one of them told Trench that he was a 'loyal' quarryman, Trench was unable to refute this statement; but when Trench checked with Young, Young insisted that the man came from a 'disloyal' family. Trench requested that the reasons for awarding a 'D' should be clarified; but on 8 June he assured Lord Penrhyn that he would not accept any more applications for the Tregarth cottages until 11 June, when the identity of 'the good men' would be made known[42].

In May 1901 the Penrhyn Choir had fund-raising engagements in London, Halifax, Bradford, Stockton-on-Tees, South Bank, Middlesbrough and West Hartlepool. On 9 May the

Morning Leader printed a letter from the Rev W. W. Lloyd, secretary of the Penrhyn Relief Fund, who thanked the editor for a donation of £100 and offered to secure 'clean, comfortable and cheap lodgings' for visitors wishing to enjoy Bethesda's beautiful scenery and bracing air. On 22 May a 'crowded meeting' was held at the Memorial Hall in London under the chairmanship of Robert Blatchford, the socialist journalist and author of *Merrie England*. According to the *North Wales Chronicle* of the following day, there were songs from the Bethesda Ladies' Choir; and unanimous endorsement was given to a motion, proposed by Keir Hardie with the support of J. Mitchell and G. N. Barnes, which blamed Lord Penrhyn for 'the stoppage and the great distress in the district' on the ground that the quarrymen were willing to accept arbitration. According to the *Liverpool Courier*, D. R. Daniel said that some men would go back but that the great majority were prepared to fight to the bitter end. Pete Curran described Lord Penrhyn as the 'Czar of Bethesda', and said that the men had suffered under tyranny of a 'most perfidious character'. There were cheers for W. J. Parry when he asked whether the dispute was to end with the men starved into submission or with the tyrant driven out of the country.

At a mass meeting in Bethesda reported by the *Manchester Guardian* on 28 May, a reference to Colonel Ruck's promise of police protection was greeted with a 'tremendous outburst of hooting and laughter'. Edward Griffiths, secretary of the Quarry Committee, said that the stewards' attempts to induce men to seek re-admission were causing division even within families; and he urged the men to go back as a body or not at all. The 650 men at this meeting passed the following resolution, which was also approved by 700 men at a meeting in Cardiff:

> In the face of Mr Young's notice inviting some of us to the Quarry on the 11th of next month while still refusing to recognise any of our real grievances especially the right of combination acknowledged by the law of the land and the best employers in the kingdom, that having regard to our fidelities to the cause of labour and loyalty to one another we cannot do otherwise than continue

our struggle till we secure an honourable settlement.

The Bethesda meeting was sceptical of rumours that between 1,500 and 1,800 men would resume work; and in fact Young commented privately that the small attendance of 650 'ought to put some pluck into the 375' who had sent in their names[43].

On 1 June the *Liverpool Daily Post* described the harassment faced by the officials when they returned home from the quarry. They were regularly greeted with hooting and the beating of tin cans, and at Whitsun the crowds were increased by men home on holiday. Those who applied for work were having second thoughts, and many of them wrote to the Quarry Committee enclosing their tickets of re-admission. An emergency meeting of the Standing Joint Police Committee in Bangor considered a request from the management that troops and extra police should be sent to Bethesda; and Colonel Ruck reported that Sergeant Owen had said he could not hope to control the 'unruly elements' in the town. The committee rejected the request for troops, but agreed to provide extra police; and between forty and sixty policemen were taken to Bethesda in brakes from Bangor. On 3 June the *Manchester Guardian* reported that the police were preventing the use of the public road in order to stop crowds from following the officials; and David Lloyd George, being appealed to by telegram, replied that they had no right to do this. A surprise visit by the police resulted in twelve summonses against men and women living in Bethesda; and the *Manchester Guardian* of 5 June carried a report of their trial. Hugh Vincent for the prosecution observed that in this row, 'as in many others, the women at Bethesda were worse than the men'. P. C. Hugh Thomas gave evidence that the crowd was unmanageable and that 'filthy language' was used; and Richard Dennis said that they shouted 'bradwyr' (traitors), 'cynffonwyr' (tail-waggers) and 'Judases'. William George for the defence alleged that when a stone was thrown at a policeman he lost his temper and drew his truncheon on the crowd. John Machno Williams was fined £1 with costs on each of two charges, and one of the women was fined 10s with costs of 5s; but the charges of obstruction were dismissed. After the trial a public meeting was held in the Bethesda Market Hall to protest at the importation of extra police. The Rev T. Griffiths, the Bethesda Congregational minister, said that a blow had been struck at Bethesda's good name, and asked if this was because it was a Nonconformist community. The crowds had gathered, he said, to see

> the strangest sight ever seen – a steward working – (loud laughter) – and escorted home by lifeguards. (Laughter)

Appealing for good behaviour, the Rev. W. W. Lloyd reminded the audience that those taken to the cells during the soldiers' time in Bangor had included some soldiers but no quarrymen[44]. In the meantime Young was sorting the applications for readmission on the following system:

> L = Loyal, DL = Disloyal, VDL = Very Disloyal, GW = Good Worker, Fair or FW = Fair Worker, Middling = Middling Worker, Smart = Smart Worker, Bad = Bad Worker, VGW = Very Good Worker, Poor W = Poor Worker.

On some applications Young wrote a curt 'No', and others were later withdrawn because of intimidation[45].

On the eagerly-awaited morning of 11 June 1901, the usual journalists assembled to gather material for their eyewitness accounts. On 12 June the *Manchester Guardian* reported that some of the men were on their way at 5 a.m., and the rest set out about 7 a.m.:

> All the district was astir very early, and crowds of men, women and children congregated in the roads near the quarry entrances at Pont Twr and Coedyparc, and they hooted and laughed derisively at the men passing into the quarry.

There was a contingent from the Rhiwlas district, but three or four of them turned back. There were few constables in evidence, and the number of men returning was estimated at 400; only 100 of these were quarrymen, and a few were elderly, but some were members of the N.W.Q.U. After 7 a.m. the crowds dispersed, and apart from a few strikers walking about the streets 'the place was as peaceful as usual'. Soon afterwards, however, Lord Penrhyn and his son Edward rode through

Bethesda and on to the quarry, where a large number of workers assembled to meet them. Without dismounting, Lord Penrhyn welcomed the men back to the quarry and thanked them for having the courage to show that they were determined to work as free men in defiance of opposition. He also thanked the officials who, by working as quarrymen for the previous month, had given the lie to allegations that officials knew nothing about the technical processes of quarry work. He concluded by saying that the men need no longer fear the kind of tyranny that they all knew had existed among them. Lord Penrhyn's speech was loudly cheered.

At the end of the day's work it was announced that wages were to be increased by 5 per cent; and each man, as he left the quarry, received the gift of a gold sovereign. According to one account Young had telephoned the chief clerk William Gray on 10 June to ask if it would be possible to get this money in time; but the local manager David Davies, who was 'quite ignorant that there was any intention on the part of Lord Penrhyn to do anything of the kind', recalled the gift as 'an absolutely spontaneous action' taken by Lord Penrhyn 'on the spur of the moment when he saw the men before him'. According to Davies, it was late in the day when Gray returned to Bethesda by train, having obtained £650 in gold from the bank[46]. On the evening of 11 June a crowd of 2,000 marched through Bethesda to the Market Hall behind a banner inscribed 'Be faithful to your fellow workmen'. In a packed meeting W. H. Williams admitted that they were keenly disappointed at what had happened; and Mrs Elizabeth Williams, who had been fined for shouting and booing, was cheered as she came on to the platform. D. R. Daniel referred to Bethesda's 'black book of traitors', and urged the audience to remember that character was worth much more than a sovereign. It was suggested that printed notices saying 'Nid oes bradwr yn y tŷ hwn' (There is no traitor in this house) should be displayed in windows, and the suggestion was greeted with loud cheers. The Rev W. W. Lloyd exhorted the men to work for unity, lest the community should be disgraced and divided by family feuds.

7
Civil War: 1901

After the re-opening of the quarry Lord Penrhyn received a number of congratulatory letters. One of these, written on 12 June and signed 'D. Jones', referred to his 'decisive victory over the disaffected section of the workforce, who now knew that they had a man of 'grit and firmness to deal with'[1]. On 13 June even A. M. Thompson of the *Clarion* was writing to W. J. Parry as if he believed the struggle to be over:

> All the papers declare the strike to be virtually ended. Even the *Morning Leader* says, 'The strike at the Penrhyn Quarry is practically at an end. 1300 men are at work and all is reported quiet'. Will you write to me to 29 St Anne's Road, Brixton, London S.W. for me to receive it on Monday, saying what is the exact state of affairs.

Parry answered this letter on 14 June with a firm contradiction:

> Young floods the newspapers with lies, and the 1300–1800 is one of the latter. . . . The Union Lodge here have a correct list of the lock-out men who have returned to work, Quarrymen, boys, and labourers, and they come to 264. In addition to this there are about 200, including officials, old men and yard men who continued to work. I believe I am correct in saying that all told they don't exceed 450 quarrymen (and the bulk inferior quarrymen).

These statements in a private letter were meant to ensure that the *Clarion* went on with its fund-raising activities, but Parry did not object when the *Clarion* on 22 June printed a modified version of this letter under the heading 'A Check to Labour'.

The letter continued as follows:

> We must not lower our banner now. It must be a fight to the death with this tyrant. He will stoop to anything to gain his end. He has brought down the traitor's price from 30 pieces of silver to 20. He

> gave each of the men who returned to work and those who had continued to work during the lock-out a gold sovereign. Who but Lord Penrhyn would have done this? His friends say he is a good sportsman, but evidently he can strike below the belt. I do hope the papers and unions will come out strong and continue their support. The men still are as determined as ever. It will be difficult to help them from returning home from South Wales and England, where they work, to thrash, if not kill, these traitors.

In the printed version the *Clarion* replaced the words 'thrash, if not kill' with the word 'punish'.

Lord Penrhyn's solicitors Carter, Vincent and Jones wrote to the editor of the *Clarion* complaining that the article printed on 22 June contained improper and incorrect statements; and on 27 July the *Clarion* published an apology, a withdrawal, and an expression of regret. On 1 July, however, when he issued a second appeal for funds, W. J. Parry launched another vehement attack on Lord Penrhyn:

> Lord Penrhyn appears fully determined to refuse to his men their just demands. He will not concede to them their full right to combine, and to select whom they like to lay their complaints before him and the management; he will not give them the control of their own Sick Benefit Club and the right to select their own Medical Attendant; he will not reinstate the leaders of the men who claim to have been unjustly discharged, because of the part they took in pleading the cause of the workmen before his Lordship and the management; he persists in his refusal to do away with his present Contract System at the Quarry; he still retains the objectionable penalties for trifling breaches of Rules . . . . He has made up his mind to use Wealth, Position, Police, yes, and even the Military, and a Subservient Press, to try and crush the men, to starve them, if possible, into submission . . . . We appeal on behalf of innocent Children and helpless Women (the death rate among whom has already gone up), and on behalf of brave men – who have turned their back upon happy homes, and wives and children, fathers and mothers, for months together, to carry on the struggle, as they hope to a glorious finish. We earnestly appeal to all to come to the rescue with their Silver and Gold to fight the tyranny that Wealth and Rank and Bribery tries to set up as a permanent power

> in a district that has been beautified by Nature, by Education, and by Religion, but which now one Tyrannical Feudal Lord makes desolate and hellish.

The charges which Parry made in this appeal were cited by Lord Penrhyn's lawyers in the 1903 libel case; and when he was challenged on the rising death-rate he explained that he had meant this not seriously 'but as a bit of satire'. Besides making these statements in the appeal, however, W. J. Parry wrote another letter to A. M. Thompson on 7 July; and on 13 July the *Clarion* published this under the heading 'The Crime at Bethesda'. Once again Parry accused Lord Penrhyn of causing an increase in the death-rate:

> Matters are moving fast here, and the police are losing their heads. I prefer to believe this to believing that they are acting as they do to justify Lord Penrhyn's demand for the military. Last night they used their batons; at least, one inspector did . . .
>
> Lord Penrhyn can congratulate himself upon the rise in the death-rate here already, and there is no need for thinning them with the military, unless he is dissatisfied with the rise.
>
> Death Rate in the Parish of Bethesda in 1900
>
> General 26.8 in the 1,000, as compared with 25.3 in 1899.
>
> Infants under one year, 210.0 in the 1,000, as compared with 155.0 in 1899.
>
> Old people over 65, 8.2 in the 1,000, as compared with 6.7 in 1899.
>
> Does not this speak something? It will have no effect upon a tyrant, but I trust it will on the British public and the British working man.

Lord Penrhyn's solicitors wrote to W. J. Parry about the statements he had made in these three publications; and Parry's solicitors Lloyd George and George replied on 25 July that their client could not withdraw or apologise as his words were 'an honest expression of his opinions' on Lord Penrhyn as 'an employer of labour'. Parry's figures for deaths among people over 65 were certainly inaccurate, since the figure for 1899 was 9 in the 1,000 and the rate actually went down thereafter; but in any case, as Lord Penrhyn's counsel Sir Edward Clarke pointed out at the trial, the strike did not begin until 22 November and could thus affect only the last six months of 1900[2].

On the day following the re-opening of the quarry 'thick cloud enveloped the mountain ranges', and the *Manchester Guardian* reported that protest demonstrations were inhibited by the heavy rain. 'Traitor' notices were already being circulated, however, and began to appear in strikers' windows. The mass meeting of 15 June was comparatively quiet, and reflected the divisions of loyalty which were now emerging. A man whose father had resumed work said that he wanted to go back but would rather starve than do so without the others. Another speaker said that he had as much respect for the Pennant family as those who had returned, but that he would not return until all the men were re-accepted[3]. Young investigated allegations by the Rev R. T. Jones that a boycott was preventing those who had resumed work from getting provisions. He told Lord Penrhyn on 20 June that these allegations were further proof of 'the untruthfulness of the people and the silly way in which vicars and others' believed all they heard; but he also reported that the strikers were discussing how they could 'force Lord Penrhyn to take back all the men in a body'. On 21 June Young informed Lord Penrhyn that his wife had scarlet fever and had been taken to the Fever Hospital; she was to remain there for the next seven weeks. On 26 June Young told Lady Penrhyn, who organised the admission of quarrymen to a convalescent home in Rhyl, that he had investigated all those who had applied; six had proved to be 'most disloyal', but he had four 'most deserving cases' who would be given tickets. He reported that tickets had previously been given to 'many real bad men', including one who had spoken 'very violently' at the last mass meeting; and he undertook to make enquiries and keep full records in future[4].

On 29 June the *Clarion* observed that nearly four months had passed since Dangle's reports about the 'tyranny of the lord of Penrhyn' over 'Desolate Bethesda'. In that time £1,000 had been collected for the *Clarion* relief fund, and contrary to reports in the 'capitalist press' the struggle was still continuing.

Having walked through Bethesda and seen in 'hundreds of windows' the inscription 'NID OES BRADWR YN Y TY HWN', a correspondent signing himself 'Krypto' reported:

> In my ignorance of the language I thought this meant 'Apartments to Let', but my first inquiry was answered with a translation of the legend, which in plain English is, 'There is no traitor in this house'.

Krypto said that a procession planned for 22 June had been called off because of rain, but that 'upwards of 1,000' had assembled for a mass meeting whose message was 'No surrender'. He claimed that the strikers had the support of most people in Bethesda, including 'the professional classes, the tradespeople, the everyday labourers, aye and even the policemen'; the only exceptions were some who had business dealings with Lord Penrhyn and a few who were affected by the loss of trade. Krypto identified Tregarth, about two miles from Bethesda, as the main centre of Anglicanism and the source of 'Lord Penrhyn's 264 blacklegs'; and he recalled how Lord Penrhyn had eulogised these men and given them a sovereign each, 'whilst doubtless despising them in his heart for the treacherous sneaks' they were. He added that only 90 of the 264 were skilled quarrymen, and that the only additions to their number had been one man and the 'old mare' on which he rode to work. Contributions to the relief fund had been declining, but after the appearance of this article they began to increase again.

On 8 July the *Star* reported a speech made in Battersea Park by John Burns M.P., who said that the Penrhyn strikers were fighting for the right to combine and for the removal of the 'brutal contract system'. Also on 8 July the *Manchester Guardian* reported that notices had been posted in the Bethesda area with the heading 'Processions – Police Caution'. These referred to a procession which had taken place on 29 June on the road from Bethesda to Tregarth, Sling and Mynydd Llandegai:

> Continued hooting of a hostile nature was indulged in . . . . Threatening language was used, and stones thrown at dwelling-houses by some of the persons forming the procession, and the gen-

> eral character of the assembly was calculated to endanger the public peace.

The notices, which had been signed by Colonel Ruck on 3 July, warned that anyone taking part in such a procession in future could be charged with a serious offence.

The same issue of the *Manchester Guardian* reported that the Caernarfon magistrates had heard a number of cases arising from the Penrhyn dispute, and had committed five of the accused to the Assizes on charges of intimidation. These men, who were defended by William George, lived in the village of Rhiwlas; and police witnesses related how a crowd had assailed three Rhiwlas men with hooting, booing, beating of tin cans, and shouts of 'Tails' and 'Boers'. In the trial at Caernarfon Assizes, which was reported by the *Manchester Guardian* on 15 July, another seven defendants were charged with

> unlawfully following John Evans with more than two persons in a disorderly fashion, with a view to compelling him to abstain from working in the employment of Lord Penrhyn, at Bethesda, on 11th June.

After an absence of half an hour the jury delivered the following verdict on these seven:

> While condemning the demonstrations which have taken place at Bethesda, we find that the defendants were not proved guilty.

The five original defendants were also acquitted, because there was no evidence to support the charges.

On 18 July the *Liverpool Mercury* reported that Mr Justice Grantham, speaking at Beaumaris Assizes, had strongly condemned the displaying in some Bethesda windows of notices saying 'No traitors here' and 'Death is better than shame'. On 30 June R.C. Trench had mentioned these notices in a letter to Lord Penrhyn:

> I am going to give notice tomorrow to those people in Ogwen who had another kind of notice in their window, and shall have a look around Bethesda and see if I can find any more. I think one or two notices to quit and perhaps a written caution here and there, on

> the strength of a report that there is molesting or a display of notice, will have good effect.

In July the *Manchester Guardian* reported four cases in which eviction notices had been served. On 27 June John Roberts of Tregarth, a former quarryman now working at Penmaenmawr, was given notice on the ground that he had not paid the rent due in November and May. On the same date notice was served on Mrs Margaret Roberts of Braichmelyn, who had been under notice to quit before and now owed rent from November 1899. On 1 July notice was served on William Davies of Maescaradog, who owed 10s rent and was said to be a man the quarry management would not take back under any circumstances. On the same date notice was served on a quarryman's widow now married to Geoffrey Jones, an ex-quarryman whose brother Henry was chairman of the mass meetings. The displaying of a 'Traitor Notice' in the window of Mrs Jones' house at Ogwen had been reported by the Rev W. Morgan and by John Jones of Ogwen Cottage; and the reporter observed that this was the sole reason for her eviction, there being 'no question of rent' in this case. On 24 July Trench reported that while most houses in Cefnan, where several notices were displayed, would not become Lord Penrhyn's property until their leases expired, he had identified one whose lease had expired already. Having learned that the tenant was working in Llanberis, Trench told his wife that, unless she took down the notice and promised not to display it again, her husband would receive a notice to quit as soon as he arrived home. Trench reported to Lord Penrhyn that she had for some time refused to give this promise, but that she had done so 'at last'[5].

The strikers' weekly procession through the streets of Bethesda commonly began at 5 p.m. on Saturday. With reference to that of 27 July, Young later wrote to Lord Penrhyn:

> It was really bad on Saturday night and witnessed by Mr Kneeshaw and Col Ruck till after 11 p.m. The police were powerless to move the crowd for about two hours.

On 28 July Young informed Lord Penrhyn that the workmen

and officials had 'on their own initiative' drawn up a petition requesting more protection for themselves and their families; they intended to send copies to Colonel Ruck, to the magistrates, and to the Standing Joint Police Committee. Young added:

> I feel fairly confident our 600 will stick to work. The quarrymen's average wage last month was 6s 1¾d a day and it will take considerable rioting to force them away from such wages.

The phrase 'our 600' does not indicate the number of men working; it is an allusion, interesting for the light it throws on Young's psychology, to the 'noble six hundred' of Tennyson's 'The Charge of the Light Brigade'. Many strikers were now returning from South Wales, where the Miners' Executive Committee had declared a three-day holiday. On 31 July Young reported to Lord Penrhyn that some two hundred strikers had arrived in Bethesda about 6 a.m. the previous day, 'just as the men were going to work'. Because of the threats made during that encounter, telegrams were sent requesting military assistance; and in the evening a police constable had his head 'cut open with a stone' in an incident at Rachub.

The troops sent to the area were listed by the *Liverpool Courier* of 1 August as 64 men of the Dragoon Guards (Queen's Bays) under Captain Herron, 200 men of the North and South Staffordshires and East Yorkshires under Captain Ewington, and a contingent of Lancers; and according to the *Manchester Guardian* of the same date the Queen's Bays were billeted at St Paul's Schools in Bangor and some of the infantry at the National Schools in Bethesda. Some of the troops arrived in Bethesda about 2 a.m. on 31 July; and at 6 a.m. Young went up to the quarry with the workmen 'to encourage them'. All the men turned up, and Young said that they seemed 'quite plucky and determined'. Writing at 5 p.m. the same day, he reported that the town had been 'quite quiet' since the troops' arrival; and he told Lord Penrhyn that there was no need for him to return to the area. Young had said earlier that he anticipated 'extra rioting' during the coming Bank Holiday weekend; but he now observed that the management could 'do but little', since responsibility for maintaining order lay with Colonel Ruck.

On 1 August Young told Lord Penrhyn that all the men remained 'firmly' at work, and that they were unlikely to give in now that the soldiers were in Bethesda. He said that the local people were 'more against the police than anything', and that the weakness of the magistrates gave indirect encouragment to rioting. He was finding the newspapers reluctant to print his point of view, although the *Times* was an exception; and he was also conscious, as he told Lord Penrhyn, that 'the slate trade in the country' was 'getting worse and worse'. While most commentators ignored such issues, the strike was in fact encouraging foreign competition and thus hastening the decline of the industry[6]. On 3 August the *North Wales Chronicle* reported an angry meeting of the working quarrymen on the Red Lion gallery under the presidency of Robert Jones of Tregarth. Addressing the meeting, Melancthon Williams of Tregarth referred to reports in the *Manchester Guardian*, the *Liverpool Courier* and the *Liverpool Daily Post* which contained 'shameful lies' about them. The following statement was drawn up:

> There is no semblance of truth in what you published in your issue of today with regard to the quarrymen now at work in the Penrhyn Quarry that they have held a meeting to consider a proposal to cease working; on the contrary we are perfectly contented with Lord Penrhyn's terms, which we know to be as favourable as those at any other quarry, and we are determined to continue working.

This statement, with the signatures of eight quarrymen, was sent to the three offending newspapers.

As the Bank Holiday approached more strikers returned from Liverpool, Manchester and South Wales, and additional troops were brought into Bethesda. Journalists too descended on the town; and the events of Saturday 3 August were extensively reported, for example by the *Carnarvon and Denbigh Herald* of 9 August. 'Some 40 or 50 dragoons' were brought up from Bangor by train; and a crowd cheered them as they made their way, with 'horses ready saddled and arms at hand', from the station to a nearby yard. '120 infantry, also under arms', were stationed half a mile away 'on the side of the main street'. From the porch of the Douglas Arms Hotel three Bangor magistrates observed the scene, consulting frequently with Colonel Ruck. The streets 'presented a lively appearance', hundreds of people having come from Bangor, Caernarfon, Llanberis, Ffestiniog and elsewhere; but the 'residents of Bethesda', although they 'chatted amicably enough with the soldiers and even with the police', had a 'determined, dogged, and resentful look' which showed how much they resented this 'needless display of force'. Train after train came into Bethesda station, bringing 'sturdy lads' home from the 'Glamorganshire and Lancashire collieries'. As the crowds gathered towards 5 p.m. at the bottom of the village, Henry Jones and W. H. Williams urged them to 'maintain their character as peaceful citizens'. A procession of 1,200 to 1,300 people, 'with numerous brand new banners floating in the breeze', then marched through the town, silent at first and later singing not 'inflammatory doggerel' or martial songs but 'their own hymn tunes'; and as they passed the National Schools to 'the magnificent strains of Crugybar', the soldiers 'doffed their caps and stood bareheaded as a mark of respect'.

After the procession there was an open-air meeting attended by some 4,000 to 5,000 people. The principal speaker was Keir Hardie, who accused the government of 'ignorance' said that the soldiers had been sent to Bethesda 'to protect blacklegs and landlords, the sacred animals of Great Britain'. He assured the quarrymen of 'further financial support', and promised that when they were victorious he would 'come again and help them to put their political organisation in order'. Young's view of the proceedings was that

> owing to the fact that half the Lancers were promenading Bethesda there was practically no disturbance by order of the Committee, just to pretend that the Military is not needed.

He was confident that such tactics would not prevent the Penrhyn quarrymen from working; but he hoped that Colonel Ruck and Henry Kneeshaw, chairman of the Standing Joint Police Committee, would be able to keep the soldiers in the area to ensure peace[7]. On 5 August the Home Secretary Charles

Ritchie answered questions in the House of Commons about the use of troops in Bethesda. He said that the Home Office had received through the Chief Constable a petition from a number of workmen who claimed that they and their families were in danger; but he explained that the troops had been requisitioned by a magistrate, and that the Home Office had played no part in the decision to send them. William Jones and other members expressed some indignation at the use of troops, emphasising that the strikers had sung not 'riotous songs' but hymns, and that the soldiers had 'uncovered' as the procession marched by[8].

The magistrates continued to try cases of riot and assault; but conflicts of evidence made prosecution difficult; and punishments were usually light. On 10 August the *Liverpool Weekly Mercury* reported the case of Daniel Jones, one of the rioters fined in November 1900, who on 6 August had been charged before the Bangor magistrates with an assault on Rowland Jones. Hugh Vincent for the procecution said that on Sunday 4 August, when Rowland Jones encountered Daniel Jones and two others, Daniel Jones had said, 'You have taken my place in the quarry', and struck him a 'violent blow in the mouth, breaking one of his teeth'. This statement was greeted with laughter in court, and William George for the defence maintained that Daniel Jones had struck Rowland Jones only after the latter had kicked him; but the magistrate, Henry Lewis, fined Daniel Jones 20s with costs. Writing to Lord Penrhyn after the trial, Young commented:

> I fear fines paid by the Union will not have a deterrent effect – but on the whole considering the large number of strikers I think it is fairly quiet now . . . . This extra rioting will, I hope, die out again by the end of the week when all those from South Wales have gone there again. After this there is no holiday until Xmas I think so some may begin to think of returning to work, but I am not in a sanguine mood just now. Not one workman has been intimidated into leaving so far[9].

On 10 August Young told Lord Penrhyn that, although the Lancers were to remain, forty of the infantry had left the previous day and the rest were to leave the following Monday; he attributed this to the 'harrying' questions which had been asked in the House of Commons. The quarrymen who lived at Rachub and Mynydd Llandegai had to face 'hooting etc' every day; and Young had sent evidence about this to Hugh Vincent to see if further prosecutions were feasible. At the same time, he reported that the quarry had produced about 2,400 tons of slates since the re-opening.

On 16 August, the *Carnarvon and Denbigh Herald* commented on a recent meeting of the Standing Joint Police Committee, at which the use of troops in Bethesda was discussed. Being responsible for the preservation of law and order in the county, the Chief Constable had decided to seek military aid because of 'open threats' on the one hand and 'fears' on the other; and the requisition had been signed by Henry Kneeshaw, who was a magistrate and chairman of the sub-committee appointed to deal with 'the Bethesda difficulty'. D. P. Williams made it clear that the sub-committee had had nothing to do with this decision; but motions from J. R. Pritchard and W. J. Parry condemning the person who authorised 'the introduction of the military' were ruled out of order. Being advised by the Chief Constable that 'more police protection must be obtained at once', the Committee decided to appoint 100 special constables for Bethesda rather than borrow constables from other places. In the House of Commons on 17 August David Lloyd George asked the Home Secretary if his attention had been drawn to the fact that the members of the sub-committee had dissociated themselves from the decision to requisition military aid; but Ritchie pointed out that military aid had been requisitioned not by the sub-committee but by the magistrate who had the power to do so[10].

On 30 August Young told Lord Penrhyn that he had agreed to give an interview to Charles Sheridan Jones of the *Daily Chronicle*, who had taken rooms in Bethesda. When Jones had finished his enquiries in the town, Young would take him round the quarry; and he would explain, if the question came up, that the management did not intend 'to employ anything like the old number of men'. In future the normal team for a bargain would be two partners and a journeyman; and Young believed that with 400 fewer quarrymen than before they could produce almost as much slate and employ more labourers and bad-rockmen. He claimed that monthly production had risen from 5½ to 8½ tons per man, chiefly because of the two-partner system and the elimination of waiting at the waterbalances. On 4 September, after the interview with Sheridan Jones, Young reported that he had found him the 'most ardent Socialist Trade Unionist' he had yet met, 'worse even in a way than Clement Edwards'. Jones declared that if the quarrymen at work were not old men and boys, they were the least efficient workers; and Young pointed out that output per man was '60% more . . . than previous to the strike'. Jones said that a worker should be free to present a complaint in whatever way he wanted; and when Young claimed that men had this freedom he and Jones argued at length 'to no purpose'. Young told Jones that he 'had evidently come down with a brief for the Trades Unions'; but, after 'hammering away at him for three hours', he 'got home at 8 p.m. very depressed indeed and could not sleep'. On 5 September Young wrote to Lord Penrhyn again, saying that he needed a holiday:

> Today owing to the strain of yesterday and the gale all night my head feels bruised all over – but after lunch I will write a report of my interview with C. Sheridan Jones – it has depressed me very much, but I dare say it is only because I don't feel well – and I'm disappointed more men don't apply.

Preparations were being made for Lord Penrhyn's libel case against W. J. Parry, but Young commented:

> I want you to leave the W.J.P. affair as much as possible to Mr Vincent as it somehow quite unnerves me[11].

On 30 August the *Daily News* reported that the officers and men of the Queen's Bays, 'being thoroughly tired of idling away their time', had on 28 August organised a military tournament in aid of the Carnarvonshire and Anglesey Infirmary. The military sports were held in Penrhyn Park, 'by kind permission of the Right Honourable Lord Penrhyn', and the *Daily News* saw this as 'a finishing touch to the comedy'. The *Liverpool Echo* of 29 August said that some 3,000 people enjoyed an entertainment 'such as most of them never and few had rarely seen'. The programme included wrestling on barebacked horses, boxing between two of the troopers, and a series of tent-pegging competitions; and it concluded with a 'weird and exciting episode descriptive of a typical fight between British cavalry and Dervishes'. The total receipts at the gate were £80. Although he was suffering from gastric catarrh, Young arranged for Captain Herron and 'his fifty-five men' to have lunch at the Royal Hotel in Capel Curig, which was owned by Lord Penrhyn. They were to have 'a good solid cold lunch, drive back to the quarry 'in time for 3 p.m. blast', spend '1½ to 2 hours' at the quarry, and then drive 'right down to Bangor'. On 18 September Young told Lord Penrhyn that Captain Herron was 'a very nice man indeed', and that the arrangements had gone 'without a hitch'; he had also discovered that Lieutenant Rumbold's father had been a councillor of Young's old school, Brighton College. Young feared, however, that the troops might be sent away the following week; and since that would be 'a most regrettable move' he suggested Lord Penrhyn might tell Colonel Ruck that 'some of the ringleaders' were being given notice to quit, and that the troops ought to be retained for 'moral support'. In the event the Queen's Bays stayed until October.

A private meeting of the N.W.Q.U. executive early in August was told that the funds already guaranteed would be enough to maintain the struggle for another two years; and on 2 September the *Liverpool Courier* reported that 'the outlook for a settlement' was 'locally regarded as absolutely hopeless'. The Trades Union Congress, meeting at the Albert Hall in September, condemned the introduction of troops and pledged the delegates 'to secure regular and adequate financial help for the men to continue their courageous struggle'. At this meeting D. R. Daniel, whom the *Daily News* of 4 September described as 'frail featured, with laughing blue eyes', made

> a touching little speech, full of gratitude for help accorded, and

> pathetically appreciative of the devotion and self-sacrifice of the brave community in Bethesda.

Daniel said that there was no more need for soldiers in the streets of Bethesda than 'in the drawing-room of Lord Penrhyn'. Henry Jones, 'looking as solemn as a judge', made an eloquent speech in Welsh 'which when interpreted brought many a round of sympathetic cheers'. The *Daily News* concluded that British trade unionists were watching with admiration 'the mournful struggle beside the great hole in the mountain'.

W. J. Parry's book on the lockout of 1900–1901 appeared in August, and quickly became for many people the authoritative account of the dispute. On 26 September Young published, in response to questions from Herbert Bridge of the Christian Social Reform League, a factual pamphlet entitled *The Penrhyn Quarry Dispute;* but this was no sufficient answer to Parry's impassioned and imaginative narrative. On 24 September the *Daily Chronicle* carried a report from Bethesda under the heading 'How will it end?' Noting that there was 'little surface expression of poverty in Bethesda', the reporter observed that 'the quiet rows of cottages, with their neat exteriors', gave no clue to the sufferings of the inhabitants. The article gave portraits of a 'rebellious quarryman' named John Daniel Jones and of a Mrs Salt who before the dispute had lived by doing laundry for the quarrymen. The phrase that rang in the correspondent's ears was 'I dread the winter'. Bethesda was now so quiet that eight of the extra police stationed there were withdrawn, as were the Liverpool policemen stationed in Bangor and elsewhere[12]. At the beginning of October the Bangor magistrates decided that the 'soldiery' too should return to their normal duties; and the *Daily Chronicle* of 3 October, reporting that the cavalry had gone back to Aldershot, concluded that the trouble was now 'practically ended'.

It was by no means ended in terms of relations between the Penrhyn estate and its tenants. On 2 October the estate agent R. C. Trench reported that he had visited a row of twenty-six houses at Llwybrmain on Mynydd Llandegai, which had been built in pairs by the tenants and their 'antecedents', and were 'with only one or two exceptions very clean and tidy'. Since all the leases had expired, the houses were now Lord Penrhyn's property; and only three of them were occupied by men working in the quarry, the occupants of most of the others being employed at Llanberis or in South Wales. Trench pointed out that, since the Llwybrmain tenants were predominantly of the 'disloyal' kind, the eviction of a few of them would give the incomers more peace than in their previous houses only if the remainder could be 'made to behave themselves'. If Lord Penrhyn wanted to convert Llwybrmain into an area where only working quarrymen might live, it would be necessary to evict almost all the tenants; but Trench understood that Tregarth was to be the place for 'well-disposed people', and one tenant was indeed moving from Llwybrmain to Tregarth. He thought on the other hand that some good might be done by a 'strong letter of caution', informing those Llwybrmain tenants who were not working in the quarry that any interference with Lord Penrhyn's quarrymen 'would result in a notice to quit'. He added that some of the tenants, such as the four members of the Oliver family, were 'a bad lot'; and he said that it would be good to get rid of these, especially if they were never to be re-admitted to the quarry.

Writing again on 5 October, Trench said that the notices already given 'had been magnified to a great extent', so that it was being reported that all who were not working in the quarry would receive such notices. On 8 October he reported that his assistant, a man named Richards, had visited Llwybrmain the previous Saturday and found 'one of those traitor notices in nearly every window'; the tenants evidently displayed them on Saturdays and removed them for the rest of the week. Trench contemplated going up to a place from which he could see the notices without being seen himself; since the houses were numbered, his list would enable him 'to identify the tenants at once'. On 9 October the *Manchester Guardian* carried a report from its Caernarfon correspondent who said that the situation in Bethesda was going from bad to worse. He explained that some tenants, who were working in South Wales and had left their wives and families at home, were being given notices to quit; and he also implied that the Llwybrmain tenants, each of whom occupied four ground-floor rooms and an attic for an annual rent of £3 10s, were expecting similar notices. Writing to Lord Penrhyn on 9 October, Trench observed that the *Manchester Guardian* account was 'rather interesting'; but he emphasised that no notices had been served in Llwybrmain '*yet*'.

A statement drawn up in reply to the *Manchester Guardian* report said that only three notices to quit had been served, and went on to describe the circumstances of each of these. The first involved a tenant occupying a house built by Lord Penrhyn, about a year earlier, 'expressly for quarrymen employed in the quarry'; the tenant had now left the quarry, and his house was required for man who was still working. The second case involved a tenant who had gone to South Wales, leaving a house 'within a quarter of a mile of the main Penrhyn entrance'; there was much demand for such houses from people employed on the estate, and it was thought undesirable that a tenant unlikely to have any further link with the estate should retain a house 'so close to Lord Penrhyn's doors'. The third case involved a tenant who was in arrears and had left the neighbourhood; his house was wanted for a man working in the quarry. Hugh Vincent was anxious to refute the *Manchester Guardian* allegations lest they should prejudice the libel case against W. J. Parry; and Trench told Lord Penrhyn that it would be better not to serve notice on the Olivers 'at present'. On 15 October Trench decided to soften the warning notice to be sent to Llwybrmain residents; they were to be told that 'while they were perfectly free to work or not as they liked', they could not remain as Lord Penrhyn's tenants 'if they annoyed their fellow workmen.'

The pressure of public opinion made it difficult for Trench to get rid of 'undesirable' tenants and create a district of 'loyal' men. On 16 October he told Lord Penrhyn of the problems he was encountering with John Jones, one of three tenants who had been given notice to leave houses in Tregarth. Jones contended that the men would be back at work in two months' time, having obtained 'better terms'; and he said that he would be away when the notice expired, and that his wife and family would not leave the house until they were 'turned into the street'. Trench believed that 'the other side' was urging people not to move, hoping to make 'great capital out of these contemplated evictions'. He added:

> Of course I *could* say to the three that I have reported their cases to you, and that you seeing that the winter is coming on have instructed me to say that the notices are to be postponed for six months.

Trench apologised for putting this to Lord Penrhyn, acknowledging that 'leniency might be taken for weakness'; but he observed that the problem was 'rather a difficult' one. Lord Penrhyn settled for 'leniency'; and on 21 October each of the three tenants received a letter saying that since a 'change of abode' in early winter might cause hardship, it had been decided that the notices should be withdrawn 'for the present'[13].

On 12 October the statement that only three notices had been served appeared in the *Manchester Guardian*, the *North Wales Chronicle*, and the Liverpool daily papers; but on 17 October the *Daily Express* and the *Liverpool Echo* printed a letter which said that thirty strikers had been given a month's notice to quit their cottages. The writer added that there had in these cases been no unpaid rent and no complaints, and suggested that the 'wholesale eviction of the men, women and children living on Lord Penrhyn's estate' was in contemplation. Lord Penrhyn consulted Charles W. Matthews and Sir Edward Clarke, the lawyers who were preparing the libel case against W. J. Parry; but they informed him on 23 October that there was no need to take action against the two newspapers. On 26 October the editor of the *Daily Express* wrote to Carter, Vincent and Jones expressing his regret at the false statements which had been printed; and on 28 October a similar apology was received from the editor of the *Liverpool Echo*.

At a mass meeting in Bethesda reported by the *Manchester Guardian* on 21 October, D. R. Daniel delivered a 'stirring address'. He described the Free Labour Association as a 'dirty and rotten concern', and went on:

> If the men who had gone to work at the Penrhyn Quarries were black before, they became covered with soot as soon as they joined hands with that society.

H. Griffith Parry reported that membership of the N.W.Q.U. had increased by about 1,000 in three months, and said that there could be 'a lasting peace' in Bethesda if Lord Penrhyn would restrict Young's authority to the port and appoint at the quarry someone who understood quarrying. Thinking probably of the flourishing Penyrorsedd Quarry managed by W. A. Darbishire, Griffith Parry spoke of Nantlle as a place where quarrymen were 'treated like men' and were therefore 'ready to fight to the bitter end for their employer'; and, after noting that the strikers were now being referred to as 'Boers', he commented:

> Well, at any rate, the Boers had proved faithful to their country and their cause.

The *Manchester Guardian* reporter said that this was 'one of the most enthusiastic meetings' the strikers had held. On 24 October the argument about military aid was renewed at a meeting of the Standing Joint Police Committee. The Rev Ceidiog Roberts ridiculed the petition in which working quarrymen claimed to go to and from the quarry 'with fear and trembling'. They hoped the Home Secretary would conclude that they resembled the Light Brigade:

> But there was no cannon to the front and only women to the right and children to the left, with youngsters in front again yelling and shouting – (laughter). If they were stormed it was only with tins. In spite of this array they boldly marched along, 'the noble 600'.

Having celebrated Bethesda as a 'self-dependent community' and a 'unique village hidden away in the Welsh hills', Ceidiog Roberts poured scorn on Lord Penrhyn's notion that 'a certain amount of booing and jeering at the expense of seceders' constituted 'a menace to the public safety'. At this date Bethesda had twenty policemen as against the five judged sufficient before the strike; and the meeting was informed that when another man had returned to work more police protection had been required because of a revival of 'hooting and following men . . . and their wives on Saturday nights[14].'

On 28 October 1901 the *Manchester Guardian* reported a visit to Bethesda by Pete Curran and Isaac Mitchell, the chairman and general secretary of the General Federation of Trade Unions. At a crowded meeting in the Market Hall, Mitchell declared that they had come to see how the strikers were likely to survive the winter, and could now go back to London and say 'that the Bethesda men, and perhaps even some of the Bethesda women – (laughter) – were all right'. Referring to the fact that Lord Penrhyn and Young had refused to see them, Mitchell said that after investigating the situation on their own they had concluded that 'the men who were out were worthy, honest and just men . . . and that it was the duty of trade unionists to assist them'; and he argued that the outlook was more hopeful than six months earlier. There was a fear that 'Lord Penrhyn might endeavour to play the part of an Irish landlord, and place some of their wives and families on the roadside'; but Lord Penrhyn should not 'carry that business too far', because 'the men of Bethesda would defend their homesteads'. Curran too gave the strikers a promise of public support; and D. R. Daniel translated the main substance of both speeches. The same issue of the *Manchester Guardian* reported that Lord Penrhyn had given orders for the withdrawal of notices to quit which had been served on some tenants who were quarrymen no longer working at the quarry; the correspondent suggested that this action showed 'his Lordship's conciliatory attitude when approached in a proper manner'.

On 28 October the Caernarfon Assizes heard charges of rioting arising from incidents in Rachub Square near Bethesda on 30 July. Many strikers had returned from South Wales earlier that day; and Owen Morris testified that the crowd in the square had been 'fearfully wild'. P.C. Edward Pierce Williams said that a 'very disorderly crowd of 250 to 300 people' had greeted the men returning from the quarry with 'threats and shouts', and that P.C. Jones had been wounded in the back of the head by a stone. He rejected charges that he had used his stick, explaining that in his district policemen other than inspectors were not allowed to carry sticks. William Hughes, a labourer, and Owen Lewis Owen, a quarryman, were sentenced to one month's imprisonment for striking a policeman; and Thomas Lewis Owen and William Owen, both quarrymen, were sentenced to a fortnight's imprisonment for throwing stones. Frank Plater, a hairdresser, was fined £5, and Robert Roberts was discharged because of insufficient evidence. After the verdict the mothers of those who had received prison sentences 'cried out hysterically, producing general upset in court'. The counsel for the defence in this case was Samuel Moss M.P.[15]

Lord Penrhyn had twelve daughters, five of whom were to remain unmarried; the last to marry was Elin, whose wedding took place in 1920[16]. In November 1901 he was involved in drawing up the marriage settlement of Ina, who was to marry Major-General Arthur Edward Sandbach on 15 January 1902. On 23 September Sandbach had replied to Lord Penrhyn's enquiries about his 'ways and means' by saying that he had a house in Montgomeryshire and a cattle estate in Jamaica, and could settle £1,500 a year on Ina. After Lord Penrhyn had given his consent to the marriage, the quarrymen proposed through Young to give Ina a present; and on this occasion their suggestion was accepted[17]. Celebrations of a different kind occurred in Bethesda on 7 November, when the two men who had been imprisoned for two weeks were released. The *Liverpool Mercury* of 8 November said that they looked well and were 'but little depressed by their incarceration'; the prison officers had apparently been 'as considerate as the rules of the prison permitted'. The men left Caernarfon by the midday train, and were met in Bethesda by a large crowd, who 'conducted a triumphal procession to Rachub square'. Now and then 'a volley of hooting by the women indicated the residence of a *bradwr*', but in general the procession was orderly; the four policemen, who without Colonel Ruck's knowledge had been assigned to accompany it, had 'nothing whatever to do'[18]. 23 November brought the release of the two men who had been imprisoned in Caernarfon for a month. Along with the two released earlier, they were 'drawn in a carriage by a large number of their comrades' to the Market Hall; they were given seats on the platform, and the assembly resolved to set up a Strikers' Defence Fund for the benefit of quarrymen involved in legal proceedings[19]. About the same date Lord Penrhyn's son, Lieutenant Charles Douglas Pennant of the Grenadier Guards, was reported missing by the War Office; but on 2 December it became known that he was a prisoner-of-war, and on 31 December a telegram was sent to say that he had been released[20].

Before the dispute the quarry had employed 2,741 men, and produced about 110,000 tons per annum. By 10 October 1901 686 men had returned to work, among them the nephew of the local union treasurer Griffith Edwards; and output was said to be running at the rate of 34,000 tons per annum[21]. At the end of November the situation was reviewed at a special meeting of the Standing Joint Police Committee, which Lord Penrhyn did not attend. Colonel Ruck said that there had been 'booing and shouting and disturbances', besides 'a good deal of window breaking', and that he was therefore compelled to retain twenty-one policemen in Bethesda. W. J. Parry remarked that window-breaking was common elsewhere, but R. O. Jones responded that six windows had been broken in his own district only 'the other day'. Rejecting W. J. Parry's argument that there would be 'more quietness' if the Bethesda police force were reduced to ten, the committee passed a motion asking the Home Office to sanction an increase[22]. On 3 December the *Liverpool Courier* reported that an 'outrageous and murderous assault' had been committed 'not 300 yards from Mr Parry's own door'. The victim was 'a harmless, innocent man, 63 years old'; and he was attacked 'without any warning' by 'seven stalwart ruffians' who 'rushed on to him, knocked him down, opened his head', and 'brutally kicked him'. He crawled home 'covered with blood'; and the reporter noted that 'there was no policeman near'. On 4 December the *Liverpool Daily Post* reported that Elizabeth

Griffiths of Caellwyngrydd had been fined 5s with costs for using indecent and abusive language towards a policeman who was escorting a workman home from Penrhyn Quarry. The decline in relations between the police and the strikers is documented in the evidence collected by an inquiry initiated on 23 October 1902. Sergeant Owen, who had been so popular in November 1900, testified on 28 November 1902 that the strikers had become resentful after the re-opening of the quarry in June 1901, when the police had to protect those who resumed work. Sergeant Owen said that if he now attempted to attend a mass meeting he 'would be very soon chucked out'; and he added that even 'an angel from heaven' could not hope to satisfy the contending factions.

The *Clarion* had urged the General Federation of Trade Unions to give 'sustained and systematic support to the men until the close of the strike'; and the *Clarion* relief fund had collected almost £2,000 in the nine months of its existence; in addition, the paper had helped to organise concerts all over the country by the quarrymen's choir, which brought in 'perhaps thousands of pounds more'. On 30 November the *Barnsley Chronicle* reported that the 'Welsh singers' were to visit Barnsley, and that the relief committee was paying an average sum of 6s 8d per fortnight in 'upwards of 700 cases of distress'; but on the same day it was announced that the *Clarion* relief fund was to close at the end of the year. The detachment of the Queen's Bays which had served in Bangor sailed in November for South Africa; and Lord Penrhyn sent the commanding officer £25 to buy 'luxuries' for his men during the voyage. Just before Christmas, Thomas Pierce asked Young to thank Lord Penrhyn for the £15 he had received some weeks earlier after the burning of his hayhouse[23]. Many of the strikers forfeited not only wages and jobs but also sick pay and pensions; and there was confusion about the relative significance of local and national issues in the dispute. William Mosses of the United Pattern Makers Association argued that the strike affected 'only a handful of men in a comparatively unimportant industry, and situated in an isolated and almost inaccessible district'; he considered that 'their defeat or victory would make no appreciable difference in the growth (or otherwise) of democratic opinion'. Mosses also observed that Lord Penrhyn had not violated the letter of the law, since like all employers 'of his stamp' he had the best of legal advice[24].

Early in December it was announced that the Hon W. W. Vivian was to retire after twenty-one years as manager of Dinorwic Quarry. The *Carnarvon and Denbigh Herald* of 6 December called him 'the scion of a distinguished Welsh family' and recalled that he had introduced new rules and regulations:

> These were distasteful to the easy-going and conservative quarrymen; and a six months strike resulted. Ultimately, the men not being well-organised, were defeated.

Management thereafter had been strict, but also 'intelligent and sympathetic', and though wages had not been high, a genuine attempt had been made to provide regular employment and redress real grievances. Vivian had spoken up for the Welsh people when they were disparaged; and he had won the approval of his employees by putting on a 'a suit of quarrymen's togs' and going to the sheds to learn 'the whole art and mystery of producing slates for the market'. He was succeeded by the assistant general manager Ernest Neele, who had once been superintendant of the Chester and Holyhead district of the L.N.W.R. On 9 December Young commented:

> At Dinorwic, if Mr Vivian leaves the helm visibly, he will for some time yet be a directing influence[25].

On 10 December Vivian wrote to Lord Penrhyn, saying that Neele fully realised the importance of keeping up the 'existing kindly feeling' between the two managements. Vivian regarded Lord Penrhyn with 'regard, respect, and as one of the few thinkers left in poor old England'; and he attributed the country's economic decline to trade union representatives, 'unwise labour legislation', and an 'ill-balanced and sensation mongering press'[26].

As Christmas approached there were fears that the return of the quarrymen who had left the area would bring renewed violence. Lord Penrhyn wrote to Colonel Ruck requesting extra protection for the working quarrymen; and on 21 December Colonel Ruck replied that he had doubled the police force, and that the magistrates would probably allow him to seek outside assistance if this proved necessary. He asked Lord Penrhyn to advise the quarrymen to keep away from the main street on Saturdays and avoid 'anything in the shape of provocation'; and Lord Penrhyn replied that the men had been urged to refrain from any behaviour that might provide an excuse for violence. Lord Penrhyn added, however, that he shared the men's feelings that it was

> disgraceful that mob rule should dominate to such an extent as to make it dangerous for women to go shopping in the main street of Bethesda after dark[27].

Just before Christmas two special trains brought about 1,000 men back to Bethesda from South Wales and elsewhere. On Christmas Eve *Yr Herald Cymraeg* published a letter from 'Methodist', who asked if the mass meetings had

> any object further than congregating to eulogise one another and to glorify in the fact that they [were] being called Boers;

he argued that the quarrymen's cause was

> too important a matter to come together to hold useless meetings only to lead them further astray.

As the town made ready for fresh scenes of rioting, members of the Pennant family exchanged the usual Christmas letters. Alan, the son of Edward Douglas Pennant, wrote to Lord Penrhyn from Sholebrook Lodge near Wicken:

> My dear Grandpapa,
>
> Thank you very much for Baron Munchhausen. I am reading it now, it is very good, so exciting and funny. We went to a Christmas tree at File house. When first we got there we had tea. After tea we had the tree, it was a lovely one. I got a knife, a football, a train and a butterfly. After the tree there were fireworks and some of the rockets went so high that Dad could see them from the garden.
>
> Give my love to Granny.
>
> Ever your loving Alan[28].

8
Violent Bethesda: 1902

Events in Bethesda during the first days after Christmas 1901 included a mass meeting attended by 1,800 people and a demonstration at which attendance was reduced by heavy rain. The relief committee distributed £900 in additional relief, giving 10s each to heads of families, 5s each to single adult strikers, and 2s 6d each to strikers under seventeen[1]. Although extra police had been drafted into the area, the situation remained peaceful until Tuesday 31 December; but on that day the town Ben Tillett had called 'crimeless Bethesda' was overrun by violence. The windows of the Victoria Hotel and the Waterloo Inn were smashed because they had served 'traitors' with drink; and the windows of twenty-six houses inhabited by working quarrymen were also broken[2]. Colonel Ruck hurried to Bethesda to direct police operations; but according to the *Carnarvon and Denbigh Herald* of 3 January 1902 the first hours of New Year's Day saw 'terror and misrule' in control of the High Street, where 'the seething mass swept like a human torrent in various directions, carrying everything before it'. Large stones were thrown into the house of Richard Hughes, the contractor involved in earlier riots; and there were attacks on houses in Gordon Terrace, Mountain View, Brynteg Street, Coetmor Mount, and Penybryn.

At a hastily-convened meeting in Bangor on 1 January three magistrates, after hearing evidence from Colonel Ruck, signed the order for 40 cavalry and 100 infantry to be brought into the area; and Colonel Ruck returned to Bethesda, accompanied by a magistrate who was prepared to read the Riot Act. On the Wednesday afternoon, before the troops had arrived, there was another serious disturbance as the men left the quarry; stones were thrown, the police were unable to maintain order, and according to the *Times* of 3 January working quarrymen had to plunge into the river Ogwen to escape their assailants. A company of the Staffordshire Regiment reached Bethesda about 4 a.m. on Thursday 2 January; and two troops of the 3rd Provisional Regiment of Hussars reached Bangor about 3 p.m. the same day, having travelled by special train with their horses in cattle trucks[3]. The infantry was billeted at the Glanogwen National Schools in Bethesda, the cavalry at the goods yard of Bangor railway station.

About 4 p.m. on 2 January the people of Bethesda were startled to find Lord Penrhyn and E. A. Young in their midst. The *Times* reported that they were 'vigorously hooted at', and the *Carnarvon and Denbigh Herald* claimed that when they reached Bethesda railway station they drove off in a 'closed carriage'. The Liberal M.P. William Jones protested strongly to Colonel Ruck about Lord Penrhyn's 'provocative action in parading the streets in the present excited condition of the quarrymen'. On 4 January, however, the *Liverpool Courier* and the *Manchester Guardian* rejected accounts of a 'hostile reception' for Lord Penrhyn and his manager; and on 10 January the *Carnarvon and Denbigh Herald* printed an official statement which had been issued some days earlier from Port Penrhyn:

> Not the slightest incivility was shown to them as they walked quietly through the main street of Bethesda about 4 p.m. on Thursday and as a matter of fact Lord Penrhyn was most respectfully saluted by many of the bystanders. Not a sound of hooting was heard anywhere except from one or two small children who made some dubious noises near the railway station.

The statement also denied both the report that Lord Penrhyn and Young had entered 'a closed carriage', and the earlier report that working quarrymen had been forced on 1 January to take refuge on the Ogwen; these lies, it said, were designed to 'stimulate excitement and raise the hopes of the rioters'.

There was some disturbance after 4 p.m. on 2 January when the quarrymen finished work; but in the evening there was a quieter atmosphere, which Colonel Ruck attributed to heavy rain. On 3 January Colonel Ruck reported to the Under-Secretary of State at the Home Office that when the quarrymen finished work the cavalry would be on duty where the trouble had occurred the previous day. He said that the rioters' object was to frighten the working quarrymen by breaking as many windows as possible before the majority of the strikers left the district at the end of the holiday; and he explained that the scattered nature of the area made it hard for the police to know where an attack was to be made.

On Saturday 4 January, which was the quarrymen's monthly pay day, extra police were brought in, and public houses were ordered to close at 9 p.m. The Cavalry were on duty, and according to the *Manchester Courier* of 6 January they were issued with fifty rounds each of ball ammunition. Continuous rain in the morning cooled the strikers' enthusiasm; but some 500 men and 100 women and children joined the afternoon procession, cheering William Jones M.P. and booing as they passed the police station. Contemporary drawings show the Welsh inscriptions on the banners: 'There is no traitor in this crowd', 'Better die a soldier than live a traitor', 'Be faithful to your fellow-workmen'. At a mass meeting in the evening, Henry Jones said that he feared 'the hands had overruled the other powers'; but a voice from the crowd replied, 'Not half enough'. William Jones M.P. made a plea for arbitration, offering the slogan 'Na chais iawn ond o gymod' (Seek no right save through concord); he urged that if the working quarrymen came out, their 'old fellow workmen' should 'be reconciled to them and take the earliest opportunity of applying the principle of conciliation'. On 6 January the *Manchester Guardian* commented that the strikers were clearly embittered by the knowledge that no favourable settlement was in sight, since the number of men working was sufficient to make the quarry profitable.

Welsh hymns were sung at Bethesda station on 6 January as some 600 strikers left by special train for South Wales; and the *Manchester Evening Mail* of 6 January noted the prevailing atmosphere of respectability and joviality. The calm which descended on Bethesda after this exodus was celebrated on 7 January by the *Manchester Courier:*

> The wild career of the river down the picturesque valley was the only thing to relieve the dull monotony . . . and the thought of the troops being stationed in the village appeared altogether ludicrous.

On 7 January the magistrates began hearing the many cases arising from the New Year disturbances. David Thomas was fined 20s with costs for incitement to disorderly conduct, and Owen Owen was fined 5s with costs for throwing stones[4]. At a concert given in Denbigh by the Penrhyn Choir the Rev W. W. Lloyd declared that there was not a 'particle of truth' in the allegations of 'riotous conduct'; he claimed that the police had unnecessarily 'wired for assistance' after 'an innocent demonstration on the part of thirty young persons, who in the usual manner celebrated the coming of the New Year'[5]. On 10 January the *Daily Chronicle* reported that the Staffordshire Regiment was to be withdrawn but that the Hussars were to remain. In a statement printed by the same newspaper, Young spoke of the injuries sustained by working quarrymen during the 'disgraceful riots', and described in detail the damage done to a house occupied by two district nurses; but he also pointed out that the number at work was increasing, another thirty having returned in December.

The *Cambrian News* of 10 January blamed the riots on the men's leaders, who had scandalously obscured and misrepresented the whole situation'. The 'conciliation' which these leaders advocated meant simply that the working quarrymen would be driven out of the quarry and then 'pelted'; but Lord Penrhyn, whose refusal to allow the coercion of non-unionists had prompted the strike, would not consent to their being coerced now. On 11 January the *North Wales Chronicle* reported a meeting of workmen and officials, at which they congratulated the Hon Ina Douglas Pennant on her approaching marriage; they asked her to accept a 'tea kettle and candelabra' as expression of their 'attachment and respect for Lord and Lady Penrhyn and family', from whom they had 'always received in health and in sickness the greatest possible kindness and consideration'. On 11 January Trench reported that all the tenants who had contributed to the wedding present were to be sent pieces of the cake, which had cost £218[6]. At the January meeting of the N.W.Q.U. it was reported that membership was increasing, Nantlle alone having 1,000 members; and all lodges were urged to help with the organisation of Labour Day, where the guests would include Mabon (William Abraham), J. Bryn Roberts M.P., and the 'Bethesda Choir'[7].

The *Liverpool Mercury* of 13 January said that Bethesda was returning to 'its quiet, not to say its lethargic, condition', and noted that 'nearly everyone of the Noncomformist secessionist quarrymen' had joined the Anglican church, partly because of intimidation and partly because of the welcome extended by the 'Church party'. A fuller picture was given by a correspondent from the *North Wales Observer and Express*, whose report was printed on 17 January. His journey from the 'narrow, crowded Bangor streets' to the 'great slate hills' would have taken only fifteen minutes by train; but it took forty minutes by road, and the driver was reluctant to talk because the little grey mare pulling the post-car had 'a dash of vice in her blood'. Bethesda was described as a 'conglomeration of scattered hamlets and villages'; and the High Street from which the roads to these villages started was said to have 'smart business establishments, small dwelling houses, inns, and open spaces' jostling one another in 'delightful inconsequence'. The correspondent had timed his visit so as to arrive at 4.30 p.m. or 'pudding-time', when the quarrymen stopped work for the day; and he found the police and the Hussars already stationed to protect them. Observing that the working quarrymen could be described as 'secessionists' or 'loyal workers', 'traitors' or 'honest men', he recounted how thirty of them, escorted front and rear by 'stalwart constables', were received with boos which culminated in such a 'mighty howl' that 'a stranger might be forgiven' for harbouring 'fears of violence and bloodshed'. As the police hustled their 'frightened convoy' round the corner, a dozen troopers carried out a flanking movement to cover their retreat. While the Hussars were returning to their quarters, some of the strikers shouted insults at them; but these, being 'Welsh of the Welsh', were fortunately not understood. Some of the strikers told the reporter what they were demanding: abolition of the contract system, a new set of rules displaying some 'humane spirit', and a management capable of 'a little human sympathy'. Noting that the men had said nothing of socialism or unionism, the reporter meditated as the Bangor train carried him away from the 'slate hills':

> Could not . . . the waste of the last fourteen months in Bethesda have been obviated by bringing into the early stages of the negotiations – just a little human sympathy?

In January 1902 Pantdreiniog Quarry, which had claimed to have an 'abundant supply of labour at a reasonable cost', was said to be suffering becase of the resumption of work at Penrhyn[8]. The village of Tregarth was the home of many 'loyal' workmen, and Young tried to prevent 'disloyal' people from settling there. Strenuous efforts were made to prevent William Williams of Rachub from opening a business in Tregarth, on the ground that he was 'one of W. J. Parry's right hand men in all agitations', and would make the village 'like Caellwyngrydd and Bethesda'[9]. On 22 January the 7.25 p.m. train from Bangor, which was carrying men, women and children, was met on its arrival in Tregarth by a huge crowd of men. In the ensuing 'free fight' several of the combatants were hurled on to the lines between the carriages, 'one woman sustaining a severe cut on her head'. According to the *Liverpool Daily Post*, the police were helpless; and the train was delayed twenty minutes before the line was cleared. This incident took place on the last day of the quarry month, which was 'always a critical period in times of dispute'; and it prompted the Hussar officers, whose headquarters were in Bangor, to go Bethesda and take charge of the detachment stationed there.

When the Standing Joint Police Committee met on 24 January, most of its members were of the opinion that the situation in Bethesda had deteriorated. Issard Davies proposed the creation of a new police district comprising the urban district of Bethesda and parts of the adjoining rural districts; and in arguing for this proposal he said that 'occasional outbursts had developed into organised riots' which were 'premeditated and preconcerted'. When W. J. Parry disputed this, Davies maintained that the strikers' houses had been untouched on New Year's Eve because 'lights were exhibited' in their windows 'so that people should pass them'[10]. Writing to Henry Kneeshaw on 8 January, the Home Secretary had said that he would 'strongly deprecate a policy of relying on the Military' for the maintenance of order; instead, he recommended that extra police should be brought in from other forces, and that if this source was exhausted a force of special constables should be created. This letter was placed before the Standing Joint Police Committee, and on 30 January Kneeshaw told the Home Secretary that despite the resolution of August 1901 no special constables had been sworn in. The Home Secretary's letter was passed to the Bangor magistrates for their consideration, and on 1 February Kneeshaw sent a copy of it to his friend Lord Penrhyn. After the incident at Tregarth station, however, the level of violence declined for a time. The cavalry and some of the imported policemen were withdrawn;[11] and the strikers pressed ahead with their plan, first reported in the *Manchester Guardian* of 18 January, of going to Newfoundland in the spring to work in the slate quarries there.

In the euphoria of St David's Day 1901 Lord Penrhyn had agreed to be president of the National Eisteddfod; but some of the quarrymen now threatened to boycott it if he took part, and he therefore decided to resign. His decision received much publicity and was widely regretted, but it was noted that he had donated £100 towards the expenses[12]. A mass meeting early in February, which was well attended despite a heavy snowstorm, heard from John O. Williams of Tregarth a re-statement of some of the men's demands: the right of combination, the right to use the dinner-hour as they chose, and the right to have a holiday on Labour Day. There was some excitement over an 'intervention' by Caernarfonshire County Council, which had appointed D. P. Williams and Ephraim Wood as mediators[13]. The County Council proposed a meeting between Lord Penrhyn and men 'lately employed at the quarry'; but Lord Penrhyn's asthma prevented this from taking place. Williams and Wood had a meeting with Young on 15 February; but this meeting, which was 'purely friendly and unofficial', produced no result. Subsequent attempts to arrange a meeting between the mediators and Lord Penrhyn were unsuccessful, because Wood was ill and Williams had to accompany his invalid wife to the south of France. On 7 March Williams explained these difficulties to Lord Penrhyn and to Henry Jones, expressing the hope that the meeting could take place later; but the postponement proved to be indefinite[14].

Evidence that the Penrhyn Choir was an effective publicity agent is afforded by the speech of a Dr Parker, who paid tribute after a concert in the City Temple to men who 'found all the reward they needed in being allowed to sing to the congregation'; Dr Parker was convinced that if Lord Penrhyn could hear them sing 'his heart would soften towards them'. The Penrhyn Choir did not of course sing 'without fee or reward', since its object was to rise money for the Relief Fund; but the concert which aroused Dr Parker's enthusiasm was in fact given by the Garw Male Voice Society from South Wales[15]. Another asset the strikers tried to exploit was the potentiality of Bethesda as a tourist centre. On 22 February the *Manchester Guardian* carried an advertisement headed 'Excursion to Bethesda':

> A novel holiday, which should prove particularly acceptable to trade unionists . . . the object being to assist the dependants of the Bethesda quarrymen.

The week-long excursion had been arranged to begin on 17 May, and the total cost including 'rail and steamship fares, food and housing' would be 30s from Manchester and 27s 6d from Liverpool. A programme written by the Rev W. W. Lloyd described the proposed rambles, celebrated the beauty of the district, and gave a brief history of the dispute; and readers were invited to enjoy a short holiday and at the same time help a 'deserving community' suffering 'through no fault of their own'.

On 17 February 1902 H. P. Meares submitted his resignation in a letter to Lord Penrhyn:

> Herewith I send you my resignation, private circumstances make it advisable that I should do so, and it will be with deep regret that I shall leave your service.

According to the *Liverpool Mercury* of 19 March, Meares' decision was caused by his wife's ill-health; it seems possible that the strains of the dispute, which involved both her husband and her brother, had become too much for her. In his resignation letter Meares said that he had no prospect of future employment, and would be glad of any help Lord Penrhyn could offer; but he eventually found work in Glasgow. Meares' departure caused some dismay among the working quarrymen, who feared that drastic changes were about to take place. On 14 March Young wrote to Lord Penrhyn, asking him to go up to the quarry:

> There is an uneasy feeling up there at the news of Mr Meares' leaving as they fear that it is 1874 over again and that they may be thrown over after all.

Young had spoken to fourteen of the leading men; and David D. Davies, on being appointed local manager, had 'cried like a child' at the thought of his new responsibilities. Young concluded:

> Nothing but your presence will ensure things keeping right as the announcement has come upon them just when they are in a highly nervous condition as to Easter.

An announcement in the press sought to assure the men that Meares' resignation did not imply any change of policy:

> The internal management of the quarry will, as heretofore, be conducted by the three setters, one of whom, Mr David D. Davies, has been appointed local manager, directly responsible to Mr E. A. Young the chief manager[16].

In another announcement, Young had pointed out that the numbers employed had been rising steadily since 11 June 1901.

In January and February the quarry had taken on 43 men, including 12 slatemakers; and with a total of 800 men at work, production was now at the rate of over 36,000 tons per annum[17]. Writing privately to Lord Penrhyn, Young expressed the hope that this 'little notice' might encourage some of the men who wanted to resume work.

The logbooks of Bethesda schools give some impression of the dispute's effect on everyday life. The logbook of Glanogwen National Girls' School recorded on 1 November 1900 that many girls arrived late 'owing to disturbance in the quarry', on 11 November 1900 that attendance was 'not quite so good owing to the disturbed state of the district', and on 23 and 25 November 1900 that several girls had withdrawn because their families were leaving the area. On 15 July 1901 an Inspector's Report said that this school was 'remarkably well organised and disciplined'; but on 18 October 1901 the Head Teacher reported that several girls had transferred to the Cefnfaes and Carneddi Schools, 'owing to speeches by ministers at the Cefnfaes concert'. On 7 November 1901 the Head Teacher of Carneddi gave his pupils a holiday, and thirteen girls thereupon 'absented themselves' from Glanogwen in order to 'join the procession who escorted the boys home who were released from Carnarvon Gaol'. Glanogwen's numbers were 'still further reduced' by the withdrawal of four girls in April 1902; but it was said that attendance was generally 'excellent'.

The Gerlan National School had a Coronation Committee headed by the Rev R. J. Jones, one of Lord Penrhyn's most devoted supporters; and all pupils received copies of a 'splendid Coronation Medal' given by Lord Penrhyn. Attendance at Gerlan was affected, however, not only by sheepshearing on the local farms but also by such events as the quarrymen's release from Caernarfon Prison; the logbook entry for 8 November 1901 records that those who absented themselves on that occasion were 'severely reprimanded' the following morning. Gerlan was not a loyalist area, and an entry for July 1902 records that children from Carneddi School were going round the houses of Gerlan pupils to 'entreat and persuade' them to transfer. The admission and discharge register of the Llanllechid National School also indicates that some pupils moved to British schools during the dispute; and an entry for September 1901 records that William Williams, born in 1891, moved to a British school because there were 'too many cynffonwyr' at Llanllechid.

The logbook of the Bethesda British School recorded that very few children were present on the morning of 6 November, when the quarrymen went to Bangor to 'accompany the sixteen men who had warrants'. On 7 December 1900 the Head Teacher noted that the average weekly attendance had dropped from 317 to 292, and observed that many pupils were 'taking advantage of the Lock Out in the Quarry'. Later entries, however, show the average weekly attendance for 1901 as 297, and that for eleven months of 1902 as 316; and on 11 November 1902 the Head Teacher commented, 'the attendance has been excellent during the strike: 92 per cent'. The Head Teacher of the Carneddi British School recorded on 2 September 1903 that the 'bad feeling caused by the Strike between Strikers and Secessionists' had prompted 'some half-dozen children' to move to 'Church Schools'. He continued:

> I am grateful that, with one exception, the children of Strikers and Secessionists fraternise together. I have repeatedly warned the children that I will not tolerate any molesting and they seem to have reacted accordingly. But some parents seem to apprehend danger as it comes, and remove their children. Some have removed from the neighbourhood, others are over age and leave. Our losses are about ten in all.

The logbook of the Cefnfaes British School recorded on 6 November 1900 that the school had been closed for the day because of the 'general unrest throughout the neighbourhood'. The Head Teacher commented:

> All the workmen left the quarry this morning and not one half of the scholars presented themselves here. So after waiting till 9.55 a.m. lest H.M.I.s might call all the children were dismissed for the day. The teachers too were very desirous of going down to Bangor with the workmen as I found out after the children had been dismissed.

The school was closed again on 13 November because the teachers were 'anxious to go down to Bangor because of the trial of the quarrymen'; and on 22 November it was noted that attendance had become somewhat irregular, 'probably owing to the cessation of work at the Quarry'. The logbook of the Cefnfaes night school, opened on 30 October 1895 at the 'earnest request of several boys and young men', recorded on 26 November 1900 that many young men had 'gone elsewhere to look for work', on 14 January 1901 that only two adults had attended, and on 14 February 1901 that only five pupils were present because of a meeting 'in connection with the Strike in Glanogwen Boys' Schoolroom'. Entries in this logbook ceased after 27 February 1902, probably because the night school had been temporarily closed[18].

As Easter approached, there were fears that the holiday would bring a repetition of the New Year riots; and early in March some of the quarrymen were already asking for more police protection. On 6 March Owen Parry of Cefnan reported that after he had gone to bed

> showers of stones were thrown on the roof of the house from the front and the back of the house, at the same time, the attackers were shouting to him to come out to be killed, declaring that if he was not a corpse before the morning, that every soul of them would be killed before Easter.

Before dispersing, the crowd had smashed the windows of his kitchen. On 7 March H. C. Meares, who did not leave until the end of May, sent a report to the Deputy Chief Constable about two workers, John Jones and Griffith Griffiths of Brynteg Street. These men were met near their homes every evening by 'a crowd of men, women and children', who hooted, yelled and called them 'all manner of names'; and the crowd was becoming 'more insolent day by day'. The districts where these incidents occurred were strongholds of the strikers; but no district was entirely homogeneous, and this made policing more difficult.

On 12 March Young wrote to Thomas Lewis, the chairman of the Bangor magistrates, enclosing an English translation of a letter one of his workmen had received from his daughter in

South Wales. This letter, which resembled letters received before the Christmas holiday, reported the threats being uttered both against the working quarrymen and against the police; and Young urged that adequate precautions should be taken to prevent more riots[19]. On 19 March the *Liverpool Mercury* carried a grim report under the heading 'Great Distress at Bethesda', claiming among other things that the townspeople could not pay their rates and that the Bethesda Café had been empty since 31 December 'because of the disturbances'. A very different picture had been presented in January by a reporter from the *North Wales Observer and Express*, who found 'no evidence of poverty or need', and saw shops which were 'well and extensively stocked' and maintained 'an air of health and prosperity'. According to that witness, many of the townspeople were 'well and comfortably dressed', with 'good macintoshes and smart brown leggings'; the younger women were 'daintily and tastefully apparelled', and no hunger was apparent on any countenance. One of the strikers had told him that union funds supplemented by outside contributions met all needs, and that no-one was forced back to work by poverty. Both reports were no doubt overstated, but the contrast between them suggests that the incidence of hardship was increasing[20].

On 20 March 1902 the *Manchester Guardian* printed Lord Penrhyn's speech to the working quarrymen, in which he promised that there would be no negotiations behind their backs and that he would not 'give any of them away'. He also assured them that if his son had to take over he too would regard as friends all those who had been 'faithful and friendly'. Referring to the 'agitators', he said that many of them would never work in the quarry again:

> They might possibly wish to do so, but you must not think that I am going to put you at their mercy.

As far as Penrhyn Quarry was concerned, the strikers would to take a 'back seat'. Edward Douglas Pennant, who was received with cheers, said that he thoroughly concurred in everything his father had done; and Young told the men that Lord Penrhyn had acceded to their request that a friendly society in Tregarth be called the Penrhyn Society. Lord Penrhyn's speech was read by the quarrymen working in South Wales, and a letter sent from Aberdare on 20 March gives some hint of their feelings at this time:

> I find from today's paper that Lord Penrhyn promises to be *true* to those who have been so to him. There is some anxiety here as to whether Mr Meares resigned or was dismissed. I have seen John Williams, Ynys, and another man, D. Williams, collecting. He said that a settlement was at the door and everything will be right again very soon. The great drawback, he says, is to find some peaceful means between both parties for the future – because those who are out of work say that they can never look upon, nor do anything for those now working[21].

This letter was signed 'Henry', and was addressed to the writer's parents in Bethesda.

On 26 March it was announced that Colonel Ruck had drafted into Bethesda, in readiness for Easter, an additional force of sixty policemen and twenty-five mounted policemen. Most of these men came from England; and all were to be quartered in the Bethesda Café, which had been specially fitted up by a Bangor tradesman. Colonel Ruck said that the district was quiet apart from 'the casual smashing of windows', but that the working quarrymen still needed protection to pass through the High Street. Many Bethesda tradesmen were refusing to supply the workers, and as a result trade was being diverted to Tregarth[22]. On 27 March Young told Lord Penrhyn that David Davies saw nothing of 'the nervousness among the men which was very visible before Christmas'; and he attributed the men's confidence to Lord Penrhyn's speech at the quarry. He reported that some quarrymen had, in their desire to resume work, moved out of 'disturbed' districts and taken lodgings in Bangor; and he expressed the hope that more men would return to the quarry after Easter. In February 1902 output reached the unprecedented rate of 36,500 tons per annum; and although little or no work was done during the *trannoeth*, the average daily wage was 6s 9d per man[23].

In the spring of 1902 the N.W.Q.U. president W. W. Jones, commonly known as 'Cyrus', made a fund-raising visit to America; Cyrus, who was a Methodist deacon, represented the dispute as a national struggle between Welsh quarrymen and tyrannical English authority[24]. Because of Lord Penrhyn's libel suit against him, W. J. Parry went to London to see his lawyers; at this stage he was being represented by W. S. Robson and David Lloyd George, though the latter was to be replaced by his brother William. Parry protested to the Home Secretary about the drafting of extra policemen into Bethesda; and he declared that Lord Penrhyn, by persuading men to 'desert their old comrades', had 'sown the seeds of discord and hatred in Bethesda for many a long year to come'. Dismissing Lord Penrhyn's speech at the quarry as a 'mass of feudal arrogance', he pinned his hopes on 'compulsory arbitation'[25].

Fewer of the strikers returned to North Wales at Easter than at Christmas; and this fact, together with the presence of mounted policemen, made the holiday period quieter than had been feared. At a mass meeting reported by the *Manchester Guardian* on 1 April, Henry Jones recalled that Lord Penrhyn, in a 'recent memorable speech', had excluded some men from all hope of returning to work; but he said that while he 'recognised himself as being among the number', this was 'quite immaterial' to him. Telegrams were sent to the quarrymen employed in Tonypandy and Penarth, with the message, 'Be firm, men, and come back to the paradise of workmen and reject the "back seats" of the traitors'. The strikers' demands were set out yet again: a representative committee, a return to work *en masse,* changes in the contract system, a new attitude to discipline, and a free use of the dinner hour. Isaac Mitchell of the General Federation of Trade Unions was greeted with applause when he said that the strike would never have begun if Lord Penrhyn had been as conciliatory at the outset as he had now become, since not 1 per cent of the strikers had any connection with the Independent Labour Party or the Social Democratic Federation.

On 1 April Young told Lord Penrhyn that there had been

only minor disturbances, and that the strikers' tone was 'much less jubilant and more subdued'; he also reported that a Nantlle quarryman and his two sons were about to start work at Penrhyn[26]. On 5 April the extra police were withdrawn from Bethesda; and at the end of the holiday about 150 quarrymen left for South Wales, 60 of them for the first time[27]. Further consideration was given to the plan for a new police district of 6,623 acres with a population of 9,021; and J. Menzies, managing director of the Alexandra and Cefndu quarries, said that the rate would be about 2s in the £1. W. J. Parry observed that they would then have to 'employ the military to collect the rates'; and a decision on the plan was deferred for three months[28]. The cost of poor relief in Caernarfonshire rose from £1,556 in the year ending April 1901 to £1,663 in the year ending April 1902; and Bethesda was described in the latter month as an 'impoverished and largely depopulated district'. The increase was connected both with the impact of the dispute and with the declining prosperity of the slate trade; but current opinion attributed much 'ordinary pauperism' to drunkenness, and the Chairman of the Board of Guardians welcomed the government's declared intention of improving the licensing laws[29].

On 21 April 1902 Trench informed Lord Penrhyn that six men, all of whom he believed to be striking quarrymen, had been caught by the gamekeepers setting fire to gorse and heather near Bryn on the Penrhyn estate. Hugh Vincent said that the case was 'a clear one', which if tried could lead to a sentence of one month's imprisonment with hard labour; but he suggested that, if Lord Penrhyn did not want to take 'extreme measures', it might be thought sufficient on this occasion to send a warning letter. This advice, which was acted on, may have been influenced by the publicity given to an earlier case in which J. O'Brien had been charged with stealing branches from ornamental barberry trees near Aber railway station. The *North Wales Observer and Express* had commented that O'Brien 'from his name should have known something of the sacredness of a landlord and his belongings', and that Lord Penrhyn would recover his 'well-preserved berries' while 'Patrick' ate his 'skilly'[30].

During the annual Labour Day celebrations in Caernarfon at the beginning of May, the workers of the Llanberis area forgot their 'happy condition of material comfort' in thinking of 'the injustice and misery amongst their brethren on the other side of the Elidir[31]. The Llanberis men benefited from the reduced quantity of Penrhyn slates on the market; but that contraction of output also stimulated imports of foreign slates, which rose from 25,529 tons in 1895 to 119,805 tons in 1903. These imports came partly from the U.S.A. but chiefly from France, where long hours and low wages resulted in cheaper products which were often durable and of good quality[32]. In his Labour Day speech the N.W.Q.U. president declared that the 'purely local aspect' of the strike was being swallowed up in the wider issue:

> Have working men the right to ask their employers for terms of employment, or have they not? Are they to go to work upon no other terms than the employer may be pleased to offer them?

The union's membership was growing; but £10,323 of its £13,836 gross receipts was devoted to strike allowances and expenses for the Bethesda Lodge[33].

For the visit to Bangor and Caernarfon in May 1902 by the Prince and Princess of Wales, Colonel Ruck drafted about 130 extra policemen into each town[34]. Lord Penrhyn decided not to offer the royal couple hospitality, because he feared that W. J. Parry might arrange to have the libel case heard at that time; and arrangements were made for them to stay at Vaynol, half-way between Bangor and Caernarfon. The 'squire of Vaynol' was George Assheton Smith, who had inherited the estate and the Dinorwic Quarry in 1859. He was of a 'somewhat retiring disposition', and had turned down several public offices; but his vast wealth and 'liberal mind' made him responsive to 'the claims of charity', and he incurred much less hostility than Lord Penrhyn. In 1888 he had married the daughter of Colin Stanhope Jones; and responsibility for the entertainment of the royal visitors fell chiefly on her shoulders[35]. On 23 April Mrs Assheton Smith invited Lord Penrhyn to join the weekend party at Vaynol from 10 to 12 May. She explained that 'in a weak moment' she had agreed to provide rooms for some of those receiving degrees; and she went on:

> Added to this, they are just commencing to *paper* the rooms the Royalties are to occupy, so I suppose it will end in their having to sleep on the floor! in rooms smelling strongly of paint![36]

Lord Penrhyn, who could never have approached such an occasion in this relaxed way, did not take up the invitation.

The main event of the royal visit was the installation of the Prince of Wales as Chancellor of the University of Wales, which was to take place in Caernarfon on 9 May. On that day the Penrhyn Quarry workers were given a half-holiday, and similar arrangements were made for those employed at Port Penrhyn. Having watched the royal couple's arrival in Bangor, Trench told Lord Penrhyn that 'the yellow carriages and greys looked very pretty'[37]. The *Liverpool Daily Post* of 10 May reported that despite the presence of mounted police congestion in the streets of Bangor had caused a half-hour delay; and from this the paper deduced that 'the Celt' was a 'firm supporter of the royal race'. A contingent of Penrhyn Quarry strikers had marched into Bangor for the occasion, and

> as the Royal cortège passed they hoisted aloft a large banner bearing the words 'Hearty Welcome to the Prince and Princess from Desolate Bethesda'.

After the royal couple had departed for Caernarfon, the Penrhyn workmen returned to the quarry; and according to the *Daily Chronicle* of 12 May this was 'a cause of comment in the district', since the whole day was being observed elsewhere as a 'general holiday'.

Assheton Smith gave '5,000 employees' a holiday on full pay; and according to the *North Wales Observer and Express* of 9 May he presented every workman over twenty with 4s. The installation ceremony took place not in Caernarfon Castle but in a pavilion with a corrugated iron roof; and U.C.N.W. students in the audience caused some offence by singing 'Goodbye Dolly' and other popular songs. On 10 May the royal couple drove through Caernarfon with the Assheton Smiths to visit 'the celebrated Dinorwic Quarry', which as a result of the Penrhyn dispute was now employing over 3,000 men. The visitors were entertained by a large blast which detonated over 70,000 tons of material, some of it good slate; and after an impromptu concert by the quarrymen they returned on the quarry railway to Port Dinorwic. On Sunday 11 May the Bishop of Bangor conducted a special service in the private chapel at Vaynol.

On 14 May Trench sought instructions from Lord Penrhyn about a house in Llwybrmain whose occupant, a widow named Mrs Williams, had just died. Since the lease had expired about twenty-five years earlier, the house was Lord Penrhyn's property; and an application for it had been submitted by the widow's son. This son was W. H. Williams, the financial secretary of the union; and he was able to say that he had always lived in the house, which had been built by his father, and that he had himself spent £56 on improving it. Williams, whom Trench described as a 'sharp middle-aged man' and as 'clean' and 'respectable looking', had worked in the quarry for thirty-four years, but had not returned after the strike of 1896–7. Trench explained to him that Lord Penrhyn would prefer

> a man living in the house working for him, to a man whose sympathies were out and out with those who had left the quarry and were on strike;

but Williams argued that others who were on strike had been allowed to maintain their tenancies. Knowing that Williams was 'an important man on the other side' and that 'great interest' would be taken in the result of his application, Trench explained to Lord Penrhyn that although Williams was 'practically the leader of the strike' he was nonetheless 'a moderate man' as far as his speeches went. He pointed out, too, that although Williams could be removed from the estate he could not be removed from the district. Recognising that the case was 'a sort of test', Trench recommended 'in the interests of peace' that Williams should be granted the tenancy; and Lord Penrhyn seems to have accepted this advice[38].

Whatever policy Trench might follow over tenancies, Young and David Davies were determined to prevent 'undesirable' workmen from returning to the quarry; and for this purpose they maintained an 'excluded list' and a 'bad list', largely made up of men who had acted as 'agitators'. Those who were denied employment in this way naturally resented the management's willingness to employ men whose work had been affected by drink; but such problems were sometimes treated quite leniently, as in the case of a Tregarth quarryman named Thomas Jones. Having returned to work on 27 May 1901, he was absent without leave for substantial periods in September and November. After being suspended for a time, he was given 'one more chance' on 26 December, but was in difficulties again a few months later. David Davies commented:

> I cannot plead for the man, but I will give him his due. He is one of the best quarrymen in Penrhyn Quarry. Never gives any trouble while he is at work. It is really a pity he cannot be reformed.

A pencilled note by Young indicates that on 10 June 1902 Thomas Jones was 'given another chance'[39].

As the Whitsun holiday approached, threats from the strikers became numerous, especially in the Caellwyngrydd and Mynydd Llandegai districts; and on 16 May Lord Penrhyn informed Colonel Ruck that a special train was expected in Bethesda the following day and that a mass meeting was to be held on Whit Monday. He expressed satisfaction with Colonel Ruck's undertaking to provide 'protection to the extent of his power'; but he strongly objected to Colonel Ruck's statement that 'nearly all the more serious disturbances' were caused by the appearance in the Bethesda streets of working quarrymen and their families. He accepted that some of the workmen were 'injudicious from time to time'; but he said that most of them were 'peaceful men', and that they were entitled to 'simple protection' against those who visited Bethesda for the purpose of 'threatening and abusing and assaulting them'[40]. According to the *Liverpool Daily Post* of 20 May, only about 200 to 300 of the strikers actually returned for the Whitsun holidays, and so no extra police were needed. At the mass meeting on 19 May W. H.

Williams claimed that the principles they had fought for were already won, but urged the younger men to look for work so that funds could be preserved for the older strikers. D. R. Daniel said that although they had won the sympathy of the socialists they were not being 'engineered' by them; and he asked who, apart from the Free Labour Association, was on the side of Lord Penrhyn[41]. On 27 May two strikers, William Williams and Owen Williams, were charged in Bangor with maliciously damaging the house of a working quarryman named John Davies by throwing stones and smashing the windows; they were ordered to pay 10s damages[42].

The national and international events of 1902 evoked from the people of Bethesda responses coloured by the dispute. Late in May, while Henry Jones was on a fund-raising trip to New York, John Edwards J.P. presided over a meeting in the Market Hall, at which J. Ogwen Owen proposed the following resolution:

> That this meeting express their deep regret for their inability to celebrate in a worthy manner the Coronation of his Majesty, because of the sad state of things in the district owing to the dispute at Penrhyn Quarry.

This resolution was carried, after the meeting had accepted a suggestion from the Rev W. W. Lloyd that some words be added to remind Edward VII of the loyal welcome he had received as Prince of Wales[43]. Around the same time Lord Penrhyn paid a visit to the quarry, where he told the men that they would have a full day's paid holiday for the Coronation. On 3 June the *Manchester Guardian* reported that the working quarrymen, whose number was now over 900, had celebrated the end of the South African War by firing hundreds of rock cannon in the lower part of the quarry so that the noise could be heard 'for miles around'. On 6 June the *North Wales Observer and Express* described the strikers' reaction to the same event:

> Desolate Bethesda showed a subdued sense of joy and elation when the rocket rose from Coetmor Hall to tell the countryside that the great South African strike was over. And there was felt a tinge of envy.

The reporter contrasted the general 'jubilation' occasioned by the coming of peace with 'the want, the misery, the dismembered families, the mental disquietude' which characterised the 'square mile of mountain and valley' around Bethesda.

On his departure from the quarry, H. P. Meares was presented with a 'handsome testimonial, and a purse containing gold'. On 7 June *The Candid Friend* gave a double portrait of Lord and Lady Penrhyn, whom it described as a 'domestic couple' bearing the 'sign-manual of eminent respectability'. The article stated that they divided their time between Mortimer House, which had a 'dreary' exterior but was 'stately and comfortable' within, and Penrhyn Castle, where they entertained 'most hospitably' in the autumn. The working quarrymen, somewhat injudiciously, celebrated the anniversary of the quarry's re-opening with a display of bunting; and this so enraged the strikers that calls had to be made to Bangor and Caernarfon for police reinforcements[44]. On 12 June some of the working quarrymen tried to join the funeral procession of two former Penrhyn quarrymen, Robert Hughes and Owen Williams, who had been killed in a pit disaster at Vochriw Colliery in South Wales; but they had to leave 'on account of the threatening aspect of the others'[45].

Relations between Lord Penrhyn and George Assheton Smith were disturbed by rumours that a new section of Dinorwic Quarry was to be opened, at the request of the Prince of Wales, to employ hundreds of Penrhyn Quarry strikers. On 17 June Lord Penrhyn wrote to Assheton Smith about what he called 'a very serious (to me) bit of mischief', suggesting that it must be a 'sort of long chance card played by the agitators to keep their game alive'. Assheton Smith replied on 19 June, saying that it was wonderful what lies were spread to 'gain an end', and that he was writing to his manager E. Neele instructing him to issue the 'fullest contradiction'[46]. A report published in the *Liverpool Echo* on 19 June said that about 400 strikers who had applied to Dinorwic had been told that they would be called on if there were vacancies, but that it might be two years or more before this happened. On 20 June the *Liverpool Mercury* told its readers that the 3,000 workers at Dinorwic were to be given two days' holiday for the Coronation, together with a grant of 6s for every adult and 4s for every boy. The Rev W. W. Lloyd of the Penrhyn Relief Fund planned to distribute 500 lbs of cake to the schools in celebration of the Coronation; but the Rev W. Morgan of St Anne's Church in Bethesda informed him that Lord Penrhyn 'with his usual generosity' was 'providing the treat all round at his own expense', so that the children would have 'an abundance of everything'[47].

Although the Coronation was postponed so that the King could undergo an operation, he signified his wish that planned celebrations should go ahead; and on 27 June the *Manchester Guardian* reported that a 'special 5 per cent bonus' was to be added to the Penrhyn quarrymen's wagebills for the current month. At a mass meeting reported by *Yr Herald Cymraeg* on 1 July, Henry Jones condemned some of the women for encouraging their husbands to return to work; and William Thomas Jones, who had just returned from South Wales, complained that some of the Bethesda men there were not supporting the struggle. On 4 July the Rev W. W. Lloyd told the *Clarion* that the strikers might have to endure another winter, and begged their friends not to 'forsake them now' lest they should 'succumb through sheer want'. On 9 July the *Liverpool Echo* announced that the 'historic labour contest' in Bethesda had ended; and D. R. Daniel had to send telegrams contradicting this report to the various centres where strikers had found work[48]. In the *Liverpool Echo* of 10 July Young commented that as far as Lord Penrhyn was concerned the strike had been settled on 11 June 1901, and that no negotiations had taken place since then.

On 12 July a striker named David Williams wrote to his parents from Rhaiadr in Radnorshire, where he had found work:

> I have not much news to tell you, but that the Bethesda boys are very uneasy here. There is a cheap train from here on August 1 and it is very likely that I shall come home. What I mean to say is this, that my father should apply for work for me at the quarry. It is pos-

> sible that all of them will go there very soon, and therefore I find that this is the only chance for me. Remember not to tell anyone because there are so many working here.

As this letter was being written, the *Gentlewoman* of 12 July was telling its readers that Lord and Lady Penrhyn were holding garden parties on Wednesdays at Mortimer House, where tea was served under the trees and 'smart London society' appeared 'in their best dresses'. This theme was taken up on 13 August by the *Tatler*, which referred to Lady Penrhyn as a 'well-known London hostess' and to Lord Penrhyn as a 'tall, spare man of decided character' who was a 'constant patron of the turf'. Their home at Mortimer House was said to be 'just out of Belgrave Square', and to be unusual among fashionable London houses in having a garden; and Penrhyn Castle was described as 'a veritable museum . . . crammed full of costly art treasures'.

At a meeting of the Standing Joint Police Committee on 24 July, Colonel Ruck reported that, although he had reduced the police force in Bethesda by ten constables after 24 May, certain offences were occurring after dark so that he needed more men on night duty. W. J. Parry pointed out that no constable was now needed to escort the men home from the quarry[49]. On 10 July Lord Penrhyn had written to Colonel Ruck complaining that intimidation was increasing and that the strikers and their 'partisans' were becoming 'more violent in their demeanour and proceedings', especially in Mynydd Llandegai. He reminded Colonel Ruck that military assistance had been needed during the summer of 1901, and pointed out that a growing number of strikers were 'loafing about the locality'[50].

In the House of Commons on 6 August William Jones said that the King, having received a petition from a 'non-political organisation' asking him to intercede, had sent a sympathetic reply and suggested forwarding the petition to the Board of Trade. Gerald Balfour, speaking as President of the Board of Trade, identified the organisation as the Swindon and District Trades Council, and pointed out that the Board of Trade had received no application from either party to the dispute. Keir

Hardie attributed the men's failure to apply to their painful experience over an earlier attempt[51]. On 12 August *Y Genedl Gymreig* observed that this exchange had caused surprise and disappointment among the strikers. In August 1902 the management received numerous applications for work, and many men were taken on at the quarry; for that reason and because trade was brisk, full-time working was resumed at Port Penrhyn, where the staff had been on a five-day week. Bethesda was said to be quiet, and the extra police who had been brought in for the holiday were withdrawn[52].

At this stage the N.W.Q.U. was trying to obtain a weekly levy from its other lodges for the support of the Penrhyn men. The vote in favour of such a levy was 332 to 38 in Dinorwic, but only 282 to 191 in Ffestiniog. Elsewhere the men of Alexandra Quarry voted to give 6d a month for three months, those of Moeltryfan voted by 202 to 148 to give 3d a month, and those of Dolwyddelan voted to give 3d a week. Despite the industry's temporary prosperity, there was no general enthusiasm for the continuation of the strike[53]. Having paid a short visit to Bethesda, Mabon reported in Cardiff on 27 August that funds were running out, and urged all trade unions to give the strikers 'liberal assistance'[54].

At the end of August about 1,600 men attended a mass meeting in Bethesda, many of them having come home either for this meeting or for the Eisteddfod in Bangor. Henry Jones told them that they had enough money for a month, but that they might have to fight on without outside support. Although the prospect looked bleak, the meeting endorsed the strikers' ten conditions for a settlement: 'representation' in laying complaints before management, a return to work *en masse*, freedom to use the dinner-hour as they thought best, a minimum wage of 4s 2d a day, abolition of the contract system, better treatment from officials, amendment of the rules of discipline, acknowledgement of Labour day, registration of the sick club, and payment of wages fortnightly instead of monthly. After the chairman had read telegrams of support from ex-quarrymen now working elsewhere, a 'workman from the body of the hall' suggested another appeal to Lord Penrhyn; and the chairman on behalf of the Committee then proposed the following resolution:

> That this meeting respectfully asks Lord Penrhyn if he would be prepared to accept the services of Mr Balfour, the Prime Minister, or the Earl of Rosebery, or both, as conciliators, with the object of honourably terminating this unhappy dispute.

After some discussion, this resolution was 'put to the meeting and carried unanimously'[55].

Lord Penrhyn received a copy of the resolution while he was staying with a shooting party at Glan Conway near Bettws y Coed. He had sent some grouse to J. E. Vincent, who was visiting the 'lonely village' of Drayton near Abingdon; and Vincent wrote on 31 August that he had considered showing them for an 'honest penny', but had concluded that where wages averaged 10s a week 'a peepshow would not pay'[56]. From Glan Conway Lord Penrhyn wrote to Henry Jones on 3 September, reiterating his refusal to recognise the 'Quarry Committee' and saying that, as he had not deprived the men of their right of combination as set out in the 1897 settlement, he declined to avail himself of the services of 'either of the gentlemen named'[57].

In the meantime Lloyd George had been seeking further support for the strikers from the T.U.C. On 3 September he wrote to his wife:

> I've been to the Trades Union Congress to plead for the Bethesda Quarrymen. They suspended the standing orders to enable me to do so. Gave me a fine reception and passed a resolution unanimously to support them. I think they have been saved. But very severe things were said about Daniel I am sorry to say. Unions that had paid £10 a week regularly refused balance sheets saying how the money was being spent[58].

The T.U.C. sent word to Bethesda that the bricklayers, the London compositors, and the Printing Machinemen's Society had agreed to make large grants for the benefit of the Penrhyn strikers. When the T.U.C. message was reported to the next mass meeting W. H. Williams said that it was not only 'an encouragement' but also a warning that the trade unions would not support 'young men who idled their time away in Bethesda instead of getting work elsewhere'. Williams stressed the need for a 'peaceful and honourable' resolution of the conflict; and when the men had considered Lord Penrhyn's predictable response to their earlier message, they not only re-affirmed their demands but also expressed their desire to bring the 'present deplorable dispute' to an end. With this object in view, they decided to ask Lord Penrhyn if he would be prepared to meet Henry Jones, R. J. Prichard, R. J. Jones and Griffith Edwards as their representatives[59].

Noting the men's professed desire for a 'peaceful and honourable' settlement, Lord Penrhyn responded on 10 September that the behaviour of many of the strikers was anything but peaceful: assaults were committed, windows were broken, 'disgraceful and abusive language' was used, and men, women and children were 'followed, molested and stoned'. In these circumstances, Lord Penrhyn said, he would postpone any further reply[60]. The situation was already dangerous because of the many strikers who had returned from South Wales; and this letter had an inflammatory effect. The next mass meeting passed a resolution regretting that Lord Penrhyn, instead of enquiring into the causes of the dispute in a 'conciliatory spirit', had emphasised 'petty offences' of a type committed by both parties. When Lord Penrhyn's letter was read out, it was received with 'fierce hooting and cries of "Let's go to Bangor to settle them"'.

The crowd made for the railway station, but was diverted from boarding a train by the arrival from Bangor of Owen Tyndwr, a marker who lived between Bethesda and Tregarth. It was customary to keep departing passengers out of the station until the arriving passengers had left it; but one of the crowd spotted Tyndwr and his wife, and the cry of 'Bradwyr' was raised. Tyndwr was thrown to the ground, and was saved only by a railway porter whom the crowd mistook for a policeman. He and his wife were pushed into the station-master's office; and when the crowd returned to break into the office, the station-master managed to smuggle the couple into a train bound for Tregarth. Meanwhile about 2,000 people were parading in the High Street; and although fifty extra policemen were brought in, much damage was done to the Victoria Hotel and the house of a quarry official before the arrival of mounted police from Bangor restored order. In Bangor itself there were frequent fights in the High Street, and police drafted in from Lancashire made a number of arrests. A few days earlier three men had been injured in an incident at Port Penrhyn; and on the Saturday evening there was an exchange of abuse between 'secessionists' in their cottage gardens at Tregarth and strikers travelling by train to Bethesda. The men arrested at Bangor included some working quarrymen; and one of these, David Jones, was fined £2 10s and bound over for assaulting a striker[61].

On 19 September the newspapers reported that Henry Jones had received a letter from Lord Penrhyn, in which he agreed to meet the four representatives named by the mass meeting, on condition that all demands for the restoration of the Quarry Committee were abandoned. Lord Penrhyn stipulated that 'Mr Towell and Mr D. Rhys' should attend as shorthand-writer and writer respectively, and that the proceedings should be treated as private until Lord Penrhyn's reply had been communicated to the deputation[62]. According to his wife, George Assheton Smith was 'a bit huffy' that Lord Penrhyn had not consulted him about the resolution of the dispute. On 20 September 1902 she wrote to Lord Penrhyn that after the Dinorwic strike the leaders had been taken back with a warning of what would happen if they did not 'keep matters smooth'. She hoped that, 'if this should be the only stumbling block to a settlement', Lord Penrhyn would take the strike leaders back on the same terms. Acknowledging that it was hard to explain what she meant, she continued:

> I'm sure manner and the way things are said go a long way with the Welsh – they are not downright like the North Country folk.

Lord Penrhyn pointed out that some of the Dinorwic strike leaders had not been taken back; and on 26 September Mrs Assheton Smith admitted the unreliability of her source:

> *I* think George has forgotten what the terms of the settlement were, but that is what *he* thinks.

Responding to Lord Penrhyn's arguments on what he regarded as the central issue, she commented:

> Yes, I believe people who know nothing about it, *do* think you are obstinate about that Quarry Committee but I perfectly realise that you can't possibly give in to them[63].

The strikers expressed pleasure that Lord Penrhyn was prepared to meet their representatives, and declared that they only wanted to have a 'a free hand' to elect their representatives and appoint their deputations in their own way. All hopes of a settlement were dashed, however, by a further letter from Lord Penrhyn, in which he claimed that the strikers were trying to resurrect the 'Quarry Committee', set out once again the terms of the 1897 agreement, and concluded that there was little to be gained from further discussion[64]. With the return of many strikers to South Wales the situation in Bethesda had become more peaceful, and the imported policemen had left; but attention was increasingly focussed on the hardships being endured by the people of Bethesda. The £300 per week from the trade unions gave the unemployed strikers only 10s each, and the relief committee's funds were diminishing. Even the choirs had been unemployed for several weeks; and little money was coming into the Bethesda shops, as most of the working quarrymen lived and shopped elsewhere. The families which remained in Bethesda were those of old and middle-aged men who had become freeholders and could not leave without sacrificing their savings.

On 22 September the *Daily Chronicle* reminded its readers of the harsh conditions which had existed in the quarry in 1899. A former employee recalled how they were forced to stay in the blasting sheds and then punished for making tea there, and how they were watched by 'detectives'

> until they felt they could not so much as exchange a joke or look over their shoulders in safety.

On 25 November the *Daily News* reported that Lord Penrhyn was building cottages on an 'extensive scale', and that these cottages were being let by the month to men prepared to work in the quarry. The 'new cottages' at Tregarth, which had cost Lord Penrhyn £5,000, were much sought after; and a new race of quarrymen was being raised who 'from the first realised their 'absolute dependency on Lord Penrhyn's pleasure'. The recruiting of middle-aged and elderly workers continued, and even those in their eighties were not necessarily excluded. On 6 October David Davies wrote to Young about William Thomas of Caellwyngrydd:

> I know nothing against him except his extreme age. He owns to eighty-one years, but I think he is more, for he used to tell me before the strike that he was over eighty years of age.

Young's comment was simply, 'Accept'. On the same day David Davies told Young that he thought they should maintain their policy of reporting small injuries to the Assistant Inspector of Mines, especially when they were taking on so many men not used to the work. Even the strikers who were coming back to the quarry, Davies added, had

> pinched themselves to such an extent that were they to meet with a slight accident after coming in their injuries might be a long while healing[65].

While many of the strikers went hungry, Lord Penrhyn's lawyers were preparing for the Penrhyn v Parry libel case, which at this stage was expected to be heard in London in November. The case was in fact to be delayed until March 1903; but on 28 October Lord Penrhyn sent a cheque for £500 to meet witnesses' expenses. About the same time he sent £2,000 to his London agent L. W. Byrne, who had offices in the Strand; and the total cost to date was estimated at £2,798. Writing to a London firm of auditors named Smith and Whinney, Young said that the libel action was 'to be heard earlier than expected'; and he added that William Gray and himself were 'busy every day preparing the same'[66].

9
The End of the Strike: 1903

During the course of the dispute third parties frequently attempted to promote a settlement. John Whiting of Leeds, who was a friend of Lord Penrhyn, approached George Cadbury, the cocoa tycoon and principal shareholder of the *Daily News*, in the hope of persuading him to moderate his paper's attacks. In reply Cadbury acknowledged that Lord Penrhyn was highly regarded 'as a man', and expressed his desire to help 'the patient and . . . truly good men of Bethesda'; but he sent Whiting a copy of R. S. Rowntree's *Poverty*, explaining that it described the plight of 'six or seven million' people in Britain and arguing that the way forward was 'combination against those who paid starvation wages'. He described the manager of the *Daily News* as 'one of the most noble men' he had ever met, and the paper itself as a force for 'National Righteousness'; and he pointed out that its circulation had increased substantially under its new ownership. (Lloyd George had been so much involved in the takeover that on 8 January 1901 he called the paper 'my *Daily News*'[1].) Cadbury concluded by saying that although he was anxious to be a 'peacemaker' he could see no advantage in his meeting with Lord Penrhyn. Lord Penrhyn himself, writing to Whiting on 6 November 1902, was equally sceptical. While he recognised Whiting's good intentions, he could not reconcile Cadbury's professed role as 'peacemaker' with the articles printed in his paper; and in view of the 'gratuitous insults' heaped upon himself by the *Daily News* he agreed with Cadbury that an interview between them would serve no useful purpose[2].

Press coverage of the dispute was clearly influenced by the conviction, most notably expressed by the founder of the *Daily*

Mail, that readers liked 'a good hate'[3]. On 10 November 1902 the editor of *Gwalia* Robert Williams wrote to Lord Penrhyn suggesting that two causes, apart from 'the machinations of the strike leaders and certain outsiders', largely accounted for the continuance of the strike. The first cause was that press representatives from the *Times* downwards derived their views from 'the W. J. Parry set and the Quarrymen's Union officials', and sought to publish everything that was 'encouraging to or in the interests of the men'; the only exceptions were the *Cambrian News*, which was published in Aberystwyth, and the *North Wales Chronicle*, which was 'rarely heard of outside Bangor and then only by a select class'. The other cause was the financial help from outside, which was 'entirely obtained by maligning and mis-representing' Lord Penrhyn; and Williams therefore suggested that Lord Penrhyn might give an interview to one of the leading London papers. On 11 November 1902 Lord Penrhyn replied that he was 'practically debarred' from making any statement to the press because of the imminent libel case, and that he would therefore have to let the facts speak for themselves[4].

Reynolds' News, the weekly newspaper owned by the cooperative movement, claimed on 14 December 1902 that its readers had contributed about £800 to the quarrymen's cause. Explaining that some 1,300 quarrymen were working in South Wales and elsewere, and that others had been driven back to the quarry 'by despair and starvation', the paper made a plea for the 700 to 800 men who depended on union allowances, and for the aged and infirm men who were no longer entitled to these. On 15 December the *Liverpool Echo* reported that Keir Hardie, speaking in Holborn Town Hall at a concert by 'the Bethesda Choir', had denied the right of an 'obstinate man who dwelt in a castle' to stop '3,000 quarrymen' from working because they would not submit unconditionally to his terms. He argued that 'the right to work must be given to every man', and that the state must take over 'not merely the hills of Wales, but the land of the whole country'; and he blamed the people for sending 'landlords and their nominees' to parliament, so that 'landlordism' was protected and labour was 'trampled underfoot'. On 17 December the *Daily News* reported a 'lantern lecture' given by C. Sheridan Jones to the Bethnal Green Liberal and Radical Club under the title 'What I saw at Bethesda: the struggle of a race against one man'. Sheridan Jones said that when he visited Bethesda on 25 September 1902 the union funds were depleted and the relief committee had made no distribution for six weeks; but he claimed that the *Daily News* had saved the men 'within a month'. As an example of the tyranny exercised by the management, he reported that men had been dismissed 'for speaking to an official without taking off their hats'. On 20 December it was reported that seventeen M.P.s had contributed a total of £321 15s to the Central Relief Committee of Penrhyn Quarry; according to the *Daily News*, John E. Ellis had given £100.

As Christmas approached, Colonel Ruck drafted extra police into Bethesda to prepare for the strikers' return from South Wales[5]. On Christmas Eve the *Manchester Guardian* reported that the 'long-standing quarrel among the Bethesda quarrymen' was affecting 'the lives of the schoolboys of the district' and 'embittering their comradeship'. A working quarryman having complained that his son was being molested by other pupils at Carneddi British School, the Head Teacher had given the boy permission to arrive late and leave early; but the boy had nonetheless been assaulted by three others. He had subsequently moved to a school in Rachub; and although the assault was acknowledged, the case had been dismissed on the payment of costs.

Christmas 1902 was relatively quiet in Bethesda; and a special grant from the London relief committee ensured that every family had a Christmas dinner[6]. On 26 December the *Carnarvon and Denbigh Herald* reported that the town's poverty was concealed from the 'casual observer' because the Rev W. W. Lloyd had distributed 'bales of old and new clothing and boots' which had been 'sent to the sufferers'. About 200 strikers came home for the holiday, and the reporter described them as 'a strong, burly, healthy looking and determined set of men'. On their first Christmas, Thomas Roberts told the mass meeting, they had had an offer to go back 'except six', and on this third Christmas they had an offer to go back 'except 600'; but everyone who was still out had 'a clear conscience'. Young wrote to Lord Penrhyn on 27 December:

> Last night it was so quiet in Bethesda that we are doubtful what took place – I hear there was a Mass Meeting at 5.30 but chiefly women and those who have attended all along.

On a rumour that the strikers had resolved to stay out for another two years, Young commented that if true this would be 'useful as a reason for evictions should they be found necessary'. Having visited the quarry on 26 December and 'come down with the workmen', he reported that he had spoken to 'as many men as possible' and that 'they all seemed quite radiant and not in fear of any disturbance'; and he added that he planned to attend 'their 6 p.m. Welsh service at St Anne's Church' on Sunday 28 December[7].

On 27 December 1902 the *North Wales Chronicle* considered the bearing of the Taff Vale judgment on the Penrhyn Dispute. The Taff Vale Railway Company had successfully sued the Amalgamated Society of Railway Servants for £30,000 damages and costs, and the judgement had been upheld by the House of Lords; the effect was to restrict trade union activity and thus impel the unions into a closer alliance with the socialists for the sake of parliamentary representation. Besides comparing the railway company with Lord Penrhyn, the *North Wales Chronicle* condemned the Bethesda strikers for throwing insulting phrases such as 'bradwr diawl' (devilish traitor) at those 'honest quarrymen' who preferred to live by their toil 'rather than by the charity of English socialist organisations'.

On 29 December the *Daily News* observed that the holidays and extra travelling facilities had brought a few hundred of the strikers home from South Wales and from England, but that 'the proportion which came was considerably smaller than on other occasions of public holiday'. The paper referred also to recent street collections in Bethnal Green, where £84 had been taken; £64 of this had been in coppers, 'and the bulk of the coppers in farthings'. Also on 29 December the *Liverpool Courier* reported that 'more than sixty of the strikers' had signified their intention of applying for work; but Young's letters offer no confirmation of this report. On 31 December the *Times,* surveying the year's events in Wales, commented on the 'disability' many pupils suffered in having a poor knowledge of English because of 'the "patriotic" folly of their parents'; and about the same time a visitor to Bethesda named Isabella Wilson wrote to Lord Penrhyn, saying that 'half the trouble' there had been caused by the 'bilingual state of affairs'[8].

On 2 January 1903 the *Irish Independent* reported from Bethesda that there had been 'no riots' and 'no collapse', and that fears of surrender were unjustified; it also noted that the *Daily News* still kept a correspondent 'on the spot to record the incidents of the fight', and that the *Times* had sent 'a special correspondent to state the case from Lord Penrhyn's point of view'. All the papers emphasised that over Christmas 1902 the police had nothing to do; and on 9 January the *Daily Chronicle* described New Year's Eve as a sad and sorrowful time with

> a heavy-hearted group of less than a hundred people congregated round the church gates in that dreary midnight hour.

The crowd was so quiet that between 2 a.m. and 3 a.m. the extra police were sent back to their homes. On 6 January Young told Lord Penrhyn that 'five more quarrymen' had applied for work; four had been accepted, but one had been refused because he was 'one of those left out in 1897 convicted for theft at Bettwsycoed'. In the same letter Young reported that 958 men were now working at the quarry, 427 of them being in the mills and 531 outside[9].

Although the men's leaders continued to express confidence in the union's financial position, many of the strikers decided to take their wives and families with them to South Wales; and on 6 January the *Liverpool Echo* described the atmosphere on the day of their departure. There was no singing on this occasion, and the women and children who were staying in Bethesda looked on with 'drawn faces and set lips'; the cheer which they tried to raise, as the train steamed out of the station, ended in sobs. With 1,400 men away, the 700 unemployed strikers lived on union pay of 10s a week; and other families, including those of widows, received 3s 6d a week from the relief committee. Half the shops in the High Street were closed, and those that remained open had few customers. A woman in Caellwyngrydd said that her four children had 'forgotten how to play'; and the reporter noted that their supper was 'dry bread'. On 15 January the *Star* carried a similar report of distress in Bethesda, but added that the *Daily News* fund had reached £5,000. As secretary of the London Central Committee of the Penrhyn Quarrymen's Fund, C. Sheridan Jones announced that he had sent a cheque for £100 to help provide families in Bethesda with groceries, butcher's meat, and coal.

On 5 January 1903 Lord Penrhyn wrote from Penrhyn Castle to George Assheton Smith:

> I cannot recollect the name of the book out of which you read that very funny motor car story which amused us all so much about a year ago, and I should be so glad if you could tell me what it was, as I want to give my people here the same sort of good laugh that I had when I heard it.

Lord Penrhyn noted that Assheton Smith had declined to contribute to the University College of North Wales Building Fund, and commented:

> Goodness knows the Bangor College never has been and is not now, anything like a pet lamb of mine, but nevertheless there it is, set up in our midst, and we must make the best of the situation. I do not think turning our backs on it will improve matters, but in my humble opinion will have the opposite effect (at all events for those who come after us) and it is with that feeling that I have promised to subscribe. I really and truly should have given more if I had not been afflicted by the strike.

Assheton Smith replied on 7 January, re-affirming his decision and ridiculing the arguments used by G. T. Kenyon on behalf of the College Council:

> Kenyon talks some bosh about the advantage that would be de-

rived from certain subjects being taught such as Quarrying – I told him the best school for learning Quarrying was the Quarry itself.

The sum required for the College was estimated at between £175,000 and £200,000, and in February 1903 only £11,000 had been raised. Lord Penrhyn had undertaken to pay £3,000 in instalments of £500, but these payments were not completed until after his death[10].

Writing on 12 January to the Rev Howell Roberts, who had offered to act as envoy to the strikers, Lord Penrhyn declined the offer on the ground that peace moves were futile so long as the management and the working quarrymen were being vilified. He said that he did not want to employ men who had no confidence in himself or his officials, and therefore had no intention of inviting the 'leaders of mischief' to re-enter his service. 'A number of new hands besides nearly one hundred boys' had been taken on since the re-opening of the quarry; and since the workforce before the strike had been too large, this implied 'the expulsion of some hundreds of the former employés', who had 'severed their connection' with the quarry two years earlier by 'leaving without giving any notice or assigning the slightest reason for striking'. Those now working at the quarry, he said, were happy with their terms and conditions, which were 'quite as favourable as in any other Slate Quarry'[11].

The end of January brought the publication of majority and minority reports from the committee set up by the Standing Joint Police Committee to investigate the state of affairs in Bethesda, the prosecutions undertaken by the police, and the additional police expenditure incurred in the district. The chairman of this committee was J. R. Pritchard, and the other members were Captain N. P. Stewart, D. P. Williams, J. A. Picton, J. Jones Morris, J. Issard Davies and E. R. Davies. They met for the first time in Caernarfon on 6 November 1902, and held seven further meetings, including one in Bethesda on 15 November; and they heard evidence from twenty-six members of the police force and fifty-five witnesses representing the strikers. Neither the police nor the strikers asked for legal representation, and the committee refused to allow legal representatives of Lord Penrhyn and the management to attend. When the committee wrote to Young suggesting that working quarrymen might appear as witnesses, he objected to the exclusion of solicitors and asked for a copy of the strikers' evidence; but the committee replied that they were investigating not the quarry management but the police. In the event, no evidence from working quarrymen was heard; but Colonel Ruck testified that the quarry officials had reported 852 incidents to him between 3 June 1901 and 24 December 1902. The committee also considered a substantial body of evidence from people living in Bethesda, most of which related to the alleged need for a large additional police force. Some of this evidence, including that given by Griffith Edwards on 12 November 1902, indicated the strain imposed on the police, who had to lodge either in public houses or in the houses of working quarrymen.

Those who signed the majority report said that before the enquiry they had had no conception of the strife and bitterness engendered by the dispute; and they paid tribute to the efforts made by ministers of religion and other leading inhabitants of the district. On 12 November 1902 the Rev T. Griffith, who was a Congregational minister in Bethesda, testified that Superintendant Jones had said on 3 June 1901 that all the ministers were Judases ('Judasiaid ydych chwi bob un'). The Rev Griffith claimed that although he supported the men's cause he had encouraged them to respect the law; but he said that the 'unruly crowd' who came to Bethesda on Saturday nights and at holiday times attended neither the chapels nor the quarrymen's mass meetings and were thus outside his 'sphere of influence'.

The report took a less favourable view of the part played by the quarry management, arguing that

> the method by which the complaints of the men at work were conveyed to the police by the quarry officials was calculated to do mischief, to increase the tension and deepen the ill-feeling already existing between the parties to the dispute.

The report also voiced dissatisfaction with the manner in which the police had given their evidence, especially in relation to complaints about unnecessary violence. The percentage of

convictions obtained was about 57½: 13 of the 125 prosecutions had been withdrawn, and of the remaining defendants 71 had been convicted, 39 had been discharged, and 2 had absconded. The report said that the
working quarrymen had failed to sh
the feelings of 'the late employés', and
been carried out in a way which creat
sentment among the ex-quarrymen' a
the peace. On 22 December 1902
cautioned Mrs Mary Williams for sh
and blowing a horn. He said that he h
trouble if she did not stop, but she cl

> Shut your mouth, you devil, or I will for ever prevent your husband going back to the quarry, you devil.

P.C. Owen said that, as the workmen passed, Mrs Williams knocked a pair of horseshoes together and shouted, 'It is time to go to church'. He claimed that the men he escorted were very quiet and made no display; but Griffith Edwards, the secretary of the men's Committee, had testified on 12 November that they 'used devices to make themselves appear very important people.'

The report recommended that the number of policemen stationed in Bethesda should be reduced, since the presence of a large force tended to 'irritate people', and it was unfair to deprive other districts of their protection. It suggested that Superintendant Harris should be removed from Bangor to take charge of another division, and that Sergeant Owen, who had 'done his work well under trying circumstances', should be transferred to another district where there would be less pressure. On the expenditure of £4,418 18 11 for extra police and other assistance, the report said that the charges made by other police authorities were exorbitant, and that better arrangements should be made if outside assistance was again required. It also stated that the Board of Trade should set up an enquiry with a view to resolving the conflict, and that the Government should make some 'public provision' for settling trade disputes in general.

The minority report was drafted by Issard Davies and approved by Captain Stewart, the estate agent for Assheton Smith at Vaynol. It noted that while the strikers had given evidence the working quarrymen had not, because 'the latter through their manager made it a condition that the evidence of the former should be placed at their disposal'; and it regretted the 'fatuous attitude of the manager' on this point. It said that acts of violence were now rare, and that most of the workmen had dispensed with police protection; but it recalled that there had been riots of a serious nature, during which the workmen had been in 'possible danger of their lives'. It rejected the suggestion that the police had acted in a partisan and vindictive spirit; and it observed that, when an angry and excitable crowd advocated violence, the strike leaders had protested only by pointing out the legal limits of intimidation. Like the majority report, it condemned the way in which complaints had been brought before the police; but it noted that the Chief Constable had taken action on only 6 of 852 such reports, and commented that this did not appear to show vindictiveness. The majority and minority reports agreed in considering the police expenditure excessive, and in acknowledging the 'firmness and courtesy' of Colonel Ruck[12].

On 23 January the *Daily News* noted that the majority report had confirmed its allegations against the police; but it argued that the minority report was more important, because while exonerating the police it condemned the 'exaggeration and malice' with which 'complaints against the old workmen' had been conveyed to them. The paper recalled that Young had no 'lifelong experience of quarry management', but held Lord Penrhyn himself responsible for all the 'bitterness and anger' which had arisen among 'a pious and enlightened community of workers'. On 13 February the *Times* reported that a special meeting of the Standing Joint Police Committee had adopted the majority report by fourteen votes to seven. The chairman J. Menzies was quoted in the *Carnarvon and Denbigh Herald* of the same date as saying that it was a marvel there had not been far more disturbance, and that the reports represented 'the honest opinion of those who wrote them' concerning 'evidence which was admittedly conflicting'. The *Daily News* of 13 February expressed the hope that 'the police tyranny' was now at an end. On 17 February Young gave his reaction to the reports in a letter to Lord Penrhyn:

> Fearing you may wish to look at the Police Enquiry Evidence again, I am posting it now, although I have only been able to read as far as page 78. The further I get into it, the more I rejoice that I had nothing whatever to do with it[13].

In the House of Commons on 5 March William Jones (Arfon) initiated a debate on

> the severe privations and loss arising from the struggle in the Penrhyn quarry district, the recent grave recommendation of the Carnarvonshire Standing Joint Committee in reporting thereon, and the failure to put into operation the provisions of the Conciliation Act to terminate the dispute.

In a fifty-minute speech he traced the history of the conflict from the dispute of 1896–7, which he inaccurately declared to have been resolved through the intervention of the Board of Trade. He listed the men's grievances, emphasising their desire to be represented by a freely chosen group of their fellow-workers; and he referred to Young's failure to give evidence during the recent enquiry. He spoke of the distress in Bethesda, where he had visited the men's homes and seen their 'starving children'; and he described how those who had found work in South Wales were struggling to keep two homes going:

> Many of these men had managed to save £50 or £60 and had just eked out a living spreading over these two years, and when the pinch of hunger came, they were too proud to ask for alms or relief.

More surprisingly, since the quarry was to make a profit of £28,890 in 1903, he claimed that

> Mr Young admitted himself that the output of the quarry was a failure, and it was being worked at a loss.

The motion was seconded by Bryn Roberts (Eifion), who regretted that the Conciliation Act had not been invoked. Sir Alfred Thomas (Glamorganshire East) quoted the Welsh proverb, 'Trech gwlad nag arglwydd' (The people are stronger than a lord). William Bromley Davenport (Macclesfield) pointed out that an action was pending which 'raised the whole question as to whether Lord Penrhyn had or had not refused the quarrymen the right of combination'. Gerald Balfour, the President of the Board of Trade, reminded the House that the provisions of the Conciliation Act were 'purely voluntary'. David Lloyd George (Caernarfon Boroughs) argued that responsibility for what happened in the district would rest 'to a certain degree' with those who declined to use the weapon of the Conciliation Act; and he re-iterated his claim that the quarry was on common land, and that Lord Penrhyn was using a property not his own 'for the purpose of starving out men'. Colonel Pryce-Jones (Montgomery Boroughs) claimed amid laughter that Lord Penrhyn, who was fighting for 'a very important principle', was a better employer than the majority throughout the country; and he urged that the matter should be left for Lord Penrhyn and the workmen to settle between themselves. Harold Tennant (Berwickshire) argued that Lord Penrhyn's actions were increasing the number of socialists and thus destroying 'the security of property'. When the House divided, William Jones' motion was defeated by157 votes to 127; but he was supported by the majority of his Welsh colleagues[14].

The Penrhyn v Parry libel case required Young's presence in London; and on 4 March he wrote to A. Judah of the Hotel Cecil, making reservations for himself and his colleagues:

> I shall arrive with Mr H. C. Vincent on Saturday evening 7th inst. and Mr Trevor will join us and require a bedroom on Monday night the 9th and Mr Carter will join us about 6 o'clock Tuesday morning the 10th. So you see I shall require four bedrooms and one sitting room and I beg you to be sure and arrange for same particularly *facing the river* on the fourth or fifth floor.

During the case, which began on 9 March and lasted five days, a mass of evidence was presented about the way in which the quarry had been run since the first Lord Penrhyn handed over to his son in 1885. The witnesses called by W. J. Parry included W. R. Evans, who had been dismissed from the quarry after an argument with Prichard, and John Williams and Peter Roberts, who had been sacked for infringing the safety regulations. Thomas Ellis gave evidence on the lax discipline he had discovered on his appointment as inspector; and evidence was also given by Hugh Vincent and David Davies. Lord Penrhyn and W. J. Parry spent long periods in the witness-box and were rigorously cross-examined. The counsel for the defendant sought to explain the strong language of Parry's letter to the *Clarion* by referring to the circumstances in which it was written:

> Starvation is Lord Penrhyn's weapon – his legitimate and lawful weapon – but starvation is one of the things which does not improve the choice of language; it does not make men very patient or particular in their literary style, so we must expect that, and that is one of the things we must take into consideration. But if it provokes those who have to suffer, it provokes also, I think, but not with such furious indignation, those who have to observe it, and who are seeking to relieve it.

The counsel for the plaintiff re-directed the jury's attention to the plain sense of Parry's words:

> No one can read those words without seeing that they impute to Lord Penrhyn such wicked and cynical indifference to the interests of the people by whom he is surrounded, that he would rejoice that there should be an increase in the death rate through their sufferings, and would be glad if the military were brought down to increase the number of deaths..

In his summing-up, the Lord Chief Justice told the jury that they must be satisfied either that what the defendant said was

> fair comment upon what he had the right to believe were the public acts of Lord Penrhyn in dealing with his quarrymen

or that it conveyed

> imputations of misconduct of motive or of evil intention for which there was no justification in what had gone before.

Whether the allegations were designed for publication was immaterial, since the defendant never disclaimed them and declined to apologise. The jury, having taken forty-eight minutes to consider their verdict, found for the plaintiff and awarded £500 damages. Acting on a hint from the Lord Chief Justice, they added a rider

> that, by the exercise of a little more conciliatory spirit on the part of both Lord Penrhyn and his men, happier relations might be restored at the Bethesda Quarry.

To this rider the Lord Chief Justice responded that he was 'much obliged' and that he hoped it would 'do good'.

The verdict was greeted enthusiastically by Lord Penrhyn's supporters, and he received many congratulatory letters and telegrams. William Dawson, writing from Acton Bridge, said that the 'intimate acquaintance with the Welsh workman' he had acquired through twelve years' residence in Bangor enabled him to understand what Lord Penrhyn had suffered in recent years. The ex-quarry-owner A. B. Pryce, writing from Dublin on the same date, deplored the 'evil results' which followed when 'the wildest assertions and the vilest insinuations' were 'accentuated and multiplied owing to the influence of the least admirable sections of the press'. S. Sandbach, writing to Lady Penrhyn from Abergele, asked her to congratulate her husband 'most heartily upon his grand victory over the Libellers and those scurrilous newspapers'. Lord Penrhyn's daughter Gwyneth, who was married to Sir William Quilter, wrote from Woodbridge:

> Just a line to congratulate you upon your victory. I hope that this will be the ending of the Strike – It has taught the world a great deal about you, and you will no longer be thought a tyrant etc etc. Will Mr W. J. Parry have enough money to pay up. I trust not. Now you must be once more feeling lively again and enjoying life again hunting I suppose.

The Duke of Grafton, writing from Northampton, addressed Lord Penrhyn ironically as 'Dear Tyrant' and expressed pleasure at his victory. H. O. Hughes observed that Robson, the defence counsel, had carried out Lloyd George's instructions 'con amore'; and he congratulated Lord Penrhyn on keeping his temper 'under circumstances of great provocation'. He declared that Lord Penrhyn had 'fought the battle of all employers of Labour', but wished that the rider had been omitted. One of the Mostyns of Mostyn Hall observed that he did not think the Lord Chief Justice was 'down enough on Robson'. W. Thomas, writing from Corris, expressed satisfaction at Parry's defeat:

> As a native of Bethesda and one who knows W.J.P. since 1846, and his connections in after years with the men employed at Penrhyn Quarry, I am glad that the *old fox* has lost his tail in his own trap.

George Assheton Smith thought it wrong that Parry, 'though a leading member of the Strike Committee', nonetheless 'sat on the Bench when rioters were tried'; and he also found it odd that Parry, 'while arguing the people were starving', had accepted money for his own defence. Henry Platt, writing from Llanfairfechan, advised Lord Penrhyn that he should 'go and fish', leaving his sorrows behind and renewing his strength in 'the invigorating air of Scotland'.

These congratulatory letters and telegrams were too numerous to be answered individually; and on 20 March Lord Penrhyn placed a statement in the *Liverpool Courier* and the *Liverpool Daily Post*, through which he expressed 'his sincere thanks to the senders'. On the same day the *Clarion*, while noting the verdict with regret, re-affirmed that it had withdrawn the 'personal attacks' in Parry's letters to A. M. Thompson; and Thompson himself repeated that he had 'unquestioningly assumed that these letters were designed for publication'. On 24 March forty-seven tenants and 'loyal quarrymen' from Glasinfryn and Pentir held a meeting in the Glasinfryn National School; at this meeting they approved a letter to Lord Penrhyn, in which they expressed not only their 'sincere rejoicings' at his success in the libel action but also their appreciation of his 'kindness at all times'[15]. On 28 March the workmen at the quarry drew up an address, which was reported in the *Carnarvon and Denbigh Herald* on 3 April. While congratulating Lord

Penrhyn on 'the happy result of the recent trial', they said that they required no jury to prove his 'high personal honour', his 'open-handed generosity', and his 'unswerving justice and fairness to all alike as an employer of labour'. Some of the signatories claimed to have worked in the quarry for more than fifty years.

In a letter printed by the *Times* on 21 March, Lord Penrhyn repeated the old charge that Michael Davitt had been associated in the 1880s with a scheme to take over Penrhyn Quarry and run it as a socialist enterprise. While denying that 'such a wild scheme' had ever existed, Davitt replied that the dispute had shown the dangers of allowing one man to control 'a vast source of employment'; and he re-affirmed his belief that all income from 'the soil belonging to the nation' should go 'into the coffers of the nation in order to be expended for the good of the people'[16]. Also on 21 March the *Manchester Guardian* reported that a member of the Penrhyn Choir had contracted smallpox while visiting Rugby, and after being refused admission to a workhouse hospital had travelled from Rugby to Bethesda by rail. On 23 March Trench informed Lord Penrhyn that the man was now in hospital, but that the vehicle which had taken him from Bethesda station to his home in Rachub had been used the next day for a wedding party. Surprisingly, no other case of the disease was reported [17]. Launching an appeal on behalf of W. J. Parry on 27 March, the *Daily News* said that he could not be left to struggle alone with the 'enormous liability' he had incurred after

> forty years of noble and unselfish service on behalf of the people of Bethesda in fighting for their rights and redressing their wrongs.

The newspaper put the sum required at 'a little less than £4,000'; and this suggests that Parry's expenditure had been much less than his opponent's, since Young later claimed to have spent nearly £5,000 on the case[18].

Immediately after the libel case there was some communication between Lord Penrhyn's counsel Sir Edward Clarke and W. Llewelyn Williams, the junior counsel for the defendant. What resulted from this communication was a proposal, which each side later attributed to the other, that Clarke should meet two 'representatives of the Bethesda men' who were in London for the trial. In the event he appears to have met five men, two of whom were union officials; and after the meeting terms for a settlement were drafted by the men's three legal representatives, J. H. Davies, A. Rhys Roberts and W. Llewelyn Williams. These terms included the recruiting of a workforce equal to that employed in October 1900; preference in recruitment for those who were employed at the quarry in that month; and re-admission of W. R. Evans, R. Davies, P. Roberts, J. Williams and Azariah Roberts[19]. Writing to Sir Edward Clarke on 18 March, Lord Penrhyn explained that while he appreciated the motives for the meeting, he could not entertain the proposals which had emerged from it; and he foresaw that 'non-acceptance of the conditions sought to be imposed' would bring upon him 'an increased storm of obloquy and misrepresentations'. Writing again on 24 March, he said that newspaper reports of the discussions were causing 'serious alarm' among the working quarrymen, who feared that they might 'after all find themselves placed again at the mercy of their former enemies'. He continued:

> The thousand men and boys now working are like a happy family in their relations with officials and their employer, and I will not do anything to endanger the pleasant conditions which now exist amongst the men to whom I refer, by re-admitting the strikers on terms which appear to be preferential to those which have been accepted by and been thoroughly approved by the men now working, whose contentment with them is sufficient indication of their fairness.

Lord Penrhyn added that he needed 600 fewer men than had formerly been employed, and that this fact precluded the 'wholesale re-admission of the men who struck in 1900'[20]. The news of Lord Penrhyn's reaction to the talks brought cries of outrage from the press; and a report in the *Daily News* of 26 March was headed 'Lord Penrhyn Obdurate. Again Breaks Off Negotiations'. On 30 March Young attributed this adverse publicity to 'a very stupid step of Sir Edward Clarke'.

Writing to Lord Penrhyn on 29 March, Young said that he was 'really physically unequal to a continuance of the severe strain' of the previous month, and that he needed 'a short rest'. He feared an attack of insomnia, and thought he would be of more 'permanent use' if he recuperated before overstraining himself further; and so he and his wife had taken 'rooms at Llandudno' for a fortnight starting on 31 March[21]. On 30 March, however, he went up to the quarry to 'have a chat with the men' about Sir Edward Clarke's initiative and thus relieve Lord Penrhyn of 'some of the odium' Clarke had forced upon him. In his speech to the quarrymen, Young explained that the discussions had taken place 'not only without Lord Penrhyn's authority but without his knowing anything about it'. He assured the men that Lord Penrhyn would never allow their interests to be sacrificed to those of the strikers, and that 'Lord Penrhyn himself and he alone' would decide who was to be re-admitted. At the same time, he asked the men to 'work in peace and harmony' with those strikers who did return to the quarry:

> For many weary months they have been out on strike, and possibly many bitter words have been said, and unkind acts have been done by some of them towards you, and possibly by some of you towards them. I am sure that these bitter words and unkind acts are now regretted on both sides, and I am going to ask you to forget them all, and to act towards the men returning as if they had never been said or done: in fact, let bygones be bygones, and the past forgotten.

Reporting to Lord Penrhyn after this visit, Young made it clear that he considered it a success:

> It was the happiest day I ever spent with the workmen, and the cheers they sent up when I finished with your name were heard at Ogwen Bank and in Bethesda. They quite agreed with your phrase describing them as 'a happy family', and they also endorsed my statements that they were better off under the new system of two partners instead of three. Mr D. D. Davies translated each paragraph.

In printing Young's speech on 31 March, the *Daily News* declared that Lord Penrhyn's words were untrue; and it argued that his 'latest proceedings' were typical of a man who, in his 'hard and narrow obstinacy' and his 'pathetic attachment to small intricacies', was 'curiously reminiscent of Charles I'.

On 2 April 1903 the *Blackburn Telegraph* reported that the Liberal Party had 'declared war on Lord Penrhyn'. The immediate occasion for this report was the news that Sir Henry Campbell-Bannerman was to ask the Prime Minister what steps the Government proposed to take in connection with the Penrhyn dispute, and whether the Government would give a day 'to enable the House to express its opinion on the subject'. The Prime Minister A. J. Balfour declined to give a day for such a debate; and Herbert Asquith therefore indicated that he would propose a motion condemning the Government's inaction. Writing to Lord Penrhyn, Young commented:

> It is deplorable that there should again be a debate in the House but after it is over the dispute will be just as before and surely more men will come back.

He added that he expected eleven or twelve men to start soon, and that although there might be some 'silly speeches' the mass meeting on Easter Monday would be 'very flat'; Bethesda was 'quiet and likely to remain so', and in any case Colonel Ruck had promised 'protection'[22]. Most newspapers interpreted the debate as a political manoeuvre rather than an attempt to influence labour relations or the Penrhyn dispute. The *Sunday Special* predicted that it would bring together Herbert Asquith, Sir Edward Grey, and 'supremely ably young Radicals like Mr Lloyd George'; and it argued that 'the sufferings of the Bethesda quarrymen' would be 'a strong card for the Liberals to play at the General Election', and that

> Penrhyn and Taff Vale should succeed in uniting all sections of the Labour movement with the main body of Liberalism.

Speaking to an audience of about 2,000 Liberals in Newcastle-on-Tyne on 5 April, Lloyd George found much support for his denunciation of Lord Penrhyn. He described how the quarry had fallen a century before into the hands of 'a rich slave owner from Jamaica'; and he declared that it had been 'run upon slave-driving principles' ever since. He claimed that parts of the quarry were on common land; and with reference to the current dispute he said that no struggle in labour history had revealed 'such tenacity' and 'such unflinching courage'[23]. On 6 April the *Sun*, whose motto was 'If you see it in the *Sun* it is so', passed judgment on the dispute in verse:

> Laws grind the poor, and rich men rule the law:
> Penrhyn doth prove this is no idle saw.

On the same day Evan R. Davies, solicitor and Town Clerk of Pwllheli, wrote to John Gibson, editor of the *Cambrian News*, suggesting that he might use his influence to 'pave the way for a settlement', since it was 'evident that Lord Penrhyn set great store' by his views. On 7 April Gibson replied from Aberystwyth, disclaiming any influence with Lord Penrhyn and arguing that Lloyd George's Newcastle speech had made a settlement impossible. He criticised William Jones for speaking of the men's leaders as 'Gods' and of Lord Penrhyn and Young as 'devils'; and he described the *Daily News* and the *Daily Chronicle* as

> low-down gutter raking journals, ready to eat any amount of filth in order to pander to the 'Labour' party.

He noted that the Liberal opposition was moving a vote of censure in order to 'bespatter Lord Penrhyn with mud'; but he said that such a vote would not alter the situation. The only course now was for Lloyd George, William Jones and 'the London Swine papers' to alter their attitude: Lord Penrhyn had won, and the men's leaders would be discredited by the final result. As for the 'promoters' of the conflict, they cared no more for the quarrymen than Davies and himself cared 'for so many midsummer flies'[24]. Writing to Lord Penrhyn on 6 April, Oliver and Alice Scatcherd praised his 'fine fight' for freedom; and they said that the 'brave editor' of the *Cambrian News*, who was their personal friend', had had 'sorrow to face all his life', but had never allowed it to weaken his will or his conscience'. Replying to this letter on 8 April, Lord Penrhyn wrote:

> If the stand I have made against trades union coercion and intimidation of my men and myself really does any good for the cause of free labour, I shall some day feel fully rewarded.

In a postscript he added a tribute to John Gibson:

> I have long felt greatly indebted to Mr Gibson for his disinterested defence of one who was a total stranger to him, and I quite appreciate what you say about his sterling character[25].

Easter 1903 was fairly quiet in Bethesda, despite the fact that large numbers of men came home from South Wales. About 1,200 attended the mass meeting on 13 April, and when Henry Jones put the question 'Did they intend going to work with traitors, or would they stand like men?' there were cries of 'Stand'. The men said that they would 'stand by' their 'past resolution' until they received 'fair terms'; but they were willing to submit the whole dispute to 'any gentleman of impartial judgment', such as 'the Prime Minister, Mr Chamberlain, or Lord James of Hereford'. William Jones M.P. said that the dispute had risen into

> the sphere of party politics, and was fast becoming a subject of grave national importance, watched as it was by all the civilised world.

Ellis Griffiths M.P. was greeted with cheers when he said that Lord Penrhyn's heart might be 'as hard as the rock which he claimed to own, and as cold as the snow which covered it', but that the quarrymen were not his property. W. H. Williams again warned those who had stayed in Bethesda that they should 'seek employment immediately'[26]. The *Daily Chronicle* of 14 April commented that all the men attending the meeting were 'respectable-looking', but that most of them showed signs of poverty and want. The same issue reported a characteristic speech by Lloyd George, in which he said that Penrhyn Quarry 'once belonged to the whole of the community' but was 'now under the landlord's control.'

At the Independent Labour Party conference in York on 14 April it was argued that the Party's M.P.s had been neglecting 'such vital questions as the Bethesda case', while the Liberal Front Bench 'were burning with zeal to deal with it'; but Keir Hardie replied that they had given 'practical sympathy' throughout the strike, whereas the Liberals were making 'a pretence of coming to the rescue' now that countrywide interest had been aroused[27]. On 16 April Bernard Shaw wrote to the *Daily News*, saying that the outcry against Lord Penrhyn seemed to him as 'impertinent' as it was 'unconstitutional'. The enfranchisement of the working class had resulted in 'an overwhelming vote in favour of the party of aristocracy and property'; and while the Liberal vote might be deemed 'anti-aristocratic' by those who saw Lords Rosebery and Spencer as opponents of the peerage, it was certainly 'as solid a property vote as the Conservative vote'. Shaw said that he did not know 'any nobleman of baronial rank, officer by profession and educated at Eton and Oxford', who was in the habit of letting working men 'confer with him on equal terms' or dictate how he should manage his estates; and since the proportion of socialists to supporters of property in the House of Commons was 'about 1 to 233', there was no justification for 'interfering with Lord Penrhyn', and working men had only themselves to blame for their situation.

At the annual meeting of the Standing Joint Police Committee in April 1903, Colonel Ruck confirmed J. R. Pritchard's statement that summonses had recently been issued by strikers and private persons against working quarrymen, as well as by working quarrymen against strikers; and he expressed the view that those employed in the quarry were becoming 'more aggressive' that they had been[28]. On 15 April Trench reported that 148 cottages on the estate were occupied by strikers, 81 of these having been built by the estate and 67 by the tenants or their predecessors. The rents varied from £2 to £8 per annum; but only three houses with land cost over £5, and only one of these cost £8. On 23 April Trench explained that while the new Tregarth cottages were let only to working quarrymen, he served notices to quit on all who were in arrears, whether they were at work or on strike. When they applied for rent the estate officers did not know who was working and who was not; but when further enquiry had been made, more pressure was put on those who were at work, because they were in a better position to pay. Trench added that he tried not to press tenants 'unduly or harshly', but that if he did not constantly remind them about their rents, they would get further into debt[29].

Because of the forthcoming debate in the House of Commons, the Bishop of Bangor asked the Rev R. J. Jones, vicar of Glanogwen, to report on the state of Bethesda; and the vicar's information reached Lord Penrhyn on 25 and 26 April. He reported that the new shops opened in Bethesda include 'a provision and greengrocer's largely supplying luxuries such as bananas, tomatoes, apples, pears, grapes'; this, he said, had 'taken the place of Mr W. J. Parry's ironmongery shops'. Another shop of the same kind had 'opened under Bank Chambers'; and a butcher's shop 'almost opposite Waterloo Hotel High Street' had presumably been successful, since the owner had married during the Easter holiday. Two tobacconist's shops had been opened, one at the bottom of the High Street and the other next door to Gwalia Stores; and a small general dealer's had been opened the previous month 'almost opposite Bethesda Chapel'. So far as the vicar knew, 'not a single shop or public house' had been closed during the strike. One butcher 'had to arrange with his creditors', but this was 'largely due to the opinions he held on the question of the strike', and in any case he was continuing with his business. The vicar claimed that large quantities of lamb and veal were sold at Easter, and that the seven butchers 'in a large way of business' on the High Street appeared, 'judging from the number of carcases exposed for sale', to be 'doing just as good a trade as ever'. The income of those on strike consisted of

> the amount paid per man from the union every month coupled with a supplementary dole from the relief fund, and in some cases from members of the choir and from those working in South Wales;

and the vicar estimated that, since there were often two or three breadwinners in a family, this provided a weekly average of

'£1 or £1 5s' for each household. He also referred to the sum of about £3,000 which had been raised for the purpose of building 'a large vestry hall' and installing a new organ at the Jerusalem Chapel. The vicar concluded by saying that he was writing in confidence, and that his name should not be mentioned since he wished to live on in Bethesda 'and be of some use'[30].

When the House of Commons debated the dispute on 27 April, the spectators included Lord Penrhyn and Sir Edward Clarke. The *Daily News* of 28 April described the expression on Lord Penrhyn's 'long, narrow face' as one of 'melancholy and want of alertness'; and *Punch* on 6 May said that he heard himself discussed 'as if he were no more sensitive than a block of his own slate hewn from the quarry at Bethesda'. The motion, that it was the Government's duty to put the Conciliation Act into operation, was proposed by Herbert Asquith (Fifeshire East) and seconded by William Jones (Arfon): and it was supported by Ellis Griffith (Anglesey), David Lloyd George (Caernarfon Boroughs), Bryn Roberts (Eifion) and Thomas Burt (Morpeth). The Government was defended by the President of the Board of Trade Gerald Balfour (Leeds Central), Vicary Gibbs (Hertfordshire St Albans), William Bromley Davenport (Cheshire Macclesfield), James Lowther (Kent Thanet) and the Prime Minister A. J. Balfour (Manchester East).

Asquith described Bethesda before the dispute as 'a prosperous and well-ordered community', and argued that the Government could end the strike by using its powers under the Conciliation Act. William Jones suggested that the scarcity of Welsh slates occasioned by the dispute was causing the market to be flooded with German, French and American exports which might be hard to dislodge. He also reported that in the course of the dispute 100 ex-quarrymen had died, 200 had emigrated to Canada, about 200 had found permanent employment elsewhere in Wales, and 500 had returned to the quarry; and he said that Welsh quarrymen had contributed £1,000 to the Relief Fund. Ellis Griffith described Lord Penrhyn as a 'very obstinate man', and Bryn Roberts condemned his policy as 'harsh and tyrannical'. Gerald Balfour said that the Board of Trade had declined to use its powers under the Conciliation Act because it saw no prospect whatever of success; and he argued that the national importance of the dispute had been exaggerated. Thomas Burt of the Independent Labour Party praised the quarrymen as a 'sober and law-abiding' body, and said that despite extreme temptation there had been 'no serious crime' in the locality; he claimed that the conflict was paralysing the trade of the whole country, and that it raised questions about the rights of private property in land. William Bromley Davenport defended Lord Penrhyn's opposition to the Quarry Committee, and described how its interference with management had damaged the quarry's profitability and the interests of non-unionists; and he argued that the men at work should not be dispossessed to make way for 'the agitators and their victims'. A. J. Balfour re-iterated that the Conciliation Act did not provide for the compulsory settlement of disputes, and that the Government could intervene only where there was some prospect of a settlement. The motion was defeated by 316 votes to 182[31].

The *Liverpool Courier* of 28 April belittled the Liberals' efforts in the debate, saying that their 'partisan tactics' would not help the quarrymen. Suggestions that the Ffestiniog men were out of sympathy with the Bethesda strikers led to a meeting in Blaenau Ffestiniog, at which the following resolution won unanimous support:

> That this meeting of quarrymen of the Oakeley Quarry and of the Llechwedd Quarry, consisting of over 2,000 workmen, wish to express their most emphatic protest, in the strongest manner possible, against the unfounded upbraidings brought against us in the English Press as being antagonistic to the Quarrymen's Union, and hence among the supporters of Lord Penrhyn; but rather wish to declare that we are now in the fullest sympathy with the Bethesda workmen who now strike so gallantly for their rights[32].

In an attempt to counteract the flood of anti-Penrhyn feeling, Lord Penrhyn and Young published a pamphlet setting out the rules of the quarry. In a final statement Lord Penrhyn said that his quarry was open to 'unionists and non-unionists alike', and continued:

> I never have done, and I do not intend to do, anything to prevent my employés from becoming members of the Union, if they wish to do so. All that I stipulate is that those men who do not wish to do so should be left free to exercise their own judgment, without coercion or intimidation. The terms and conditions of labour at my quarry are as fair, and the wages as good as, if not better than, those of any quarry in north Wales. . . . I am ready to admit into the quarry any suitable man who will work there contentedly[33].

This pamphlet was widely circulated, slate merchants and other firms from Brentford to Aberdeen being sent up to 100 copies each[34].

On 29 April the *Liverpool Courier* reported that the Bangor magistrates had commented on the role the women of Bethesda were playing in the dispute. Anne Jane Parry, the wife of a working quarryman, alleged that Mrs Thomas Williams, the wife of a striker, had thrown stones at her and incited some children to do the same, crying out 'Kill her'; Mrs Parry's husband had seen the incident, but had not gone to the rescue because he would have been treated in the same way. The magistrates dismissed the charge of assault and battery against Mrs Williams, but commented that 'things might have gone more smoothly' in Bethesda if the women had behaved differently. The same issue of the *Liverpool Courier* reported a meeting at the Queen's Hall in London organised by the Welsh Support Committee, a fund-raising body belatedly founded in April 1903. Lloyd George, whose speech was received with enthusiasm, expressed pride in the 'gallant stand' of his countrymen, and said that

> the man who could date his letter from four separate mansions concerning disputes, which involved starvation to his men, was not on a level with his workmen.

A total of £48 10s was collected during the meeting.

On 1 May 1903 the *Sun* published a colourful article by C. Sheridan Jones under the title 'The Tragedy of Bethesda'. Sheridan Jones portrayed 'the Master' as a 'fanatic' who resembled Charles I and believed in 'the divine right of the landlord'; and he presented 'the Men' as 'Roundheads dressed in shoddy' who were 'reticent to a fault', sang hymns in the 'quiet mountain passes' and the 'shady lanes', and needed 'more boxing lessons and fewer Bible classes'. Sheridan Jones declared that a 'powerful agitation' was being organised against Lord Penrhyn, and that he was 'rapidly exhausting the patience of the nation'. The Labour Day meeting of 1903 was held at Bleanau Ffestiniog, 'under the depressing influence of a persistent downpour of rain, typical of the district'. Over £16,500 had been disbursed in strike pay, but there was a cash balance of £491, and the financial position was said to be satisfactory. The Conciliation Act was described as 'absolutely worthless'; and the president, W. W. Jones, urged the trade unions to fight the powers arrayed against them by returning seventy Labour M.P.s 'of Mabon's type'. In the afternoon there was a brassband procession through the town; and then the quarrymen held a meeting in the Assembly Rooms, where W. H. Williams and D. R. Daniel were re-elected as financial secretary and organising secretary respectively[35].

On 21 May activity at the quarry was suspended, in deference to the still-powerful superstition that working on Ascension Day led to accidents. On the same day the *Daily News* published a poem entitled 'An Open Letter to Lord Penrhyn', in which Ernest Rhys contrasted the creative labours of the quarrymen with the destructive actions of their employer:

> Every man that mines the slate
> In the mountains, builds the State:
> Every man that breaks with men
> Rends and wrecks the State again.

On 22 May Trench informed Lord Penrhyn that the Bethesda Café was to be auctioned, and suggested that 'if going cheap' it should be bought for the estate, since 'it would be a pity to let some one else get a real bargain'; but on 25 May he reported that the Café had been bought at a price of £780 'for some Methodist prayer meeting syndicate', and that 'at that price it was best left alone'[36]. At a mass meeting held in Bethesda at the beginning of June, the men re-affirmed their determination to continue the struggle; but the suggestion that they should go to the quarry and bring out the secessionists was 'received with roars of laughter'[37].

On 12 June Trench wrote to Lord Penrhyn about a widow who was in arrears with her rent and had refused to take quarrymen as lodgers. He explained that an earlier attempt to evict her had been frustrated when she paid the arrears, and that a formal order would be needed because she declined to leave unless she was 'turned into the streets'. He recalled that working quarrymen had been reluctant to live in Llwybrmain, and that some had begged to be moved from there to Tregarth; but he said that the housing situation was becoming easier, despite the fact that men 'imported' to the quarry applied for houses 'at once'. Houses were being let to widows only if they agreed to take lodgers; but Trench hoped to avoid large-scale eviction, since that might mean empty houses afterwards. He concluded by observing that, if the 'Co-op Quarry business' came to anything, there would no doubt be a 'clearing out' of any Penrhyn estate tenants associated with it[38]. The Pantdreiniog Quarry, which had been re-opened by W. J. Parry, was employing 99 men; and the Co-operative Union had plans for operating it in conjunction with quarries on Moel Faban and at Tanybwlch[39]. On 14 June Young told Lord Penrhyn that he had had 'a chat with Mr Trench' about these plans. Young considered 'the whole thing' to be 'such a rank swindle' that 'early failure was certain'; and he and Trench had agreed on a policy of silence, lest Lord Penrhyn should appear to be sabotaging a development intended for the benefit of the strikers[40]. Writing to Lord Penrhyn on 21 June, Trench said that for the present nothing would be done about those Penrhyn estate tenants who were supporting the co-operative scheme, but that if there was 'a real move' in that direction they could 'all be got rid of together'[41].

Many quarrymen had large families, and the accommodation provided was often inadequate. On 13 June Richard Roberts of Llanllechid explained to Young that although his cottage had only two bedrooms, he had a family of nine children and one nephew; he had turned the parlour into a bedroom, but it was 'small, very damp and quite unfit as such'. Roberts, his nephew, and two of his sons had returned to the quarry on what Young called 'the memorable 11 of June'; and in the two years since then they had received their share of 'the insults heaped on the returned quarrymen'. While they were reluctant to leave now that Llanllechid was 'a little quieter', Roberts' pleas to Trench for another bedroom had been answered only with promises; and unless action was taken he would be 'compelled to seek a larger house', because it was 'out of common decency to have grown up boys and girls occupying the same sleeping apartments'. On 14 June Young informed Lord Penrhyn that Trench objected to his interference with tenancy arrangements; they had arranged that Young would receive and annotate a list of the applicants for each house, but that the final selection was to be left to Trench. Young's interest in the housing question arose in part from the continuing increase in the number of men at work. On 4 July he sent Lord Penrhyn a telegram, saying:

> Thirteen applications yesterday, eleven today. Am refusing seven and accepting seventeen.

In commenting on applications for houses, Young identified those he recommended with the letter R; and while these came from both Churchmen and Nonconformists, they were always from 'loyal' workers and often from men who had returned to the quarry on 11 June 1901[42].

There was an enthusiastic welcome for Mabon when he addressed a crowded meeting in the Bethesda Market Hall on 21 June. He said that the trade unions aimed to secure a proper wage for the workman's labour, reasonable hours of work, protection of life and limb, and direct representation of labour in Parliament; and he claimed that the average standard wage in the slate industry was £5 10s or 'possibly' £5 a month, which was below the average wage of the South Wales miner[43]. This claim was challenged on 26 June by the *Cambrian News*, which claimed that the average wage was nearer £8 a month, and that wages were not among the causes of the dispute.

J. E. Ellis, acting on behalf of eleven Liberal M.P.s, appealed to the Prime Minister to use his influence to settle the dispute;

and A. J. Balfour responded by suggesting that the strikers might clarify their position in a letter to Lord Penrhyn. Henry Jones wrote to Lord Penrhyn accordingly on 26 June, stating that the men's demands were now reduced to two: they would be content to have a committee of trade unionists, who would not profess to represent any other than trade unionists, and they would be happy to resume work if Lord Penrhyn would take back those on strike in preference to new men, so far and as soon as the work of the quarry permitted. They did not want any of the men currently at work to be dispossessed, and they would use their influence to ensure that all men employed in the quarry worked peaceably together. The letter concluded by expressing the hope that the 'unhappy dispute', which had caused so much suffering, might now be brought to an end.

Replying to this letter on 29 June, Lord Penrhyn reiterated that the men were at liberty to have a committee of trade unionists, provided it did not interfere with management; and in this connection he referred to the 1897 settlement terms relating to representation. In declining to accept the second condition, he said that since he would need only 2,000 men in all and nearly 1,100 were currently at work, there would be only about 900 vacancies. These would be filled on the basis of individual applications, and in choosing suitable workmen he would to some extent be influenced by 'the line' applicants had taken during the strike. Applications for employment, he said, could be made at any time; and the men in the quarry had been working 'happily for the last two years under the terms of settlement of 1897'[44]. Having been informed of Lord Penrhyn's reply, J. E. Ellis wrote again to the Prime Minister:

> I am desired to inform you that the Bethesda quarrymen readily acted on your suggestion and approached Lord Penrhyn, but without success . . . . This unhappy struggle is to be protracted, not from business considerations, but in order that some of the men may be made to suffer for having acted in combination with their fellow workmen.

This letter was reported by the *Manchester Guardian* on 7 July.

In July 1903 the North Wales branch of the Medical Association held its annual meeting in Barmouth; and the subjects discussed included the relationship between diet and heart disease. Dr Lloyd Williams attributed the 'too large proportion of heart disease among slate quarrymen' to 'careless and injudicious feeding' over two or three generations. Tea even when weak affected the digestive organs; and in the quarry communities a diet of bread, butter and tea was producing 'debilitated and weakly men and women'. Dr Lloyd Williams said that quarrymen needed food of high nutritive value, such as 'cream, meat essences, eggs and toasted bread', together with 'milk, butter, oatmeal and greenstuffs'. He recommended that

> working men should have a solid meal in the middle of the day, and employers should seriously consider whether it was not practicable to co-operate to establish cooking and eating sheds[45].

On 25 July the *North Wales Chronicle* reported that figures supplied to the Standing Joint Police Committee showed crime to be on the increase in Caernarfonshire. Convictions, mainly for drunkenness and petty larceny, had risen from 345 in the second quarter of 1902 to 458 in the second quarter of 1903. Over the same period the number of vagrants who received poor relief had risen from 979 to 1,308; and Colonel Ruck associated this increase with the end of the South African War. Conditions in Bethesda had not yet returned to normal, and three extra policemen were still needed there. Many houses in the town were empty, and many windows had been broken. Disturbances were becoming less frequent, and those which did occur were 'principally caused by women and children'. The number of offences committed by working quarrymen and their wives was forty-eight and the number committed by strikers and their wives was forty-six.

Also on 25 July Lady Florence Douglas sent a letter 'from one kinsman to another, a Douglas to a Douglas', in which she begged Lord Penrhyn to allow the dispute to be settled by arbitration. Deploring the 'suffering and misery' which the conflict was bringing upon poor people whose life 'at the best' was 'one of labour and life long toil', Lady Florence urged her relative to be a Douglas 'tender and true, not harsh and unfeeling'. Replying to this letter on 29 July, Lord Penrhyn referred to the libel case in which W. J. Parry had been ordered to pay £500 damages. He said that 1,100 men and boys were 'working happily and contentedly' in the quarry, where relations between employer and employee were 'thoroughly friendly'; and he added that 'continual enquiries about the alleged privation and suffering among the strikers and their families' had shown newspaper statements on this subject to be 'a series of gross exaggerations'. He reminded Lady Florence of the Douglas family motto 'Mak sicker', which in this context has to mean 'Make sure of your facts'[46].

In early August there was some correspondence between Lord Penrhyn and Trench about what the latter called 'this eviction business'. Trench was convinced that the proposed eviction of one tenant in Llwybrmain and one in Bethesda would lead to 'a big fight', which would plunge the district into 'a state of turmoil once more'; and he believed that this would be 'hailed with delight by the other side', since the evictions would help to arouse sympathy and bring in funds. He also pointed out that the tenancy agreements had not been stamped, and would therefore incur £10 fines if they were produced in court. Writing from Dieppe on 13 August, Lord Penrhyn said that while no one could 'fairly' have objected to his seeking 'more desirable tenants' if the two houses had been built by the estate, the fact that they had been built on lease by predecessors of the occupants meant that evictions would expose him to 'storms of obloquy'. He therefore advised Trench to abandon the planned proceedings, and to keep quiet about the unstamped agreements. He recognised that the 'delinquent tenants' would 'indulge in a song of triumph over the withdrawal', but he concluded that this could not be helped. Trench later reported that one of the tenants had said that Lord Penrhyn would not wish to turn him out if he knew the circumstances; and he commented that this man 'absolutely neglected the house', but that many of the tenants regarded 'houses built by themselves as almost their own property'. On 22 August Trench reported that he had refused to allow tenants at Tregarth to erect a storehouse there 'to facilitate house-drinking'. Lord Penrhyn had received some praise for his refusal to have a public house in Tregarth, but Trench admitted that 'a good deal of drinking' went on in the village[47].

Towards the end of August there were further discussions about the plan to run a group of small quarries near Bethesda on a co-operative basis; and W. J. Parry, owner and manager of the Pantdreiniog Quarry which was to employ 250 men, became managing director of the co-operative[48]. On 22 August the *North Wales Chronicle* observed that this scheme was being launched amid the 'plaudits' of those journalists who had helped to prolong the dispute; and it noted that the new group wanted only 'the strongest, most active men', whereas Lord Penrhyn continued to employ 'old and faithful servants' at 'reasonable rates of remuneration'. On 25 August Lord Penrhyn served a bankruptcy petition on W. J. Parry; and on 28 August the *Manchester Guardian* invited support for one who in his old age was threatened with 'ruin and banishment from public life for an incautious expression'. An appeal which brought contributions 'from all parts of the world' raised a total of £2,508; and W. J. Parry and William George visited Lord Penrhyn's Bangor solicitors on 8 September to pay the damages and costs in full. When he returned to Bethesda station 'in a howling gale of wind and rain', Parry was met by a cheering crowd of 1,000 people, who 'took the horses out of his carriage and dragged it up the mile-long steep hill to Coetmor Hall'. In a 'rousing little speech', he thanked all those who had helped him 'in the hour of need'; and in the evening there were fireworks and bonfires[49]. Lord Penrhyn, who was at Glan Conway with a shooting party, received a telegram from Sheridan Jones which read 'Wish you good shooting but you won't bag Parry'; and he annotated it with the one word 'Cheek'[50].

The first step towards the painful conclusion of the strike was taken late in September, when the General Federation of Trade Unions informed D. R. Daniel that it proposed to end its contributions to the strike fund. The N.W.Q.U. had been affiliated to the Federation since 1899, and had subscribed at the rate of 3d per head per quarter. The union was thus entitled to draw strike pay at the rate of 2s 6d per head per week for a specified period; and these contributions had been continued for two years longer than was authorised by the constitution. Men from Penrhyn Quarry had found work in other slate quarries, in the coalmines of South Wales, and in 'the Birmingham waterworks construction'; but some of them had returned to Bethesda when their employment was terminated. Those who returned in these circumstances were given strike pay again by the N.W.Q.U., but the Management Committee of the Federation argued that this was 'contrary to the practice of all the best trade unions'. When the co-operative quarries began to offer the strikers employment at home, the Federation asked for an extra levy of 1s a week on N.W.Q.U. members in work; but the union resisted this demand, arguing that they were making sufficient sacrifices. During the month in which the Federation was preparing to end its contributions, more than 100 men left the district; but the remaining strikers continued for the time being to receive support from individual unions in other parts of the country[51].

Continuing dissatisfaction over housing conditions was reflected in an anonymous and semi-literate letter addressed to Young on 11 September:

> It is a wonder that the Inspector of Health have not found many houses especially the men now working because of the houses too small and too many kept.

The writer expressed the view that the houses 'would not be in such trouble' if they were under Young's control[52]. On 20 September Trench reported a complaint he had received from the girl in charge of Penrhyn Castle lodge about servants who returned to the Park late at night. When the maids attended dancing classes on Saturdays and other nights, it was almost 11.30 p.m. before they came through; and the farm workers were even more of a nuisance, as they were often the worse for drink. The gardeners, on the other hand, did not go out much and always came back very early[53]. The number of applications continued to rise; and on 24 September the *Manchester Guardian* quoted W. J. Parry as saying that he could not blame those who were now returning to work, since 'the only thing left to many a man was either voluntary starvation or to obtain work in the quarry'.

For most of the men, N.W.Q.U. strike pay had now been reduced to 6s a week; and on 1 October the *Manchester Guardian* reported that a vote was to be taken on the question, 'Shall the battle be continued, or are you going to give up?' The question was to be put simultaneously in a week's time at Bethesda and at Porth, Cymmer, Merthyr, Maesteg and New Tredegar in South Wales. On 2 October the *Cambrian News* poured scorn on the 600 young strikers in Bethesda who had never sought employment elsewhere. These men, it contended,

> did not mind being a burden and declined to take hints to go away in search of work. . . . They attended the weekly meetings and cheered all the statements made by the men's leaders that Lord Penrhyn was a tyrant and that the returned workmen were traitors to the innocent who carefully abstained from honest labour and lived on charity.

The ironic reference to the Light Brigade implies, as it did when the other party used it, that the comparable group in Bethesda is less heroic but equally doomed; but the confident use of this comparison by an opponent of the strike makes it clear that the tide has now turned.

At the first ordinary general meeting of North Wales Quarries Ltd, which was held early in October at the Co-operative Hall in Derby, it was announced that disputes between the Co-operative Society and its quarrymen were to be considered by a Board of Conciliation. Richard Bell M.P. reported that 195 men were working at Pantdreiniog, that Tanybwlch had been acquired, and that the purchase of Moel Faban was almost completed. These co-operative quarries were never commercially successful; but Tanybwlch and Moel Faban survived until 1911, and Pantdreiniog until 1926[54].

There was 'a good muster of the men' at the Bethesda mass meeting on Saturday 10 October, but the Market Hall was not full; the vote, taken on a show of hands, gave a majority of 452 to 76 for continuing the strike. The men at the Merthyr Tydfil meeting voted unanimously to stay out, 'even should the quarrel be prolonged till death'; and they formally resolved

> that they should continue to stand out until Lord Penrhyn would recognise the principle that the old men who had been out of employment owing to the strike should have a chance of being reinstated.

The overall result, as announced by Henry Jones at a mass meeting on Saturday 17 October, was a majority of 820 to 88 against surrender[55]. Despite this vote, however, applications for re-admission to the quarry continued; and on 23 October it was reported that another 81 men had started work in the previous three weeks[56].

At the mass meeting on Saturday 24 October, Henry Jones invited 'a free discussion'. When a motion 'that the strike should now be broken up' had been proposed and seconded, the seconder was asked if he had 'applied for admission to the quarry and been refused'; but there was applause when he insisted on his right to speak his mind without incurring 'such insinuations'. Griffith Solomon Griffith argued that they should take no decision 'without first of all endeavouring to ascertain their present position'; and the chairman said that if they decided to seek re-admission they should 'give the men in South Wales the same chance as themselves of obtaining work'. It was argued that they had taken a decision three weeks earlier and should adhere to it; but in reply it was pointed out that the number of men backing the strike had fallen from 2,800 in 1900 to 1,700 in 1901 and fewer than 900 at the start of the current month. One speaker said that they had come out 'to fight the battle of combination', and asked how they could have effective combination 'when they were divided into traitors, strikers and neutrals'.

The chairman said that he would like to return to the quarry if he could do so honourably, and referred again to the rights of 'those at a distance'. William Thomas, a man of nearly eighty, insisted that they must all abide by the decision of the majority; and he asked if the old men were 'now to be left stranded by the very men who had induced them to come out'. The proposal to seek readmission was supported by a man who said that he had 'stood loyally by the decisions of the majority', but that he 'could not forget that there were men already returned to work in the quarry whom he had begged and implored not to commence the strike'. Another speaker said he was ready to stand for three years if 'anything could be gained by doing so', but that they should not 'carry on a hopeless fight' when 'strangers' were 'taking the bread from their mouths'. A ballot was proposed, on the ground that 'men voting openly were afraid to express their honest opinion'; and although this proposal was defeated, 'a very strong minority voted in support of it'. It was decided that another vote should be taken through mass meetings in Bethesda and in South Wales[57].

On 31 October Young told Lord Penrhyn that applications during the month had numbered about ten a day, and that the 101 new men who had started work had been well received by the 'old hands'. He said that he would send a special reporter to the next mass meeting, and added, 'It is fairly evident that the end is not far off'[58]. On 2 November all strikers were informed that, because only 908 had taken part in the last vote when more than twice that number were out, a further vote would be taken on Saturday 7 November. When the Bethesda men voted on that date by a show of hands, the result was as follows:

For declaring the strike ended	192
For continuing the strike	161
Majority for surrender	31

After announcing the result, Henry Jones reminded the men that votes were being taken in South Wales also, and that the final decision 'would depend upon the aggregate and not upon the Bethesda vote alone'. In reporting this meeting, the *Manchester Guardian* commented that the men's position had become that of a beleaguered garrison forced 'either to surrender or to starve'; and while questioning Lord Penrhyn's wisdom, it acknowledged that he had shown 'remarkable force of character' in defying 'the combined influences of trade unionism, Parliamentary pressure and public opinion'[59].

On Monday 9 November thirty skilled men were taken on at the quarry; and despite the chairman's plea there were more applications for re-admission. The demand for slates was strong, and the management arranged 'an extra run of the quarry train from Bethesda to the shipping outlet at Bangor'[60]. The assumption that the dispute was over was endorsed on 13 November by the *Cambrian News*, which argued that the men's leaders had behaved unwisely 'up to the very last'. In offering advice to those who had now 'taken their fate into their hands', the editor maintained the tough line he had taken throughout the dispute:

> Let there be no more talk about 'traitors' and 'betrayal', or about 'tyrants' and 'injustice' . . . . What the returned Penrhyn quarrymen have to do is to make the business pay, and to remember that their interests and Lord Penrhyn's interests are identical.

The *Manchester Dispatch*, also assuming that the dispute was 'practically at an end', said that this news was 'sincerely welcomed at Bangor', and that the 'tradespeople of Bethesda' also had 'every reason to rejoice'. The *Pall Mall Gazette* pronounced judgement on the dispute as on a past event:

> While history continues to be at all intelligently written, the Penrhyn strike will be a landmark. It has lasted three years, and it stands as the most conspicuous case in which an employer, revolting against excessive demands on the part of a combination of his workmen, has held out against them for the right to manage his own business in his own way.

The *Daily News* reported that the strikers had 'decided to give in', and commented that no one who had 'followed the fight' could be surprised. The *North Wales Chronicle* responded to this comment with some indignation, pointing out that the

'London newspaper' which made it had consistently encouraged the strikers by prophesying 'a glorious victory for Labour'[61].

Writing to Vivian on 13 November, Young reported that another 96 men had started work at the quarry 'during the past sixteen days'; because of the pressure of work there, he was going up to the quarry daily on the '1.30 run', and returning late at night. He was also in correspondence with Trench about building more houses in Glasinfryn. At one time he had considered this site too far from the quarry; but now that two workmen's trains were running every morning instead of one, it would be possible to cater for the extra traffic arising from fifty to a hundred houses there. He recommended the building of larger houses, since those at Tregarth were in many cases too small; and in this connection he asked Trench to bear in mind that there were 'large families of eight and ten and in one case . . . thirteen'[62].

The last of the regular mass meetings was held at Bethesda Market Hall on Saturday 14 November 1903. Henry Jones recalled that the men had 'declared themselves prepared to abide by the decision of the majority', but noted that 'scores if not hundreds of them' had in the last few days sought readmission to the quarry. No 'results of voting' had arrived from South Wales; but letters had been received which advised that 'in view of the position which the men at home were in, there was no alternative but to terminate the struggle'. In the light of that advice he 'wished to make the formal announcement that nothing remained but to declare the strike at an end'. Griffith Edwards, the secretary of the Committee, said that payments from the union fund would be made the following Friday, but that those who had applied for work before the chairman's announcement would be 'debarred from applying for any of the money'. Solomon J. Griffith suggested that 'negotiations be opened with Lord Penrhyn with the view of having terms of peace defined'; but the chairman replied that it would be 'perfectly useless to approach his lordship'[63].

On 14 November 1903, from his home at 12 Goronwy Street

in Gerlan, Henry Jones sent the following letter to Lord Penrhyn:

> My Lord,
>
> It is my duty to inform you that your late quarrymen have by a majority of those who recorded their Votes determined that the struggle is now to be considered as ended.
>
> I remain My Lord
> your obedient Servant,
> Henry Jones

The reply which Lord Penrhyn sent from Penrhyn Castle on 16 November was even shorter:

> Sir,
>
> I beg to acknowledge the receipt of your letter dated 14 November.
>
> I am,
> Yours
> Penrhyn

On being informed that the men had decided to surrender, the N.W.Q.U. recorded its admiration for their struggle, and indicated that the needs of the Bethesda Lodge would be looked after during the following months[64].

10
The Aftermath: 1903–1927

The years following the dispute were cheerless ones for the people of Bethesda. Half of those who applied for work in the quarry were rejected, and many families moved away from the district for good. The defeat of the strikers left nightmarish memories, and the habit of violence lingered. The divisions in the community were perpetuated by the depressed condition of the slate trade, which worsened dramatically within a year or two of the ending of the strike. It was hard on the one hand to forget the insults and the violence, and on the other to forgive the betrayal of working-class solidarity. The town could not easily recover its former prosperity and self-sufficiency.

Even before the final collapse on 14 November letters of congratulation were being sent to Lord Penrhyn. Writing from Somerset on 12 November, Merthyr Guest praised the 'fearless, just and determined way' in which he had 'faced and beaten the destestable crew' who had sought to 'cast odium' on his 'natural and English translation of the Law of meum and tuum'. Lord Penrhyn replied on 14 November:

> If the result of the war against myself (and indirectly against other owners of property) tends to deter socialist agitators from deluding the working classes, I shall perhaps have been of some use.

Writing from London on 14 November Sir William Des Voeux said that two months in Wales had enabled him to discount 'prejudiced reports' and recognise that Lord Penrhyn was 'an exceptionally just and considerate employer'. Writing from Menai Bridge on 16 November, H. Duff recalled that the end of the 1896–7 dispute had been marred by 'misunderstanding and misrepresentation'; but he was confident that Lord Penrhyn, who had been 'insulted and abused both by educated and uneducated people in the most unparalleled manner', would have 'no further trouble' this time. Writing from Ascot on 17 November, Lord Harlech said that the strike had ended with 'a total victory' for Lord Penrhyn and 'a complete rout to Messrs Jones, Williams and not forgetting Sir E. Clarke'.

Some of the congratulatory letters came from the relatives of working quarrymen: Miss M. G. Roberts, who wrote from Penmachno on 24 November, explained that her father and her three brothers had been working in the quarry since 11 June 1901. Others came from fellow-quarry-owners: W. A. Darbishire, the owner of Penyrorsedd Quarry in Nantlle, wrote on 5 December to thank Lord Penrhyn 'in the name of all reasonable and sensible quarry owners', and added:

> If the attack had been made on me it would have been very difficult to hold our own for two years though I am quite sure we should have taken exactly the same course.

Others again came from people who had enjoyed Lord Penrhyn's patronage: the Rev R. S. Andrews, vicar of Wicken near Stoney Stratford, offered his congratulations but also complained about the 'spiritual condition' of his parish; and Edward Jones, formerly station-master in Bangor, wrote from 27 Holyhead Road to thank Lord Penrhyn for a present of game, and to express his hope that the 'unhappy strike' had come to an end 'for all time'. The thirty-four telegrams received included one from the former chief engineer H. P. Meares, one from members of the Bangor Working Men's Conservative Club, and one from Mrs Assheton Smith which read simply 'So glad thousand congratulations'[1].

The origins and progress of the dispute were the subject of much journalistic comment during the two weeks following the men's surrender. On 16 November the *Manchester Guardian* paid tribute to the 'splendid heroism and restraint' with which the strikers had demonstrated 'the principle which lies at the very root of trade unionism – the loyalty of a workman to his fellows'. On 21 November the *Times* observed that the men had

> wasted the happiness and comfort of a considerable number of years of their lives in a futile effort to obtain terms which their commonsense might have told them were out of the question.

The *Nottingham Guardian* claimed that Lord Penrhyn had 'shown the world' that socialism would not be 'brought about by intimidation'. The *Aberdeen Journal* said that trade unionism had 'received one of the most fatal blows' it could have suffered. The *Belfast News Letter* asserted that the men had been 'badly advised from the first' by 'certain Welsh members of Parliament' and by 'false prophets in the Radical Press'. The *Bristol Times* condemned the Liberal Party for treating Lord Penrhyn's 'simple determination to keep control of his own property' as if it were a 'monstrous tyranny'. The *Burton Mail* deplored the 'ghoul-like eagerness' with which 'sundry individuals' had 'sought to exploit the miseries of the men and their families for political ends'. On 20 November the *Cambrian News* implausibly blamed the dispute on the Independent Labour Party, but also offered some advice for the future:

> The danger is that a reserved, sensitive man like Lord Penrhyn, conscious of his own right desires and intentions, may not be able wholly and quickly to cast aside the memory of the past.

Despite the 'coarse and wholly unmerited abuse' he had suffered, Lord Penrhyn was exhorted to 'go freely in and out among the people and take their goodwill for granted'.

On 28 November the *Cambrian News* was happy to report that the Bethesda Market Hall, which had been the scene of the strikers' weekly meetings, was to be restored on 5 December to its original functions. On 15 December Trench informed Lord Penrhyn that men who were leaving the district after being refused work at the quarry were offering to sell their leasehold houses to the estate. Trench recommended that these should be purchased, and that £70 should be paid for one with 'about sixteen years to run'; he considered that this would be 'a quicker mode of obtaining houses than by building them and a cheaper one'[2]. Demand for slates had been high in 1903, and in spite of the continuing dispute the quarry had made a profit of £28,890[3]. On 30 December Young told Lord Penrhyn that he had spent four hours the previous day going through reports on 'the characters of a great number of applicants'; he had accepted 35 of these, and 18 had started work that morning. This brought the total workforce to 1,565; and on 7 January 1904 Young was able to report that the figure had reached 1,603[4].

On 25 January 1904 Young told Lord Penrhyn that he had been going through 'about 230 applications which were made on the celebrated 16 November', and that he intended to announce 134 refusals that night. The announcement caused renewed disorder in Bethesda, and extra police had to be brought in. On 1 February Young told Colonel Ruck that the 'additional police supervision' had had 'the desired effect' and that 'quietness prevailed in every district'; but he warned that he would be sending out 'a good many more refusals' in the next few days, and that these would 'probably increase the uneasy feeling'. On 20 February the *Manchester Guardian* quoted William Jones as saying that 1,237 skilled workmen were still shut out of the quarry because of the dispute, and that there was 'appalling distress' in Bethesda.

On 24 February 1904 Young told Lord Penrhyn that, while he would not take back anyone who had been prominent in the strike, he wanted to recruit about 500 men in addition to the 1,700 already at work; this would bring the workforce to 2,200, or 600 fewer than in 1900[5]. A breakdown of the income and expenditure for the Penrhyn Relief Fund, printed in the *Manchester Guardian* on 28 March, showed a total income of £46,763 and a total expenditure of £46,568. The income included £32,742 earned by the three choirs, £5,652 from newspaper funds, £5,646 in subscriptions from trade unions and others, and £2,471 from collections. The expenditure included £24,440 on choir expenses, over £18,500 on direct relief to strikers and their families, £2,196 on 'special distributions', and £1,228 on collectors' expenses. £15,474 of the relief had been paid through local tradesmen by means of a ticket system, with the tradesmen's bills settled fortnightly. Writing on 10 May to

Colonel W. Cornwallis at Ruthin Castle, Young agreed that 'the so-called Bethesda Choir' was 'still going all over the country'; but he said he did not think that the men refused work at the quarry were receiving anything from this source[6].

The extent to which the strike had damaged Lord Penrhyn financially had been a closely guarded secret; but on 24 April 1904 Trench wrote on this subject to Lady Penrhyn, who was temporarily in charge because her husband was receiving medical treatment:

> Now that the strike is over I hope I shall not be doing wrong in economising on the Estate as far as possible, and reducing the staff wherever there is an opportunity. While the strike was on I tried never to say anything to anyone that would make them think economy was the order of the day as the other side might have been encouraged by the idea. Early in the strike Mr Young told me he was taking the same care, but now I take it there is not the same necessity for silence and I find that while I have been away a few men have been stopped and now that no more new cottages are to be built it will mean a considerable reduction in the labour bill.

As agent for the Penrhyn estate Trench in 1904 sold some land in Bangor to the corporation, and also disposed of some property in Caernarfon. On his own account he became the tenant of a 'weekend cottage' at Ogwen Lake, from which an earlier tenant had been evicted for having a 'traitor notice' in his window during the strike. Since then it had been taken over as an annexe by A. Jones of Ogwen Lake Cottage; but he was willing to relinquish it in return for an extension to his own house. Trench explained that his residence at Lime Grove was 'so low' that it was 'rather relaxing', and that his doctor had recommended 'Ogwen air' because it was 'so bracing'; and he added that the site of his new property was 'altogether . . . one of the most delightful spots' he had ever seen[7].

At the 1904 Labour Day celebrations in Caernarfon, D. R. Daniel proclaimed that the men had been defeated but not dishonoured:

> They failed, not because the Union was ineffective, but because some of their comrades proved disloyal.

Henry Jones argued that they had been beaten in part because of

> the unfairness shown to the men by the general newspapers of the country, more particularly when it became evident that the men were fighting for a losing cause[8].

After a short period of prosperity following the dispute, the slate trade began to decline; the price of roofing slates had to be reduced, and there was stock-piling at Port Penrhyn. On 28 October 1904 Young wrote to Lord Penrhyn:

> All is well here except that no orders come in and a reduction to the level of Dinorwic prices is inevitable and wages too. I think 2½ per cent will suffice both off prices and off wages[9].

On 11 November the *Observer* alleged that there was an age-limit for admission to Penrhyn Quarry, and that this had had

> a grievous result on those elderly quarrymen who came out and remained on strike with the younger men during the recent troublous times.

Because they could not 'roam in search of employment', some of these men were making 'a gallant effort to earn a bare sustenance by hawking tea'; and it was suggested that the managers of 'the new quarries' should bear the needs of such 'veterans' in mind. With dissatisfaction mounting at Pantdreiniog, this was hardly a realistic suggestion; and by the end of 1904 two-fifths of the workforce at the co-operative quarries, including some former members of the Penrhyn Quarry Committee, had been dismissed[10].

The religious revival which began at Newquay in Cardiganshire in October 1904 reached Bethesda in the last week of November, when the Rev Hugh Hughes preached to large congregations in the Jerusalem Chapel. During the winter of 1904–5 there was a series of well-attended meetings, at which an atmosphere of religious hysteria was built up through prayers, hymns, shouts and tears. Press reports in January and February 1905 recognised that the great obstacle to spiritual regeneration in Bethesda was the heritage of bitterness and communal hostility left by the dispute; but it was claimed that the two parties were 'slowly beginning to melt into one another' under the influence of the revival[11].

On 21 January 1905 four hundred of the former Penrhyn workmen gathered in the Bethesda Market Hall with Griffith Griffiths of Gerlan in the chair. The proceedings began with a hymn, and the meeting sent the following message to Young for transmission to Lord Penrhyn:

> In the face of the straitened circumstances that have overcome us as the result of the recent dispute between us and your Lordship, as our late employer, we humbly and strongly urge your Lordship to overlook all our defects and receive back to your employment as many as possible of your late workmen, and we can never be thankful enough to your Lordship if you can see your way to grant this application.

If the supporters of this resolution genuinely expected their new humility to wash away the economic consequences of the dispute, they must have been sadly disappointed by Young's reply:

> I duly received yours of the 21st enclosing a letter to Lord Penrhyn, and in reply thereto I am instructed to say his lordship much regrets that circumstances make it impossible to accede to your request.

At a time of declining trade, there was no place in the quarry for an extra four hundred men whose individual applications had already been turned down[12].

The new atmosphere produced by the revival may also have affected Bethesda's response to the wedding of Lord Penrhyn's son Charles. Charles Douglas Pennant, who was to be killed in action on 29 October 1914, married Lady Edith Dawson on 28 January 1905; and the event was celebrated with flags and 'congratulatory mottoes' all over Bethesda. In Douglas Terrace there was an arch covered with foliage which 'attracted much attention'; and in the evening there were bonfires and firework displays at Penrhyn Quarry Hospital and in Tregarth, Rachub and Llanllechid. Whatever private reservations there may have been, these activities suggest that Bethesda was less hostile to the Pennants at this time than the history of the dispute might have led one to expect[13].

The depression in the slate industry continued, however, with slate prices falling and production costs going up; and on 2 April 1905 Young told Lord Penrhyn that he could see 'no signs of improvement in any direction'. One cause of the trouble was competition from France, where low wages enabled the quarries to undercut Welsh slates; and the situation was aggravated by foreign tariffs on Welsh slates, by the depression in the building industry, and by the increased use of tiles for roofing. On 25 April 1905 Young met representatives of the workforce and told them that the removal of the 5 per cent bonus given on 11 June 1901 had become unavoidable. He showed them the stocks of slate on the quay at Port Penrhyn; but they were well informed about the state of trade and 'accepted the reduction in good spirit', asking him to thank Lord Penrhyn for continuing the bonus so long. In May 1905, when the Ffestiniog quarries were preparing to reduce prices 10 per cent and wages 5 per cent, Young decided to reduce both poundage on slates and the tonnage price for badrock. He told the men's representatives that this would mean a 5 per cent reduction in wages; and he explained that Welsh slates were 'almost entirely' excluded from the south of England, and that about 70,000 tons had been 'dumped' in 1904 at 'very low prices'. Reduced production from 1900 to 1903 had no doubt made it easier for foreign competitors to penetrate the British market; but even if the dispute had never occurred, this depression could scarcely have been averted.

Having been warned that he was overweight and in need of exercise, Young attempted to solve the problem by taking up motoring; and on 6 June 1905 he told Lord Penrhyn that he found it 'very healthy work and beneficial to both the liver and kidneys'. He faced both the dense traffic of Sheffield and the narrow streets of York; and in the 2,000 miles of his motoring tour he had '*one* puncture only'[14]. In September 1905 a garden party was held at Penrhyn Castle; and for this 413 invitation cards were sent out, an average of two guests being expected for each card. Lord Penrhyn was well aware that he was not universally popular; and it was assumed that there would be 150 or more refusals, leaving a 'possible total' of 526 or fewer guests[15]. At the end of 1906 there was a minor scandal at Penrhyn Castle, where an investigation of the kitchen accounts led to the dismissal of the cook, Mrs Dunthorne, and occasioned a search for new tradesmen. On 26 November Trench informed Lord Penrhyn that there was 'no such thing as a Conservative butcher in Bangor'; but Hugh Vincent recommended A. J. H. Davies of Menai Bridge, who was not only a Conservative and a Churchman but also 'a good butcher'. Trench confessed apologetically that his own butcher was 'a Radical'[16].

On 18 January 1907 the *North Wales Chronicle* outlined the plans for the twenty-first anniversary of Young's appointment as Lord Penrhyn's chief agent; and on 8 February the same paper gave an account of the celebrations, which extended over two evenings. On the first evening the officials and clerks from the quarry and the port met Young at 6.30 p.m. for high tea in 'the workmen's dining hall on the quay at Port Penrhyn'. The catering was done by 'Mrs Hughes of Wicklow House', and there were tributes to Young from the chief clerk William Gray and the local manager David Davies. Having revealed that he had attended Young's twenty-first birthday party in London, Gray said that Young still showed 'the same desire to do all he could for those around him'; but he added, amid laughter, that 'possibly he now loomed larger in their eyes'. Davies referred to the repeater watch which was being presented to Young as a 'striking present', and he expressed the hope that they would all go on working together like the parts of the watch. Young replied to these jests with a serious account of the slate trade. He said that imports of French, Belgian, American and Newfoundland slates had fallen from 80,429 tons in 1904 to 33,368 tons in 1906, but that the new German tariff of 30% was damaging the Welsh slate industry, where wages were low and prices were falling. To restore the audience's spirits after this speech, he showed slides of Tanybryn, of his family, of the quarry, and of the 1894 big blast. On the following evening Young entertained the Port Penrhyn workmen in the same way, the catering being done once again by Mrs Hughes; and the men presented him with an illuminated address in appreciation of the 'very kind and considerate manner' in which he had always studied 'the welfare of all the workmen'.

On 10 March 1907 Lord Penrhyn died suddenly but peacefully from influenza at his London home of Mortimer House. When the news reached Bangor, flags were flown at half-mast from the University College of North Wales and other public buildings. Obituaries, of which there were many, spoke of his generous donations to many institutions, such as the Caernarfonshire and Anglesey Infirmary and the Society for the Care of Discharged Prisoners. Reference was made to his patronage of the National Eisteddfod, and to his encouragement of Welsh literature and art through the Cymmrodorion Society. There were many tributes to his support for Church schools, including the school at Tregarth which he had built at a cost of over £3,000. There were accounts, too, of his interest in fishing and his enthusiasm for the turf[17]. Hugh Vincent spoke of his 'goodness to the poor', and continued:

> He was the kindest, the most just, and the most generous employer, whose sole purpose in life was to find out what was right, and, having found it out as it was given him to know, to pursue it with unswerving purpose which nothing turned.

Vincent declared himself to have lost 'the best, straightest, and most loyal friend a man ever had'[18]. Edward VII sent a message of sympathy to Lady Penrhyn from Biarritz; and the workmen and officials of Penrhyn Quarry described their late employer as 'a true friend' who was 'ever anxious and solicitous' for their 'welfare and happiness'[19]. The *Daily Dispatch*, however, said that it would be 'idle to pretend' that Lord Penrhyn's death would 'cause any deep regrets in the district where he lived'. In an article entitled 'Penrhynism – and After' it celebrated the 'legal emancipation of labour' brought about by the reversal of the Taff Vale judgment in the Trades Disputes Act of 1906.

Lord Penrhyn was buried by the side of his first wife Pamela in the Church of St John the Evangelist at Wicken Park in Buckinghamshire. The Churchmen of Bangor diocese decided to perpetuate his memory by erecting a rood screen and extending the choir stalls in Bangor Cathedral[20]. The screen was built of oak and was divided into six bays, the middle two being surmounted by a carved semi-circular arch which formed the doorway. The inscription, on the lower part of the northernmost panel, reads:

To the glory of God
And in grateful and
Affectionate memory of
George Sholto Gordon
Lord Penrhyn
This screen and four
Additional stalls were
Erected by Public
Subscription in the
Year 1908[21]

On 28 February 1908 the *North Wales Chronicle* reported the unveiling of an east window to the memory of Lord Penrhyn at St Cross Church in Llanllechid. The window, designed by Sir Edward Burne-Jones, was subscribed for by tenant-farmers of all creeds on the Penrhyn estate; and the service was attended by the combined choirs of the Bethlehem Congregational Chapel, the Gilfach Baptist Chapel, and the Gatehouse Calvinistic Methodist Chapel. The inscription on the window reads:

> To the glory of God, and in memory of George Sholto Gordon Baron Penrhyn, founder of this Church, born September 30th 1836, died March 10th 1907, this window was erected as a tribute of affection and esteem by the tenants of the Penrhyn Estate, 1907.

The window was unveiled by Humphrey Ellis, chairman of the Tenants' Committee, who praised Lord Penrhyn's readiness to help and comfort those who were 'in trouble, sorrow, need, sickness, or any other adversity'[22].

Lord Penrhyn's son, Edward Sholto Douglas Pennant, succeeded to the title and took over the quarry, the castle and the estate. When he paid his first visit to Bethesda in his new role in February 1908, the *North Wales Chronicle* reported that he 'was accorded a most enthusiastic welcome'. He told the men at the quarry that his interests and theirs were identical, and that they would stand or fall together. The fortunes of the N.W.Q.U. had declined in the years after the dispute, and in 1907 it had only about 100 members in Penrhyn Quarry and only 67 in Dinorwic[23]. The financial secretary W. H. Williams decided to resign on grounds of ill-health; and this decision, though it did not take effect until a year later, was reported in the *Manchester Guardian* of 25 March 1908. In April 1908 the organising secretary, Lloyd George's friend D. R. Daniel, left to take up a new post in London[24]. At the 1908 Labour Day celebrations in Blaenau Ffestiniog, O. Ellis Jones criticised the quarrymen of North Wales for their lack of loyalty to the union[25]. W. J. Parry later commented that the men had remained loyal only so long as union money was finding its way into their pockets[26]. In 1909, however, the N.W.Q.U. entered a new era under Robert Thomas Jones of Blaenau Ffestiniog, whose decisive leadership was to bring a rapid improvement in organisation, discipline and membership figures.

On 22 September 1910, after some months of failing health, E. A. Young died at his home in Tanybryn, leaving a widow and five young sons. The obituary notices spoke of his business and organising skills, noting that these had made the quarry more efficient but had led to conflict with the workforce. Though he had been in some respects 'the best hated man in the locality', those who came to know him realised that 'his feelings were far from being so hard and bitter' as the 'disturbed imagination' of his enemies suggested. He had been closely associated with the Y.M.C.A., and had equipped a gymnasium at his own expense; the motto prominently displayed there, 'Be straightforward', had been the watchword of his own character[27]. He was also a keen sportsman, having been well-known in the football world and in his later years captain of the Bangor Golf Club.

Although he did not make any ostentatious display of his wealth, his skill in investment had made him a rich man, and he left an estate of £146,344. There is a legend in Bethesda that Young had to be buried at dead of night; but in fact he was buried in Llandegai churchyard on a Saturday afternoon, in the presence of a large gathering of mourners including the third Lord Penrhyn[28].

Despite the national celebrity which he attained through the Penrhyn dispute, W. J. Parry did not achieve his ambition of entering Parliament; but he continued to play a significant role in Caernarfonshire politics for many years. When William Jones died in 1915, Parry was much involved in the choice of his successor as Liberal candidate for Arfon; and in 1918 he was at the centre of a controversy over the choice of a Liberal candidate for the new constituency of Caernarfonshire. He was awarded a C.B.E. in 1918, and in his later years he translated sermons from English into Welsh. He died at Coetmor Hall on 1 September 1927, and was buried in the secluded churchyard of Maesygroes. He was, as his biographer put it, 'a lonely and embittered old man who had outlived his generation'[29]; but it is his account of the Penrhyn dispute, as given in the eloquent book which he published in 1901, that has guided the responses of most later historians. The evidence accumulated in the present volume should make it easier to assess the validity of Lord Penrhyn's plea, as voiced on 17 November 1903 in a letter to Sir William des Voeux:

> I *wasn't* as black as I was painted, and . . . my line was the right one[30].

Notes

Notes to Chapter 1 (pages 7-24)

1. Jean Lindsay, 'The Pennants and Jamaica 1665–1808', Parts I and II in *Transactions of the Caernarvonshire Historical Society*, 1982 and 1983.
2. A. H. Dodd, *A History of Caernarvonshire 1284–1900*, 1968, p.357.
3. Parliamentary Papers, Vol. 48, 1838, Paper 215 and E. H. Douglas Pennant, *The Pennants of Penrhyn*, 1982, p.33.
4. For a general history of the slate industry in North Wales, see Jean Lindsay, *A History of the North Wales Slate Industry*, 1974, and Dylan Pritchard, *The Slate Industry of North Wales; A Study of the Changes in Economic Organisation from 1780 to the Present Day*, unpublished thesis, University College of North Wales, 1935.
5. George Nicholson, *The Cambrian Traveller's Guide in the Principality of Wales,* 1813, p.731.
6. Hugh Derfel Hughes, 'The Penrhyn Quarry', essay presented at the Eisteddfod, 1877.
7. University College of North Wales, William Sackville West's letters, 1893–7.
8. U.C.N.W., Coetmor Papers 46 and *North Wales Gazette*, 27 January 1825.
9. *Royal Commission of Enquiry on Land in Wales and Monmouthshire*, Vol. I, 1896, Questions 12,073, 12,076-7, 12,080 and 12,083.
10. U.C.N.W., William Sackville West's letters, 1893–7.
11. U.C.N.W., Quarry Strike, 1900–1903.
12. U.C.N.W., William Sackville West's letters, 1893–7.
13. U.C.N.W., Trades Unions at Penrhyn Quarry and J. Bateman, *The Great Landowners of Great Britain and Ireland*, 1879.
14. U.C.N.W., Trades Unions at Penrhyn Quarry.
15. Cyril Parry, *Socialism in Gwynedd 1900–1920*, unpublished thesis, University of Wales, 1967, p.72.
16. U.C.N.W., Trades Unions at Penrhyn Quarry and A. H. Dodd, *A History of Caernarvonshire 1284–1900*, p.255.
17. U.C.N.W., Trades Unions at Penrhyn Quarry.
18. Census Returns, 1841.
19. Jean Lindsay, *A History of the North Wales Slate Industry*, pp.240-1.
20. J. Roose Williams, 'Quarryman's Champion', in *Transactions of the Caernarvonshire Historical Society*, 1962 and 1963.
21. *The Borough Guide to Bethesda*, n.d.
22. W. J. Parry, *The Penrhyn Lock-Out*, 1901.
23. Gwynedd Archives Service, P.Q. 98/1
24. U.C.N.W., Congratulatory letters.
25. U.C.N.W., Trades Unions at Penrhyn Quarry.
26. G.A.S., P.Q. 98/1.

27. W. R. Williams, *The Parliamentary History of the Principality of Wales 1541–1895*, 1895, p.119.
28. Morgan Richards, *Slate Quarrying and How to Make it Profitable,* n.d., p.144.
29. Jean Lindsay, *A History of the North Wales Slate Industry*, p.211. For a full account of the N.W.Q.U. see R. Merfyn Jones, *The North Wales Quarrymen 1874–1922*, 1981.
30. G.A.S., P.Q. 98/1
31. R. Merfyn Jones, *The North Wales Quarrymen 1874–1922*, pp.52-3.
32. Jean Lindsay, *A History of the North Wales Slate Industry*, p.211.
33. U.C.N.W., Trades Unions at Penrhyn Quarry.
35. Jean Lindsay, *A History of the North Wales Slate Industry*, pp.211-213.
36. U.C.N.W., Trades Unions at Penrhyn Quarry.
37. Jean Lindsay, *A History of the North Wales Slate Industry*, pp.213-214.
38. G.A.S., P.Q. Additional, unlisted. I should like to thank the depositor, Lady Janet Douglas Pennant, for permission to use uncatalogued material.
39. G.A.S., P.Q. 98/1.
40. U.C.N.W., Trades Unions at Penrhyn Quarry.
41. U.C.N.W., Letters, *North Wales Chronicle.*

Notes to Chapter 2 (pages 25-40)

1. J. Roose Williams, 'Quarryman's Champion' in *Transactions of the Caernarvonshire Historical Association*, 1964.
2. U.C.N.W., My Books.
3. U.C.N.W., Written inside the Book of Common Prayer.
4. U.C.N.W., Family letters.
5. G.A.S., P.Q. Add., unlisted, membership of the N.W.Q.U. 1874–1934.
6. G.A.S., P.Q. Add., unlisted, evidence, draft proof, of Penrhyn v Parry libel case.
7. G.A.S., Minutes of N.W.Q.U. and Minutes of Penrhyn Lodge.
8. G.A.S., P.Q. Add., unlisted, Penrhyn Quarry 1903 (pamphlet).
9. Arnold J. James and John E. Thomas, *Wales at Westminster, A History of the Parliamentary Representation of Wales 1800–1979*, 1981.
10. U.C.N.W., Letters of condolence and G.A.S., P.Q. Add., unlisted.
11. G.A.S., P.Q. Add., unlisted.
12. G.A.S., P.Q. Add., unlisted.
13. G.A.S., P.Q. Add., unlisted.
14. U.C.N.W., letters of E. A. Young.
15. U.C.N.W., letters of E. A. Young.
15. U.C.N.W., letters of E. A. Young.
17. U.C.N.W., letters of E. A. Young.
18. U.C.N.W., Papers 83.
19. *Y Faner*, 8 October 1884.
20. Cyril Parry, *Socialism in Gwynedd 1900–1920*, unpublished thesis, p.49.
21. G.A.S., P.Q. 98/1.
23. W. J. Parry, *The Penrhyn Lock-Out*, pp.35-51 and G.A.S., P.Q. Add., unlisted.

24. *Y Genedl Gymreig*, 5 March 1886, Jean Lindsay, *A History of the Slate Industry of North Wales*, pp.263-4 and U.C.N.W., William Sackville West's letters. 1885–8.
25. U.C.N.W., Congratulatory letters.
26. G.A.S., P.Q. Add., unlisted.
27. U.C.N.W., Business letters from E. A. Young.
28. G.A.S., P.Q. Add., unlisted, evidence, draft proof, of Penrhyn v Parry libel case.
29. G.A.S., P.Q. Add., unlisted and U.C.N.W., William Sackville West's letters, 1885–8.
30. U.C.N.W., Business letters from E. A. Young.
31. G.A.S., P.Q. Add., unlisted, evidence, draft proof, of Penrhyn v Parry libel case.
32. G.A.S., P.Q. Add., unlisted and U.C.N.W., Business letters from E. A. Young.
33. G.A.S., P.Q. Add., unlisted, evidence, draft proof, of Penrhyn v Parry libel case, G.A.S., XPQ 96/2 and G.A.S., P.Q. 98/1.

Notes to Chapter 3 (pages 41-60)

1. U.C.N.W., Letters of E. A. Young.
2. G.A.S., Minutes of Bethesda Lodge, N.W.Q.U., No 7 and W. J. Parry, *The Penrhyn Lock-Out*, p.53.
3. U.C.N.W., Business letters from E. A. Young and G.A.S., P.Q. Add., unlisted.
4. G.A.S., Add., unlisted.
5. Cyril Parry, *Socialism in Gwynedd 1900–1920*, unpublished thesis, pp.74-5.
6. G.A.S., P.Q. Add., unlisted.
7. *Royal Commission on Labour*, 11 February 1892 and 8 December 1891.
8. R. Merfyn Jones, *The North Wales Quarrymen 1874–1922*, pp.135-41.
9. G.A.S., P.Q. Add., unlisted.
10. U.C.N.W., Business letters from E. A. Young.
11. R. Merfyn Jones, *The North Wales Quarrymen 1874–1922*, pp.162-74.
12. U.C.N.W., Letters of E. A. Young.
13. G.A.S., P.Q. Add., unlisted.
14. N.W.Q.U., Bethesda Minute Book, 25 January 1894.
15. U.C.N.W., Letters of E. A. Young and G.A.S., P.Q. Add., unlisted.
16. G.A.S., P.Q. Add., unlisted.
17. G.A.S., P.Q. 98/1, U.C.N.W., Family letters and G.A.S., P.Q. Add., unlisted.
18. G.A.S., P.Q. Add., unlisted.
19. U.C.N.W., Letters of E. A. Young.
20. G.A.S., P.Q. Add., unlisted and U.C.N.W., Congratulatory letters.
21. G.A.S., P.Q. Add., unlisted and U.C.N.W., Quarry Strike 1896–7.

Notes to Chapter 4 (pages 61-89)

1. U.C.N.W., Letters of E. A. Young.
2. W. J. Parry, *The Penrhyn Lock-Out*, p.168 and K. O. Morgan, ed., *Lloyd George Family Letters 1885–1936*, p.109.

3. U.C.N.W., Letters of E. A. Young.
4. W. J. Parry, *The Penrhyn Lock-Out*, p.121 and U.C.N.W., Quarry Strike 1896–7.
5. U.C.N.W., Letters of E. A. Young.
6. U.C.N.W., Congratulatory letters.
7. U.C.N.W., Congratulatory letters, Letters of E. A. Young, Quarry Strike 1896–7 and Trades Unions at Penrhyn Quarry.
8. *Hansard Parliamentary Debates*, Vol. 45, 28 January 1897, J. Roose Williams, 'Quarryman's Champion' in *Transactions of the Caernarvonshire Historical Society*, 1962 and K. O. Morgan, ed., *Lloyd George Family Letters 1885–1936*, p.109.
9. U.C.N.W., Congratulatory letters, Letters of E. A. Young and Quarry Strike 1896–7.
10. G.A.S., P.Q. Add., unlisted.
11. U.C.N.W., Letters of E. A. Young.
12. U.C.N.W., Congratulatory letters and Trades Unions at Penrhyn Quarry.
13. J. Roose Williams, 'Quarryman's Champion' in *Transactions of the Caernarvonshire Historical Society*, 1965. U.C.N.W., Letters of E. A. Young and G.A.S., P.Q. Add., unlisted.
14. U.C.N.W., Letters of E. A. Young and G.A.S., P.Q. Add., unlisted.
15. G.A.S., P.Q. Add., unlisted.
16. U.C.N.W., Letters of E. A. Young.
17. G.A.S., P.Q. Add., unlisted.
18. R. Merfyn Jones, *The North Wales Quarrymen 1874–1922,* p.193.
19. G.A.S., P.Q. Add., unlisted.
20. U.C.N.W., Letters of E. A. Young.
21. G.A.S., P.Q. Add., unlisted.
22. U.C.N.W., Congratulatory letters.
23. N.W.Q.U. Minute Book 25 September 1897. and G.A.S., P.Q. Add., unlisted.
24. G.A.S., P.Q. Add., unlisted.
25. J. Roose Williams, 'Quarryman's Champion' in *Transactions of the Caernarvonshire Historical Society*, 1964.
26. G.A.S., P.Q. Add., unlisted. and U.C.N.W., Congratulatory letters.
27. U.C.N.W., Congratulatory letters.
28. G.A.S., P.Q. Add., unlisted.
29. H. A. Clegg, A. Fox and A. F. Thompson, *A History of British Trade Unionism since 1889, Vol. 1, 1889–1910*, 1964, p.213.

Notes to Chapter 5 (pages 90-102)

1. G.A.S., P.Q. Add., unlisted, P.Q. 98/1 and U.C.N.W., Letters of E. A. Young.
2. G.A.S., P.Q. Add., unlisted, P.Q. 98/1 and U.C.N.W., Letters of E. A. Young.
3. U.C.N.W., Letters of E. A. Young.
4. R. Merfyn Jones, *The North Wales Quarrymen 1874–1922*, pp.201-209.
5. U.C.N.W., Letters of E. A. Young.
6. G.A.S., P.Q. 100/41.

7. U.C.N.W., Letters of E. A. Young.
8. See James I. C. Boyd, *Narrow Gauge Railways in North Caernarvonshire, Vol. 2, The Penrhyn Quarry Railways*, 1985, pp.69-72.
9. G.A.S., P.Q. Add., unlisted and P.Q. 99/6.
10. U.C.N.W., Letters of E. A. Young and G.A.S., P.Q. Add., unlisted.
11. G.A.S., P.Q. 100/41.
12. U.C.N.W., Letters of E. A. Young; G.A.S., Minute Book 2, N.W.Q.U.

Notes to Chapter 6 (pages 103-135)

1. U.C.N.W., Family letters.
2. G.A.S., Minute Book 2, N.W.Q.U.
3. U.C.N.W., Business letters of E. A. Young.
4. G.A.S., P.Q. Add., unlisted.
5. *Hansard Parliamentary Debates*, Vol. 118, 4 March 1903, Vol. 121, 27 April 1903, R. Merfyn Jones, *The North Wales Quarrymen 1874–1922*, p.211 and Cyril Parry, *Socialism in Gwynedd 1900–1920*, unpublished thesis, p.39.
6. G.A.S., P.Q. 98/4.
7. G.A.S., P.Q. Add., unlisted and Jean Lindsay, *A History of the North Wales Slate Industry*, p.276.
8. G.A.S., P.Q. Add., unlisted.
9. U.C.N.W., Letters of E. A. Young.
10. G.A.S., P.Q. 99/6 and U.C.N.W., Quarry Strike, 1900–1903.
11. *Liverpool Courier*, 6 November 1900.
12. G.A.S., P.Q. Add., unlisted.
13. *Daily Chronicle*, 7 November 1900, *Western Mail*, 7 November 1900 and *Westminster Gazette*, 7 November 1900.
14. *Y Faner*, 5 October 1984 and G.A.S., P.Q. Add., unlisted.
15. G.A.S., P.Q. Add., unlisted.
16. *Times*, 14 November 1900.
17. U.C.N.W., Colonel Ruck letters from 1899–1904.
18. U.C.N.W., Letters of E. A. Young.
19. U.C.N.W., Letters of E. A. Young, *Liverpool Courier*, 20 November 1900 and G.A.S., P.Q. 99/6.
20. *Manchester Guardian*, 22 November 1900.
21. G.A.S., P.Q. 99/6.
22. U.C.N.W., Letters to George Livesey.
23. G.A.S., P.Q. 100/41.
24. G.A.S., Minute Book 2, N.W.Q.U.
25. U.C.N.W., Quarry Strike, 1900–1903 and Letters of E. A. Young.
26. G.A.S., P.Q. 99/6.
27. G.A.S., P.Q. 99/6.
28. U.C.N.W., Letters of E. A. Young and G.A.S., P.Q. 99/6.
29. G.A.S., P.Q. Add., unlisted.
30. G.A.S., P.Q. 99/6.
31. *Liverpool Courier*, 25 January 1901.
32. G.A.S., P.Q. 99/6.
33. *Daily News*, 13 February 1901.

34. *Liverpool Daily Post*, 13 February 1901.
35. U.C.N.W., Family letters.
36. *Times*, 24 April 1901.
37. *Manchester Guardian*, 15 April 1901.
38. G.A.S., Minute Book 2, N.W.Q.U.
39. G.A.S., P.Q. 99/6.
40. G.A.S., Add., unlisted.
41. U.C.N.W., Quarry Strike, 1900–1903.
42. U.C.N.W., Letters from R.C. Trench.
43. U.C.N.W., Letters of E. A. Young.
44. *Manchester Guardian*, 6 June 1901.
45. G.A.S., P.Q. 100/41.
46. G.A.S., P.Q. Add., unlisted.

Notes to Chapter 7 (pages 136-160)

1. U.C.N.W., Quarry Strike, 1900–1903.
2. G.A.S., P.Q. 98/1.
3. *Manchester Guardian*, 17 June 1901.
4. G.A.S., P.Q. 99/6.
5. U.C.N.W., Letters from R. C. Trench.
6. U.C.N.W., Letters of E. A. Young.
7. U.C.N.W., Letters of E. A. Young.
8. *Hansard Parliamentary Debates*, Vol. 98, 5 August 1901.
9. U.C.N.W., Letters of E. A. Young.
10. *Hansard Parliamentary Debates*, Vol. 99, 17 August 1901.
11. U.C.N.W., Letters of E. A. Young.
12. *Liverpool Daily Post*, 26 September 1901.
13. U.C.N.W., Letters from R. C. Trench and G.A.S., P.Q. Add., unlisted.
14. *Manchester Guardian*, 25 October 1901.
15. *Liverpool Mercury*, 29 October 1901 and *South Wales Daily News*, 30 October 1901.
16. E. H. Douglas Pennant, *The Pennants of Penrhyn*, pp.31-2.
17. G.A.S., P.Q. Add., unlisted and U.C.N.W., Letters of E. A. Young.
18. *Carnarvon and Denbigh Herald*, 29 November 1901.
19. *Liverpool Daily Post*, 25 November 1901.
20. U.C.N.W., Family letters.
21. U.C.N.W., Letters of E. A. Young, G.A.S., P.Q. 99/6 and 99/7 and *Liverpool Weekly Mercury*, 16 November 1901.
22. G.A.S., P.Q. 99/6 and *Carnarvon and Denbigh Herald*, 29 November 1901.
23. *Carnarvon and Denbigh Herald*, 29 November 1901 and G.A.S., P.Q. 100/41.
24. *Clarion*, 16 November 1901.
25. U.C.N.W., Letters of E. A. Young.
26. U.C.N.W., Letters to George Livesey.
27. U.C.N.W., Colonel Ruck letters from 1899–1904.
28. U.C.N.W., Family letters.

Notes to Chapter 8 (pages 161-190)

1. *Daily Mail*, 30 December 1901.
2. *Liverpool Echo*, 2 January 1902.
3. *Liverpool Daily Post*, 3 January 1902.
4. *Liverpool Daily Post*, 8 January 1902.
5. *Manchester Guardian*, 9 January 1902.
6. U.C.N.W., Letters from R. C. Trench.
7. G.A.S., Minute Book 2, N.W.Q.U.
8. G.A.S., P.Q. 100/41.
9. G.A.S., P.Q. 100/41.
10. *Manchester Guardian*, 24 January 1902 and *Liverpool Daily Post*, 24 January 1902.
11. U.C.N.W., Quarry Strike, 1900–1903, *Liverpool Mercury*, 29 January 1902 and *Liverpool Daily Post*, 4 February 1902.
12. *Liverpool Mercury*, 10 February and *Morning Leader*, 18 February 1902.
13. *Liverpool Mercury*, 10 February 1902.
14. U.C.N.W., Quarry Strike, 1900–1903 and G.A.S., N.W.Q.U., 101, 'Correspondence re Penrhyn Strike', 1896–1906.
15. *The Christian Commonwealth*, 27 February 1902.
16. U.C.N.W., Letters of E. A. Young and *North Wales Chronicle*, 15 March 1902.
17. *Liverpool Mercury*, 28 February 1902.
18. G.A.S., ES/1, Log Books, Glanogwen National Girls' School, Bethesda, 1881–1911, Cefnfaes, Evening and Day School, 1874–1954, Gerlan National School, 1872–1958, Carneddi British School, 1884–1956 and G.A.S., P.Q. Add., unlisted.
19. G.A.S., P.Q. 99/7.
20. *North Wales Observer and Express*, 17 January 1902.
21. U.C.N.W., Letters of E. A. Young and G.A.S., 100/42.
22. *Liverpool Mercury*, 26 March 1902.
23. G.A.S., P.Q. 99/7.
24. *Drych*, 27 March 1902 (American Newspaper) and *Yr Herald Cymraeg*, 18 February 1902.
25. *North Wales Observer and Express*, 28 March 1902 and G.A.S., P.Q. Minute Book 2, N.W.Q.U.
26. U.C.N.W., Letters of E. A. Young.
27. *Manchester Guardian*, 5 April 1902 and *Liverpool Echo*, 5 April 1902.
28. *Liverpool Courier*, 17 March 1902 and *Carnarvon and Denbigh Herald*, 18 April 1902.
29. *Liverpool Mercury*, 14 and 25 April 1902.
30. U.C.N.W., Letters from R. C. Trench and *North Wales Observer and Express*, 25 October 1901.
31. *North Wales Observer and Express*, 2 May 1902.
32. *Report on Slates*, 1921, Cmd. 1338.
33. *North Wales Chronicle*, 6 May 1902 and *Liverpool Courier*, 6 May 1902.
34. *Liverpool Courier*, 18 April 1902.
35. U.C.N.W., Letters from R. C. Trench and *North Wales Observer and Express*, 16 May 1902.

36. U.C.N.W., Letters to George Livesey.
37. U.C.N.W., Letters from R. C. Trench and J. Gwyn Williams, *The University College of North Wales*, 1985, p.188.
38. U.C.N.W., Letters from R. C. Trench.
39. G.A.S., P.Q. 100/42.
40. G.A.S., P.Q. 99/7.
41. *Manchester Guardian*, 20 May 1902.
42. *Liverpool Daily Post*, 28 May 1902.
43. *North Wales Observer and Express*, 30 May 1902.
44. *Liverpool Mercury*, 12 June 1902.
45. *Carnarvon and Denbigh Herald*, 13 June 1902.
46. U.C.N.W., Letters to George Livesey.
47. G.A.S., P.Q. 100/42.
48. *Carnarvon and Denbigh Herald*, 11 July 1902 and G.A.S., P.Q. 100/42.
49. *Manchester Guardian*, 25 July 1902.
50. G.A.S., P.Q. 99/7.
51. *Hansard Parliamentary Debates*, Vol. 112, 6 August 1902.
52. *Liverpool Mercury*, 14 August 1902.
53. G.A.S., Minute Book 2, N.W.Q.U.
54. *South Wales Daily News*, 28 August 1902.
55. *Times*, 1 September 1902 and *Manchester Courier*, 1 September 1902.
56. U.C.N.W., Trades Unions at Penrhyn Quarry.
57. *Liverpool Courier*, 5 September 1902.
58. K. O. Morgan, ed., *Lloyd George Family Letters 1885–1936*, p.138.
59. *Manchester Guardian*, 5 September 1902 and *Liverpool Mercury*, 8 September 1902.
60. *Liverpool Mercury*, 12 September 1902.
61. *Manchester Guardian*, 15 and 24 September 1902 and *Sheffield Telegraph*, 15 September 1902.
62. *Daily News*, 19 September 1902 and *Liverpool Daily Post*, 19 September 1902.
63. U.C.N.W., Letters to George Livesey.
64. *Liverpool Daily Post*, 25 September 1902.
65. G.A.S., P.Q. 100/42.
66. G.A.S., 100/42 and G.A.S., P.Q. Add., unlisted.

Notes to Chapter 9 (pages 191-230)

1. W. R. P. George, *Lloyd George, Backbencher*, 1983, p.327.
2. G.A.S, P.Q. 100/42.
3. R. C. K. Ensor, *England 1870–1914*, 1975, p.314.
4. U.C.N.W., Quarry Strike, 1900–1903.
5. *Liverpool Daily Post*, 18 December 1902.
6. *Morning Leader*, 24 December 1902.
7. U.C.N.W., Letters of E. A. Young and G.A.S., Minute Book 2, N.W.Q.U.
8. G.A.S., P.Q. 99/7. and U.C.N.W., Quarry Strike, 1900–1903.
9. G.A.S., P.Q. 99/7.
10. U.C.N.W., Letters to George Livesey, Letters from R. C. Trench, *North Wales Observer and Express,* 20 February 1903 and J. Gwyn

Williams, *The University College of North Wales*, p.190.
11. G.A.S., P.Q. 99/7.
12. Standing Joint Police Committee, *Minutes of Evidence and Report of the Sub-Committee Appointed to Enquire into Matters at Bethesda*, 1903.
13. G.A.S., P.Q. 99/7.
14. G.A.S., P.Q. Add., unlisted and *Hansard Parliamentary Debates*, Vol. 118, 5 March 1903.
15. U.C.N.W., Congratulatory letters.
16. *Western Mail*, 27 March 1903.
17. U.C.N.W., Letters from R. C. Trench.
18. U.C.N.W., Letters of E. A. Young.
19. *Daily News*, 26 March 1903.
20. G.A.S., P.Q. Add., unlisted.
21. U.C.N.W., Letters of E. A. Young.
22. U.C.N.W., Letters of E. A. Young.
23. *Daily News*, 6 April 1903.
24. G.A.S., P.Q. Add., unlisted.
25. U.C.N.W., Congratulatory letters.
26. *Times*, 14 April 1903.
27. *Daily Chronicle*, 15 April 1903.
28. *Liverpool Courier*, 26 September 1910 and *North Wales Chronicle*, 2 December 1910.
29. J. Roose Williams, *Quarryman's Champion: The Life and Activities of William John Parry of Coetmor*, 1978, pp.30-31.
30. U.C.N.W., Congratulatory letters.

Notes to Chapter 10 (pages 231-243)

1. U.C.N.W., Congratulatory letters.
2. U.C.N.W., Letters from R. C. Trench.
3. G.A.S., P.Q. Add., unlisted.
4. G.A.S., P.Q. 99/7.
5. G.A.S., P.Q. 99/7.
6. G.A.S., P.Q. 99/7.
7. U.C.N.W., Letters from R. C. Trench.
8. *Manchester Guardian*, 3 May 1904.
9. U.C.N.W., Business letters from E. A. Young.
10. *Manchester Guardian*, 23 November 1904 and *North Wales Chronicle*, 31 December 1904.
11. R. Merfyn Jones, *The North Wales Quarrymen 1874–1922*, pp.296-300.
12. *Manchester Guardian*, 23 January 1905 and *North Wales Chronicle*, 28 January 1905.
13. *North Wales Chronicle*, 4 February 1905.
14. U.C.N.W., Business letters from E. A. Young.
15. U.C.N.W., Garden Party List.
16. U.C.N.W., Letters from R. C. Trench.
17. *Liverpool Courier*, 12 March 1907.
18. *Manchester Guardian*, 13 March 1903.
19. *Daily Mail*, 12 March 1907 and *North Wales Observer and Express*, 20 March 1907.

20. *North Wales Observer and Express*, 20 and 22 March 1907 and *Daily Dispatch*, 12 March 1907.
21. *North Wales Chronicle*, 11 December 1908.
22. *North Wales Observer and Express*, 28 February 1908.
23. R. Merfyn Jones, *The North Wales Quarrymen 1874–1922*, pp.289-94.
24. *Manchester Guardian*, 28 April 1908.
25. *North Wales Chronicle*, 8 May 1908.
26. *Liverpool Courier*, 20 September 1910.
27. *Liverpool Courier*,23 September 1910 and *North Wales Chronicle*, 23 September 1910.
28. *Liverpool Daily Post*, 24 April 1903.
29. U.C.N.W., Letters from R. C. Trench.
30. G.A.S., P.Q. Add., unlisted.
31. *Hansard Parliamentary Debates*, Vol. 121, 27 April 1903.
32. *Daily News*, 28 April 1903.
33. *Daily Telegraph*, 28 April 1903.
34. G.A.S., P.Q. 99/7.
35. *Liverpool Mercury*, 5 May 1903.
36. *Western Mail*, 23 May 1903 and U.C.N.W., Letters from R. C. Trench.
37. *Liverpool Courier*, 2 June 1903.
38. U.C.N.W., Letters from R. C. Trench.
39. *Liverpool Courier*, 2 June 1903.
40. U.C.N.W., Business letters from E. A. Young.
41. U.C.N.W., Letters from R. C. Trench.
42. G.A.S., P.Q. 100/43 and U.C.N.W., Business letters from E. A. Young.
43. *Cambrian News*, 22 June 1903.
44. G.A.S., P.Q. 100/43-5.
45. *Manchester Guardian*, 16 July 1903.
46. U.C.N.W., Quarry Strike, 1900–1903.
47. U.C.N.W., Letters from R. C. Trench.
48. *Manchester Guardian*, 24 July 1903.
49. *Manchester Guardian*, 28 August 1903.
50. U.C.N.W., Quarry Strike, 1900–1903.
51. *Liverpool Courier*, 23 September 1903, *Manchester Guardian*, 23 September 1903 and G.A.S., Minute Book 2, N.W.Q.U.
52. G.A.S., P.Q. 100/43.
53. U.C.N.W., Letters from R. C. Trench.
54. *Manchester Guardian*, 5 October 1903 and Jean Lindsay, *A History of the North Wales Slate Industry*, pp.325, 327 and 331.
55. *Manchester Guardian*, 12 October 1903.
56. *Cambrian News*, 23 October 1903.
57. *Manchester Guardian*, 2 November 1903.
58. G.A.S., P.Q. 100/43.
59. *Manchester Guardian*, 9 November 1903.
60. *Manchester Guardian*, 10 November 1903.
61. *North Wales Chronicle*, 14 November 1903.
62. G.A.S., P.Q. 100/43.
63. *Manchester Guardian*, 16 November 1903.
64. G.A.S., Minute Book 2, N.W.Q.U.

Index